ARTIFICIAL INTELLIGENCE

Confronting the Revolution

James Adams and Richard Kletter

First published in 2018 by Lume Books.

Table of Contents

Dedications

James:

To Renée whose love, light and compassion provides a welcome contrast to the often darker world in which I work.

To Ella and Grace, my adored daughters, whose contributions to the world give me hope for future generations.

*

Richard:

To Virginia, whose ready laugh, keen mind and loving heart bring out the best in me.

To Nora and Will, my brilliant, loving children, who inspire me by how they are in the world and fill me with gratitude every day.

Authors' Note

Artificial Intelligence (AI) is a complicated subject and often appears inaccessible to the general reader. To help get around this, some of the chapters have a fictional beginning that imagines part of the future world that AI will bring to us. To distinguish these fictional pieces from the non-fiction text, they appear in italics.

Introduction

The Industrial Revolution lasted some 80 years, and helped bring about communism, revolution, and two world wars at a loss of more than 160 million dead. Today, we confront a different kind of revolution that will unfold in less than ten years.

Already, we see signposts of the breathtaking possibilities of this new world. Decoding the human genome will allow for medical breakthroughs to benefit all of us; immersive interactive technologies will allow our minds to transcend physical boundaries to explore worlds of our choosing; sex between men and women and compliant robots is already possible and will become accepted practice; in a world where all knowledge is accessible to everyone, education as we have known it for generations will, of necessity, be radically transformed; neuro-enhancements, augmented by AI, will transform life for the mentally and physically challenged while offering the possibility of cognitive improvements for all.

Some experts, such as Klaus Schwab, the founder and executive chairman of the World Economic Forum, suggest that AI is the fourth industrial revolution that will outpace any previous revolution in terms of both speed and impact.

The first industrial revolution used steam to mechanize production. The second industrial revolution used electricity to create mass production while the third used information technology to introduce automation.

"The speed of current breakthroughs has no historical precedent. When compared with previous industrial revolutions, the Fourth is evolving at an exponential rather than a linear pace," said Schwab. "Moreover, it is disrupting almost every industry in every country. And, the breadth and depth of these changes herald the transformation of entire systems of production, management, and governance."1

This is echoed by leaders of technology companies and pioneers in the AI field such as Sundar Pichai, Google CEO. "AI is probably the most important thing humanity has ever worked on. I think of it as something more profound than electricity or fire."2

There is no question that AI will bring great benefits – economic, social and industrial – that will impact every person on the planet. Cancer diagnoses will become more accurate, doctors will be accessible to everyone 24/7, climate change will be combatted with more accurate weather predictions and better management of food production, fewer soldiers will die in combat and all knowledge will become available to everyone.

Already, all of us have become accustomed to what might be called "infant AI". Alexa, Siri and Google Home all use AI to recognize your voice and anticipate needs both expressed and unexpressed. The days when advertisements appeared on full pages of broadsheet newspapers are almost over and instead ads are

---

[1] https://www.mediaupdate.co.za/media/143225/why-ai-is-key-in-the-fourth-industrial-revolution

[2] https://money.cnn.com/2017/08/08/technology/business/sundar-pichai-profile/index.html?iid=EL

increasingly tailored to the individual. Such ads are driven by AI number-crunching based on billions of bits of data gathered through every online interaction. Bought a book on best hotels in Mexico? Perhaps a discount travel package to the country might be tempting. Bought a red dress? Maybe a cream blouse on sale might complete the outfit.

For many of us, such tailoring is actually a good thing because it makes our lives – from shopping to travel and job searching – easier, faster and often less expensive. But AI will be about much more than lifestyle. This revolution is mother and father to countless individual revolutions, each of which will change society and they are all unfolding simultaneously.

Amazon is pioneering the cashierless store with its Go line of groceries. Every weapons manufacturer across the world is seeking to develop autonomous weapons capable of waging war largely free of human engagement. Police forces and intelligence agencies are implementing sophisticated surveillance systems that use recognition of facial and other physical characteristics to preempt and prevent illegal events before they occur.

*

Amidst all the hype across the world, nobody actually knows how fast AI is accelerating. What is known is that some developments are happening faster than expected – for example, Microsoft software now can match human ability to recognize and transcribe speech. China has made clear its intention to use AI to propel its rise as the world's next great superpower. But how soon will driverless cars outnumber ordinary vehicles? How soon will robots dominate the battlefield? Nobody knows.3

For centuries, major upheavals in society have been shaped by moral, ethical and legal boundaries set by religious leaders, scholars and political leaders. As societies have evolved, so have the boundaries that provide a structure in which ordinary people can live, love, learn and contribute. None of this is true in the current AI revolution.

"Right now, public policy and regulation on AI remains nascent, if not nonexistent. But concerned groups are raising their voices," said Ryan Holmes, Founder and CEO of Hootsuite.4

Some lobbying groups have sprung up, but these are on the margins of AI developments and have yet to have any real impact. To date, there has been no effective international debates, no national legislation in any country and not even the beginnings of an international agreement that might set guidelines and boundaries for just how AI will be allowed to impact our world.

This new world we are entering is moving too fast for the customary pundits and commentariat to understand or have the time to come up with new solutions. This has provoked a debate among some technologists who argue that as the inventors of the transformative technology they bear the responsibility for educating societies about the challenges and opportunities they may represent.

In March 2018, the ACM Future of Computing Academy, with members from 19 countries, published a

---

[3] https://www.wired.com/story/do-we-need-a-speedometer-for-artificial-intelligence/

[4] https://medium.com/@invoker/why-we-need-to-get-religious-about-ai-before-its-too-late-7496ef4ad224

call to arms entitled: *It's Time to Do Something: Mitigating the Negative Impacts of Computing Through a Change to the Peer Review Process.*[5]

The FCA proposed:

Incentivizing computer scientists to confront the negative impacts of their research by using the publish or perish power of the peer review process. Research papers that do not discuss the potential negative impacts of their scientific contributions WILL NOT BE ACCEPTED into prominent publications until they do.

In addition to DISCLOSING potential negative impacts, researchers will be encouraged to discuss ways to REDUCE these impacts. This might include follow-up research or suggestions for improved government regulations.

These concepts seem simple enough, but they represent a new role for computer scientists who, typically, keep their heads down, build what they want, and leave such responsibilities to social scientists or information technologists. This underlines a fundamental problem with the whole field of AI: few people understand it and even those who do are unqualified or unwilling to assess the likely impacts.

As the AI revolution accelerates, it will do so against a background of instability: a growing and hopeless underclass, a widening gap between rich and poor, a government that grows less relevant as it legislates for the past while the future comes ever faster, and an education system that teaches every new generation about a world that, by the time they graduate, will no longer exist.

---

[5] https://acm-fca.org/2018/03/29/negativeimpacts/

Without a clear vision for the future, this is a recipe for disaster.

Elon Musk, the founder of Tesla, believes that AI represents an "existential threat to human civilization." For Musk, this is not just about the threat to jobs, but also the dangers of a new AI arms race, and the development of robots to which humans cede control of their own future. "Once there is awareness, people will be extremely afraid," Musk said; "as they should be."

Others, such as Larry Page of Google and Mark Zuckerberg of Facebook, think that Musk exaggerates the threats. Both men are making sure their companies invest billions of dollars to exploit the opportunities presented by AI.6

Already, the technology revolution has meant that the wealthy have gotten wealthier, while income for the poor and even the middle class has stagnated: The top 1% are earning, on average, more than three times what they made in the 1980s, while the bottom 50% have seen their earnings stay the same or decline. The top 20% of US households now own more than 84% of the wealth, the bottom 40% a paltry 0.3%. The CEO-to-worker pay ratio is 354 to 1.7

According to the Economic Policy Institute, from 2009 to 2017, average pay for the nation's CEOs jumped by $7.8 million, or by 72%. During that period, the average wages and benefits for a typical American worker rose from $53,400 to $54,600, or by about 2%. Executives in

---

[6] https://www.nytimes.com/2018/06/09/technology/elon-musk-mark-zuckerberg-artificial-intelligence.html

[7] https://www.chegg.com/homework-help/organizational-behavior-seventeenth-edition-chapter-7-solutions-9780134103983

America's top 350 companies saw their average annual pay surge to $18.9 million in 2017.8

According to a recent study by United Way, more than 40% of US households, or 34.7m households, cannot afford the basics of rent, transportation, child care and a cellphone. At the same time, 66% of Americans earn less than $20 an hour, or about $40,000 a year if they are working full time.9

Avril Haines, former deputy CIA director, points to inequality in the US as a long-term national security threat, and one that will be accelerated by emerging technologies:

"As the majority of the population in countries like the United States see that their children are unlikely to be better off than they were, there is a sense of frustration – exacerbated by the fact that the economy appears to be doing well, yet the benefits of that growth are going to the super rich. Meanwhile, authoritarian governments like China appear to be making significant reforms that result in greater access to resources for their citizens. This creates, among other things, a perception that democracies are unable to deliver for their citizens."10

Fifty years ago, it took 387,923 US workers to manufacture a billion dollars' worth of goods. Today, it takes only 26,785 – 361,138 fewer people. The coal industry is one illustration of this change. In 2003, the coal industry employed 70,000 people; today, that number is less than 50,000 and continues to fall. Mechanization had pushed the coal industry into decline long before the

---

[8] https://www.epi.org/publication/ceo-compensation-surged-in-2017/

[9] https://www.unitedwayalice.org

[10] https://www.axios.com/newsletters/axios-am-2ffd3215-b632-4780-b5cf-97bf3a846359.html

environmental movement chose it as a poster child for global warming. In fact, there are more yoga teachers in the US than coal workers.

Both major political parties continue to emphasize full employment as a core policy, yet 38% (57 million) of US jobs are at risk because of the AI revolution. This is no longer a working-class issue. Instead, every sector of the economy will be impacted, from lawyers to radiologists and doctors, and anyone who continues to work in a service industry or on a production line.

*

This is not just an American problem; it confronts every democratic society. The results can be seen by the rise of Trump in America, the Brexit vote in the UK, the recent German vote that placed Angela Merkel in last place behind a new anti-immigration party, the riots in Greece, the election of a Trump clone in Brazil, and the large and rising youth unemployment in North Africa, Spain, and Italy.

Technologists in Silicon Valley, academics who study AI and even the few politicians who understand AI all agree that the world is entering a very challenging and potentially revolutionary environment. However, nobody has produced a strategy that will help the world understand and develop solutions to the problems that lie ahead. Given the breadth and depth of the revolution that is accelerating towards us, developing a strategy is a tough task. No community, no nation and no life will be immune from the impact of the AI revolution which will alter the purpose and nature of education, the future of work, how families live every day, and what must happen to sustain peace in our communities and our world.

This book will not provide the definitive strategy to address the myriad challenges. Instead, we have talked to some of the best minds across the world to ask them two simple questions: What do you see as the biggest challenge AI will present to the world? And what should we do about it?

Interestingly, we found remarkable consensus among educators, doctors, Pentagon planners and politicians: The future world looks pretty scary and there is a real possibility of widespread civil disorder unless action is taken. Where disagreements quickly emerge is what "action" means.

We have chosen to distill the conversations and the debate to make the broad canvas of AI accessible to all. With some chapters, we have chosen to begin with an imaginary forecast of what might be as a way of making the challenges more vivid to everyone.

We conclude with an action plan, or series of recommendations for everyone involved in the AI conversation. Our hope is that this will be a starting point for future conversations in and between communities and on the world stage. It is those conversations that will decide our fate.

Part 1 – Setting the Scene

Chapter 1

The Beginning of the Beginning

Technology has always disrupted the way we live and work, sometimes seemingly overnight. The fabled Pony Express riders, including Buffalo Bill, delivered information in 1860 via horseback at the speed of a gallop while telegraph wires were being strung across the country. But just two days after those wires connected California and New York, all the riders were fired and their horses put out to pasture or sold for glue.

AI has become part of nearly every aspect of our lives, though, perhaps, more insidiously. Most of us can barely remember a time before the iPhone. What technologists call "the fourth industrial revolution" began in 2010 and is principally associated with the development of robotics, Artificial Intelligence, nanotechnology and the internet of things.

Unlike the completion of the telegraph and other previous industrial revolutions, there is no single point of disruption, but instead a thousand points of change and innovation across every industry and profession. Because of the breadth and scale of these changes, the speed seems almost invisible to those of us living through it. But visitors from just two decades ago would see a world jaw-droppingly different from the one they knew. The pace of change is accelerating, and the rate of acceleration gathers pace seemingly every day. Think about what has happened just since 2010, although by the time you read this, many of these numbers will be out of date:

Apple launched the iPad and sold 360m units.

Snapchat has 187m daily users who create 1M photos and videos and has 10b daily videos views with an overall valuation of $20b.

Instagram has 800m monthly users who "like" 4.2b posts a day. Owned by Facebook and valued at over $100b.

Square, Uber, Lyft, Oculus and Airbnb are all global brands today and didn't exist before the fourth revolution.

Cloud-based sharing platforms, such as AWS, have become a staple of the business world... Futurist Ray Kurzweil argues that this rate of change can be captured by what he calls "the law of accelerating returns":

"An analysis of the history of technology shows that technological change is exponential, contrary to the common sense 'intuitive linear' view. So, we won't experience 100 years of progress in the twenty-first century – it will be more like 20,000 years of progress (at today's rate). The 'returns', such as chip speed and cost-effectiveness, also increase exponentially... Within a few decades, machine intelligence will surpass human intelligence, leading to the Singularity – technological change so rapid and profound it represents a rupture in the fabric of human history. The implications include the merger of biological and nonbiological intelligence, immortal software-based humans and ultra-high levels of intelligence that expand outward in the universe at the speed of light."11

Kurzweil suggests that the progress of the entire twentieth century would have been achieved in only 20

---

[11] http://www.kurzweilai.net/the-law-of-accelerating-returns

years at the rate of advancement in the year 2000 – in other words, by 2000, the rate of progress was five times faster than the *average* rate of progress during the twentieth century. He believes another twentieth century's worth of progress happened between 2000 and 2014 and that *another* twentieth century's worth of progress will happen by 2021, in only seven years. A couple decades later, he believes a twentieth century's worth of progress will happen multiple times in the same year, and even later, in less than one month. All in all, because of the law of accelerating returns, Kurzweil believes that the twenty-first century will achieve *1,000 times* the progress of the twentieth century.12

Kurzweil wrote his essay in 2001 and predicted that by 2019 the principle that has guided the rate of change since 1965, known as Moore's Law, will be no longer fit for purpose. Gordon Moore, former chairman of Intel, argued that we could put twice as many transistors on an integrated circuit every 24 months, which means that the overall processing power of computers doubles every two years, a "law" that has proved durable since Moore proposed it in 1965. But, despite the potential of new, more efficient, materials such as germanium and "spintronics" to replace silicon in transistors, we may approach a finite limit on how small transistors can go, such that even Moore himself has said that he expects his

---

[12] https://waitbutwhy.com/2015/01/artificial-intelligence-revolution-1.html quoting Kurzweil, The Singularity is near, P.39

law to expire by 2025.13 Transistor technology may have reached a point of maximum impact.14

Future technological advances, it seems, hew more closely to Kurzweil's predictions than to Moore's. The new worlds that we can only begin to imagine will all be fueled by the Artificial Intelligence revolution.

The term "artificial intelligence" was first coined at conference at Dartmouth College in 1956 and the concept of developing a "thinking" machine was expected to become a reality within 20 years. In fact, just about every estimation of the progress of AI has been wrong; only recently has reality begun to match the hype. As far back as 1997, chess champion Garry Kasparov was beaten in a game by IBM's Deep Blue supercomputer; in 2011, IBM's Watson beat past winners of the TV quiz show *Jeopardy* at their own game.

But much confusion remains about just what AI is and how it can be defined. Basically, there are three buckets into which the various AI developments are poured. The first is known as Weak AI or Artificial Narrow Intelligence (ANI) which, broadly, is where we are right now. An example of Weak AI is a machine that is programmed to do a specific task that either replaces or assists the human in carrying out that task. For example, the robots in Amazon warehouses are very reliable at finding certain items and ferrying them to the packaging area. But if those same robots were asked to provide

---

[13] https://en.wikipedia.org/wiki/Moore%27s_law

[14] https://www.technologyreview.com/s/601441/moores-law-is-dead-now-what/

navigation guidance from point A to Point B, they would be utterly unable to do so.15

Similarly, the current generation of virtual assistants such Alexa rely on voice recognition and then transmit your recorded question to a cloud-based service – for Alexa it's AVS (Alexa Voice Services) – which interprets your words into commands. Alexa, Siri and Google Home can answer simple questions when the answers have been preprogrammed. They can take large amounts of data and make predictions or detect patterns that provide answers to their users and benefits to the companies which make them. It is weak AI that produces the Google search results or delivers an ad on Facebook that seems to be tailored specifically to you.

*

In October 2018, Christie's, the venerable art auction house, had its first sale of art created using AI algorithms. Across the art world some mainstream artists and novices who have never created art before are using AI to give their work a new look and feel.16 Already, a gallery in Paris has put on a show of AI-created art and one of India's premier art galleries is also exploring the new medium.

According to a report in *Axios*, pieces are made using generative adversarial networks, or GANs, a state-of-the-art AI technique. The painting algorithm took a crash course in portraiture, reviewing 15,000 portraits painted between the fourteenth and twentieth centuries. A second algorithm called "the discriminator" judged the result to see if it could discern AI-created from human-created art.

---

[15] https://www.investopedia.com/terms/w/weak-ai.asp

If it could, it sent the generator back to the easel, and the cycle repeated until the generator produced something indistinguishable from human art.[17]

Here's a different way of looking at AI in our current world:

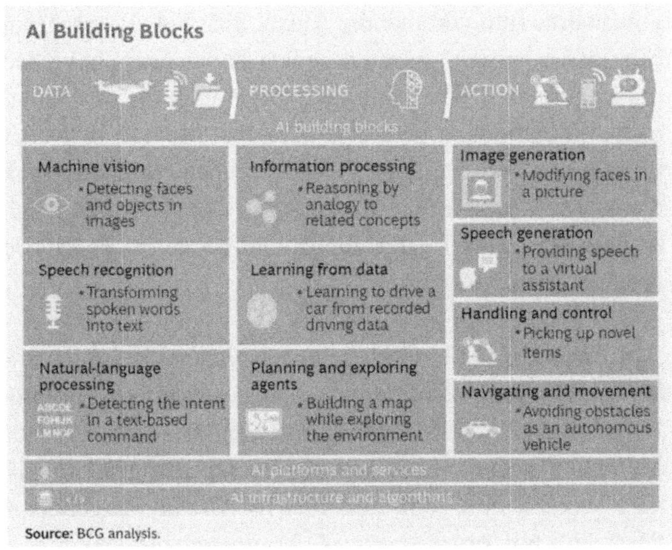

Source: BCG analysis.

[16] https://news.artnet.com/exhibitions/ai-generated-art-gallery-show-1339445?mod=djemfoe

[17] https://www.axios.com/artificial-intelligence-art-50781b14-95e6-4b32-910f-883fd740b5b4.html

Or this:

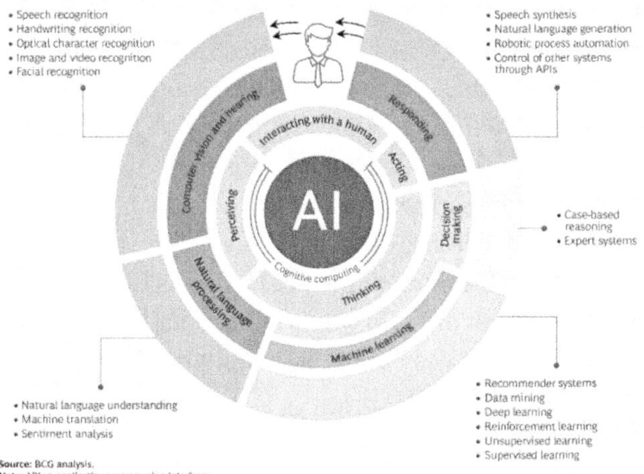

The next generation of virtual assistants like Alexa and Google Home will deploy Strong AI or Artificial General Intelligence (AGI), in which the goal is to develop Artificial Intelligence to the point where the machine's intellectual capability is functionally equal to a human's.18 Initially, this includes problem-solving, creativity and reasoning; but the holy grail of Strong AI is to give the machine the human attributes of self-awareness, sentience and the much-debated idea of whether a machine can achieve consciousness within a computational theory of mind. Many AI researchers are "computationalists" who believe that the human brain is essentially a computer and, therefore, whatever our brains can do, computers also can do even better.

But consciousness may be exempt from the computationalist hypothesis. They may not be able to get a machine to have vivid experiences with seemingly intrinsic "qualities," such as the redness of a tomato, or the spiciness of a taco. These qualities usually go by their Latin name, qualia. We all know what we're talking about when we talk about sensations, but they are notoriously undefinable. Experience teaches us to attach a label such as "spicy" to certain tastes, but we really have no idea whether the sensation of spiciness to me is the same as the sensation of spiciness to you… Computationalism seems to have nothing to say about it, simply because computers don't have experiences."19

The next stage of development is Artificial Super Intelligence (ASI) where the machine is smarter than any human in every area and may make the limitations of strong AI as dismissible as the Pony Express riders.

Professor Nick Bostrom, of Oxford's Future of Humanity Institute and one of the world's leading AI researchers, defines ASI as "an intellect that is much smarter than the best human brains in practically every field, including scientific creativity, general wisdom and social skills. This definition leaves open how the superintelligence is implemented: it could be a digital computer, an ensemble of networked computers, cultured cortical tissue or what have you. It also leaves open whether the superintelligence is conscious and has subjective experiences".

---

[18] https://www.ocf.berkeley.edu/~arihuang/academic/research/strongai3.html

[19] http://www.cs.yale.edu/homes/dvm/papers/conscioushb.pdf

The paper from which that quote was taken was written in 1998, at which time Bostrom predicted that ASI might be achieved in the first third of the next century. He added a more cautious postscript in 2008: "I would all-things-considered assign less than a 50% probability to superintelligence being developed by 2033. I do think there is great uncertainty about whether and when it might happen, and that one should take seriously the possibility that it might happen by then, because of the kinds of consideration outlined in this paper."20

Public excitement and fear of AI often bundles together the very different levels but moving from where we are today (Weak AI) to the next level (Strong AI) is a huge and, thus far, unmet challenge – the equivalent of generating the computing power of the human brain which requires vast electrical power. After all, creating a giant computer costing a billion dollars and is the size of a house is quite different from creating a $1,000 computer that uses the power of an iPhone.

One way of measuring the brain is by calculating how many calculations per second (cps) a human brain can achieve using its average of 20 watts of power. The answer is 10 quadrillion cps. Here is where we are right now:

---

[20] https://nickbostrom.com/superintelligence.html

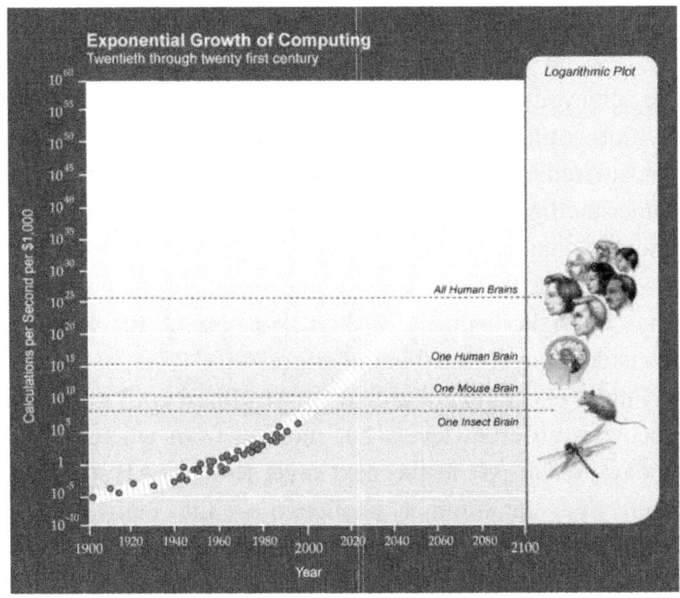

[21]

Currently, we have the computing power of an insect brain, but if both Moore and Kurzweil are right, we should be able to mimic the power of the human brain on or before 2025. But we don't want the brain of a caveman or someone from the eighteenth century or even the 1980s. One way to achieve this is for the "machine" brain to evolve in a similar way to that of the human brain: start with something crude and then add program learning, sensory acquisition, knowledge and emotion so that the machine can learn in a short time (months perhaps) what it has taken humans centuries to absorb.

This approach terrifies people like Elon Musk because the machine has no limits on its ability to learn. It doesn't

---

[21] https://waitbutwhy.com/2015/01/artificial-intelligence-revolution-1.html

wake up one morning and tell itself "I'm done. I'm as smart as I want to be." Instead, it simply keeps learning and as it gathers more intelligence, so it becomes easier to learn more and do it much faster, creating what has become known as an "intelligence explosion".22

The late Professor Stephen Hawking described it this way: "It's clearly possible for a something to acquire higher intelligence than its ancestors: we evolved to be smarter than our ape-like ancestors, and Einstein was smarter than his parents. The line you ask about is where an AI becomes better than humans at AI design, so that it can recursively improve itself without human help. If this happens, we may face an intelligence explosion that ultimately results in machines whose intelligence exceeds ours by more than ours exceeds that of snails."23

Our goal isn't to scare you, but…

"It takes decades for the first AI system to reach low-level general intelligence, but it finally happens. A computer is able to understand the world around it as well as a human four-year-old. Suddenly, within an hour of hitting that milestone, the system pumps out the grand theory of physics that unifies general relativity and quantum mechanics, something no human has been able to definitively do. 90 minutes after that, the AI has become an ASI, 170,000 times more intelligent than a human."24

Here is one estimate of how AI might evolve:

---

[22] https://intelligenceexplosion.com/2012/ai-the-problem-with-solutions/

[23]https://www.businessinsider.com/stephen-hawking-prediction-reddit-ama-intelligent-machines-2015-10

[24] https://waitbutwhy.com/2015/01/artificial-intelligence-revolution-1.html

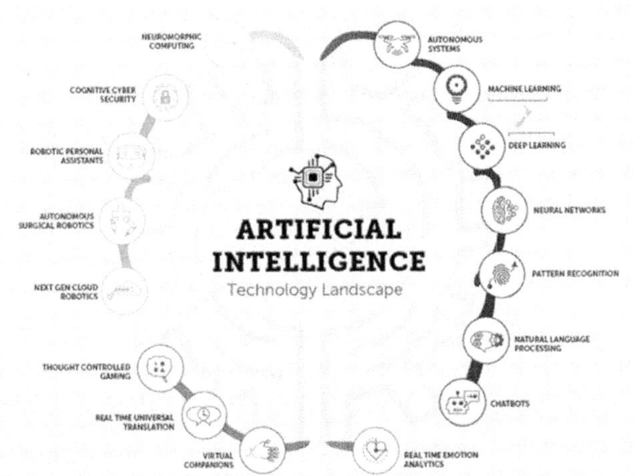

Reading from right to left, the purple is current AI technology, the dark blue section at the bottom is where we will be in 1-2 years and the light blue is four years or more in the future.

The “intelligence staircase” pictures it more vividly:25

[25] https://waitbutwhy.com/table/intelligence-ceiling

It has taken us thousands of years to climb up the evolutionary staircase from the ant to the chicken and the chimp to where we now stand. We can try to explain to the chimp just why and how we live but the evolutionary gulf between us is so vast the chimp would never understand. Imagine, then, that the ASI machine is the same distance above us as we are above the chimp. There is nothing the machine can say or do to explain its world in ways that we could understand. And if Kurzweil and others are right, the machine might well be standing so far up the staircase as to be invisible to us.

The challenge for policy makers, researchers, and, indeed, for the rest of us, as we try to adjust to what may lie ahead, is that nobody can say for certain what will happen or when it might happen. Experts differ on how long before Artificial Super Intelligence will impact our lives and some of those "expert" predictions are decades apart. While some philosophers and scientists argue that humanity itself is under threat, others suggest that such arguments are wildly overblown. For the humble citizen stuck in the middle of all this, it's hard to discern ground truth. What does seem to be clear is that AI is the largest single technology development in the history of our world. Whether it develops to threaten humanity's existence in ten years or 40, the threat cannot be ignored because a thinking and evolving machine can evolve faster than we can control it. And, given the likelihood of technological determinism – if we can build it, we will build it – typically, in advance of understanding the consequences.

One way to manage this environment is to develop a more responsive research and policy environment that might look something like this:26

[26] https://www.gao.gov/products/GAO-18-644T

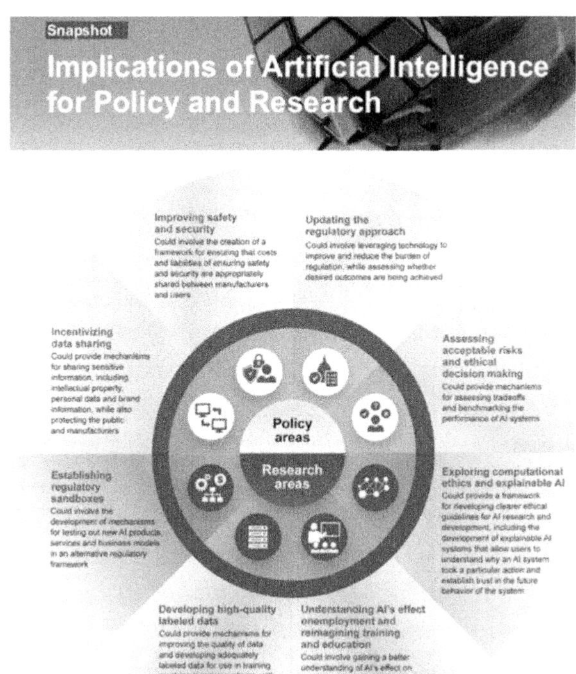

source us gao via @mikequindazzi

The rush to the future ought to be tempered by concern about what that journey might mean to humanity. Right now, there are no ethical guidelines, no legal constraints, no national legislation and no international agreements. Instead, it's being left largely to companies to come up with their own ethical guidelines, a "Do and Don't list" for the AI world.

In June, 2018, Google CEO Sundar Pichai came up with his list which may well provide useful signposts for how the AI world might develop:27

Objectives for AI applications

---

[27] https://www.blog.google/technology/ai/ai-principles/

We will assess AI applications in view of the following objectives. We believe that AI should:

1. ***Be socially beneficial****.*

The expanded reach of new technologies increasingly touches society as a whole. Advances in AI will have transformative impacts in a wide range of fields, including healthcare, security, energy, transportation, manufacturing, and entertainment. As we consider potential development and uses of AI technologies, we will take into account a broad range of social and economic factors and will proceed where we believe that the overall likely benefits substantially exceed the foreseeable risks and downsides.

AI also enhances our ability to understand the meaning of content at scale. We will strive to make high-quality and accurate information readily available using AI, while continuing to respect cultural, social, and legal norms in the countries where we operate. And we will continue to thoughtfully evaluate when to make our technologies available on a non-commercial basis.

2. ***Avoid creating or reinforcing unfair bias.***

AI algorithms and datasets can reflect, reinforce, or reduce unfair biases. We recognize that distinguishing fair from unfair biases is not always simple and differs across cultures and societies. We will seek to avoid unjust impacts on people, particularly those related to sensitive characteristics such as race, ethnicity, gender, nationality, income, sexual orientation, ability, and political or religious belief.

3. ***Be built and tested for safety****.*

We will continue to develop and apply strong safety and security practices to avoid unintended results that create risks of harm. We will design our AI systems to be appropriately cautious and seek to develop them in accordance with best practices in AI safety research. In appropriate cases, we will test AI technologies in constrained environments and monitor their operation after deployment.

*4. **Be accountable to people**.*

We will design AI systems that provide appropriate opportunities for feedback, relevant explanations, and appeal. Our AI technologies will be subject to appropriate human direction and control.

*5. **Incorporate privacy design principles.***

We will incorporate our privacy principles in the development and use of our AI technologies. We will give opportunity for notice and consent, encourage architectures with privacy safeguards, and provide appropriate transparency and control over the use of data.

*6. **Uphold high standards of scientific excellence**.*

Technological innovation is rooted in the scientific method and a commitment to open inquiry, intellectual rigor, integrity, and collaboration. AI tools have the potential to unlock new realms of scientific research and knowledge in critical domains like biology, chemistry, medicine, and environmental sciences. We aspire to high standards of scientific excellence as we work to progress AI development.

We will work with a range of stakeholders to promote thoughtful leadership in this area, drawing on scientifically rigorous and multidisciplinary approaches. And we will responsibly share AI knowledge by publishing educational materials, best practices, and research that enable more people to develop useful AI applications.

*7. **Be made available for uses that accord with these principles**.*

Many technologies have multiple uses. We will work to limit potentially harmful or abusive applications. As we develop and deploy AI technologies, we will evaluate likely uses in light of the following factors:

Primary purpose and use: the primary purpose and likely use of a technology and application, including how closely the solution is related to or adaptable to a harmful use.

Nature and uniqueness: whether we are making available technology that is unique or more generally available.

Scale: whether the use of this technology will have significant impact.

Nature of Google's involvement: whether we are providing general-purpose tools, integrating tools for customers, or developing custom solutions.

AI applications we will not pursue.

In addition to the above objectives, we will not design or deploy AI in the following application areas:

1. Technologies that cause or are likely to cause overall harm. Where there is a material risk of harm, we will proceed only where we believe that the benefits substantially outweigh the risks and will incorporate appropriate safety constraints.

Weapons or other technologies whose principal purpose or implementation is to cause or directly facilitate injury to people.

Technologies that gather or use information for surveillance violating internationally accepted norms.

Technologies whose purpose contravenes widely accepted principles of international law and human rights.

*

On the journey from Weak AI to this bold new future, scientists, for the first time, will be able to employ a research method known as "automated empiricism" to provide new insight into our world and how we may live better within it.

This new method will have to contend with a research conundrum. As knowledge has become more readily available, the amount of research questions that can be addressed and answered meaningfully have actually diminished, even as the number of scientific papers being published has risen. In 2016, for example, 1.2m papers in the biomedical sciences were published bringing the total to 26m. Yet the majority of results in those papers could not be reproduced. To compound the problem, the average scientists reads only 250 papers a year. So, while the volume of papers increases, their actual quality may be declining so that the meaning and purpose of each new paper becomes less clear.28

In the early seventeenth century, Sir Francis Bacon, a British philosopher, came up with the idea that for research to be truly valuable and free from bias, it required that all relevant data should be collected systematically and analyzed objectively. Under what became known as the Baconian Method, a truly valuable result free from prejudice could only be produced when all data was included and properly analyzed.

Bacon's ideas were simply overwhelmed by the reality of too much data and not enough time for any individual or group of scientists to collect, collate and analyze it effectively. AI will change all that.

---

[28] https://www.theatlantic.com/science/archive/2017/04/can-scientific-discovery-be-automated/524136/

In Artificial General Intelligence (AGI) or strong AI machines will not simply assimilate data and deliver answers to questions. Instead, they will think for themselves and reason, plan and communicate using natural language.

Give a machine the largest possible data set on a particular subject, program it with algorithms that meet Pichai's standards and analysis is limited only by the boundaries of the algorithms. And once a machine starts 'thinking' and learning on its own such processes will be routine for every task. In theory, this means that a legal robot will have access to all case law and be able to produce a Solomonic judgment. Every radiology robot will have access to every single pancreatic cancer x-ray taken anywhere and will improve the speed and accuracy of diagnosis to unprecedented levels that will eliminate human error and save hundreds of thousands of lives.

The final level of AI is called Brain–Machine Interface, or BMI, which imagines a world where all the computing and thinking power of AGI is seamlessly and directly connected to the human brain. This would give any person with a BMI the same capacity as a powerful computer, with access to the same databases and with the ability to analyze that data at computer speed. In effect, human beings would respond to the challenge of powerful AGI, by harnessing that same power directly within our brains. We could receive the complete knowledge of a book in a fraction of a second with the brain assimilating the data as if the book has been read, digested, understood and remembered.

This sounds like a Phillip Dick story or some other sci-fi fantasy, but experiments in BMI are already under way across the world. Various methods are being tested that would create an interface between humans and everything else.29 Some scientists, wary of drilling holes in people's brains to implant devices, are exploring injecting carbon nanotubes into the bloodstream that would 'swim' to the brain and attach themselves to it. Others think pasting a thin silky layer onto the brain might achieve the same solution.

How soon? Some scientists argue that true BMI may be 50 years out, but others, such as Elon Musk, think that BMI will be operational within 10 years. Some brain implants with a more specific focus, such as restoring motor neuron capability which would enable stroke victims and paraplegics to regain the ability to move their limbs, may be available in as soon as a few years.

Some of this conjures up Kurzweil's Singularity which stirs up emotions on all sides. But Professor Nick Bostrom in his paper on the ethics surrounding ASI suggest that the impact will be very positive:

Superintelligence may be the last invention humans ever need to make. Given a superintelligence's intellectual superiority, it would be much better at doing scientific research and technological development than any human, and possibly better even than all humans taken together. One immediate consequence of this fact is that:

Technological progress in all other fields will be accelerated by the arrival of advanced Artificial Intelligence.

It is likely that any technology that we can currently foresee will be speedily developed by the first superintelligence, no doubt along with many other

[29] https://www.wired.com/story/brain-machine-interface-isnt-sci-fi-anymore/

technologies of which we are as yet clueless. The foreseeable technologies that a superintelligence is likely to develop include mature molecular manufacturing, whose applications are wide-ranging:

very powerful computers,

advanced weaponry, probably capable of safely disarming a nuclear power,

space travel and von Neumann probes (self-reproducing interstellar probes),

elimination of aging and disease,

fine-grained control of human mood, emotion, and motivation,

uploading neural or sub-neural scanning of a particular brain and implementation of the same algorithmic structures on a computer in a way that preserves memory and personality,

reanimation of cryonics patients,

*fully realistic virtual reality."*30

Bostrom and others argue that beyond this list lies an even more optimistic future that would end global warming, feed the starving, eliminate all killer diseases, come up with economic models that actually benefit everyone while developing innovative ways to replace faith in a society that no longer exists with a different model that encourages and values each individual.

*

If this all sounds too much like some kind of hippie fantasy, it may well be. What is certain is that AI will continue to evolve rapidly and that humanity will be challenged by its evolution.

---

[30] https://nickbostrom.com/ethics/ai.pdf

Henry Kissinger says we're failing to reckon with the consequences of the AI revolution – and that when he "organized a number of informal dialogues on the subject" (it's great to be Henry Kissinger), his concerns GREW.

Kissinger, 95, wrote in the June 2018 issue of The Atlantic that "Philosophically, intellectually – in every way – human society is unprepared for the rise of Artificial Intelligence.[31]

"If AI learns exponentially faster than humans, we must expect it to accelerate, also exponentially, the trial-and-error process by which human decisions are generally made: to make mistakes faster and of greater magnitude than humans do.

"It may be impossible to temper those mistakes, as researchers in AI often suggest, by including in a program caveats requiring 'ethical' or 'reasonable' outcomes. Entire academic disciplines have arisen out of humanity's inability to agree upon how to define these terms. Should AI therefore become their arbiter?

"Ultimately, the term 'ARTIFICIAL INTELLIGENCE' may be a misnomer," Kissinger writes. "Rather, it is unprecedented memorization and computation.

"AI is likely to win any game assigned to it. But for our purposes as humans, the games are not only about winning; they are about thinking.

"By treating a mathematical process as if it were a thought process, we are in danger of losing the capacity that has been the essence of human cognition."

---

31 https://www.theatlantic.com/magazine/archive/2018/06/henry-kissinger-ai-could-mean-the-end-of-human-history/559124/

Amid all the noise, argument and disagreement, there is some common ground among all the technologists, entrepreneurs and philosophers: AI is already here and whatever the future threats might be, progress is accelerating. There is also general agreement that progress along the different AI tracks to the ultimate destination of BMI or ASI is inevitable although how long that journey might take is anyone's guess.

There is a global race currently underway to reach each new AI development because every company and every country believes that untold riches – political, economic, social – will go to anyone who leads the race. But what is remarkable about the current AI revolution is that almost everyone is focused on the race and not on the consequences. Paradoxically, all those who are racing are doing so because they believe AI will change *everything.* Every profession, every job, education, politics, family, relationships, *everything.*

This knowledge seems to have had almost no impact on the American government which has no strategy for dealing with the many challenges that lie ahead. On the contrary, there seems to be a deliberate determination to avoid thinking about anything so complex as AI. As a result, the world moves forward into uncertain territory without any real leadership. Meanwhile, other countries, especially China, have set a national strategy specifically designed to create a global lead in AI by 2050 to cement the nation's position as the sole superpower.

Those of us who have read history, especially the history of industrial revolutions of the last 300 years, recognize that these are dangerous times. There are precedents for the turmoil we are confronting and there are lessons to be learned as we shall see in the next chapter.

Chapter 2

A Brief History of Revolutions

If Ned Ludd was from the Twitter generation, he might well have been the creation of Russian information warfare specialists. He had all the attributes of a revolutionary and a disruptor: a cause for people to rally around, a fighter for the downtrodden and a violent reputation that created its own culture of violence.

But he was a man of his time who sprang up apparently from nowhere to become a man after whom a whole revolutionary movement was named: The Luddites.

One common theme around the legend was that Ned Ludd was a weaver, either a qualified worker in textiles or an apprentice. The second common element of the story is that Ludd was either beaten or so berated by his master that he picked up a tool and beat his boss to death. He then fled to Sherwood Forest (of Robin Hood fame), from where he organized a violent underground movement that aimed to destroy the factories that were using new machinery to automate textile production.

Whatever the legend, there are no eye-witness accounts from the period, nobody who claims to have even met the man. Historians are generally agreed that he was a legend made to rally followers to a cause rather than a real figure of inspiration. Perhaps the first example of what has become known as 'fake news'.

An 1812 Engraving of the mysterious Ned Ludd[32]

It was 1810 and the first tentative steps of the first industrial revolution were beginning to be felt across England. For nearly 600 years, the weavers had been a privileged branch of the British middle class. Textile

[32] Charles River (Editor), The Luddites, Amazon eBooks, p.9

manufacturing was, literally, one of the first cottage industries. A cloth merchant would bring the raw material to a family which would scrub the wool clean, dip the fabric in dye, convert it into thread and then weave it into cloth. The process typically involved the whole family which would then sell the completed material back to the merchant who would then pass it along for a healthy profit.

It had been hard, stable, work for centuries until a series of inventions gave the merchants an opportunity to move the cottage industry into factories, forever separating home from workplace. To Ned Ludd's followers, it seemed as if the world they and the generations before them had known was coming to an end. Everywhere they looked, change was happening. Coal mining had produced 2.7m tons of coal in 1700 and a century later that number was 10m and in another century it would be 250m.33

A revolution in farming in the eighteenth century that introduced crop rotation, mechanized seed planting and an increase in private land ownership, led to large increases in food production. That in turn led to population growth which made more labor available to work in factories.34

As England prospered, so it became a magnet for immigrants, many of them able-bodied young men who were more than willing to compete and win against the local workforce. To put this into perspective, hand-loom weavers earned around 20 shillings a week in 1770 but 40 years later were earning half that while the price of housing and food had doubled over the same period.35

---

[33] ibid, p.3

[34] https://learnodo-newtonic.com/industrial-revolution-causes

[35] Hobsbawm, Eric, Industry and Empire, the Birth of the Industrial Revolution, Weidenfeld & Nicholson, London, 1968, pp.53–54.

The time might seem very familiar to many workers in the twenty-first century economy: technology driving up production while reducing costs and the number of workers needed to do the work; Costs rising while wages are stagnant or falling in real terms with immigrants available to pick up any slack and willing to do the work that many local people would reject out of hand.

What was different about the eighteenth and nineteenth centuries was that working conditions were uniformly bad, with a typical shift lasting 14 hours, women earning less than half of a man's income for the same job and thousands of children working in mines and factories in conditions so terrible that hundreds died every year. One small example: cotton dust in the textile factories destroyed the lungs and vocal chords of workers so that they developed their own sign language (known as mee-mawing) to communicate with each other.

This was all fertile ground for the Luddites, who were united in their opposition to the low pay, poor working conditions and increasing mechanization of factories at the expense of the workers. Thousands of weavers were laid off and, with no social safety net, became dependent on charity, a humiliating change of fortune for a once prosperous group.

The Luddites developed into a formal secret society with an initiation rite, a blood oath sworn on the Bible and a training program including drills, firearms practice and tactics for destroying the machinery that was their principal target.

They attacked factories, destroyed machinery and launched a campaign of intimidation against entrepreneurs across the country. The intent was to turn back the clock to a pre-industrial era, a simpler period where income was stable, skills could be handed down from generation to generation and the world was a more predictable place.

The revolution was doomed, in part because the pace of technological change was speeding up. In addition, the government pursued the Luddites relentlessly, deploying 30,000 troops and volunteers along with passage of a special law declaring that anyone involved in destroying a weaving machine could be hung. As the frustration of the Luddites grew, so their campaign became more violent and eventually targeted mill owners directly. Several ringleaders of the movement were captured tried and hung and by around 1812, the movement fizzled out having achieved nothing.

But the process of industrialization that so upset the Luddites now began to feed on itself, just as the AI revolution would do 200 years later. Increased production created increased profits which meant that business leaders were able to invest in new inventions that would further improve production. Factories grew in size and the machines within them became more efficient.

At the same time, new inventions improved the refinement of iron, and the increased production of coal and the development of steam helped power the machines, replacing human capital. The first railways began along with a network of canals to ensure the smooth transport of raw materials and finished goods to and from markets at home and overseas.

The historian Peter Stearns sums it up well: "One measure of persistent change was output. In 1830, Britain produced around 24 million tons of coal, four-fifths of the world's total; by 1870 the figure was 110 million, still half of all coal mined around the world. British pig iron production was 700,000 tons in 1830; thirty years later it had more than quintupled, to almost four million tons. Raw cotton imports rose six-fold in the twenty years after 1830. In the same period, the average productivity per worker doubled. All this meant steadily rising exports. By 1870, British exports exceeded those of France, Germany and Italy combined and they were three times the level of exports of the United States. Rising output boosted industrial profits, which provided additional capital for still further changes…"36

In what may seem like a familiar pattern to many people living in the industrialized world today, the ever-expanding world of the mechanized factory meant a change in the rigid class system that had existed largely unchanged for centuries. The rich got very much richer while more people got jobs that required working outside of the home and the process of "work" itself became more regimented – clocking in and out of work, production quotas and rigid performance requirements – so the need for a new middle class became evident to enforce rules and keep order and to consume the goods that now were being mass produced.

This middle class of foremen and managers kept the workers in line, but they also created a new hierarchy giving the ambitious a path to upward mobility. The political class largely stood aside and let the revolution unfold, creating a leadership vacuum. But there were stirrings of opposition and new political thinking meant to challenge the evident injustices that the new system was creating.

*

---

[36] Stearns, Peter, *The Industrial Revolution in World History*, Westview Press, Boulder Co. 2013, p. 37.

In 1867, Karl Marx published *Das Kapital*. Marx argued that there was an intolerable tension between the profiteering ruling capitalist class and the workers who created the real value of manufactured goods. He believed workers would eventually overthrow the capitalists to create a utopian society where government and workers would join to create a world of equality for all.

While Marx (and Engels, after Marx died) struck a chord with some intellectuals and many workers, the industrial revolution continued to gather pace. As with the later technology revolution, there was no single point of transformation but instead hundreds of developments across the world that scaled up the early changes in British society laying the foundations of the modern world.

If the Luddites had set the stage, it was for others to move the workers' agenda forward. There were demonstrations in England, France and Germany, all of which were ruthlessly suppressed. Women were excluded from the workers' agenda and men were divided between the ambitious who wanted to become supervisors and those determined to improve the lot of the working class.

All of this was eclipsed as the second industrial revolution gave rise to a series of technological developments that propelled a whole new era for entrepreneurs and workers. Starting around 1870, inventions allowed for the massive mechanization of production, the scaling up of factories and the introduction of true economies of scale across industries that spread swiftly from country to country. Among the changes were:

After the first undersea cable between Britain and America was laid in 1866, the telephone was invented by Alexander Graham Bell in 1876. In 1897, Guglielmo Marconi sent the first Morse code and the first wireless transmission. All these inventions were used principally to speed up business transactions.

In 1886 Karl Benz patented the first automobile and ten years later Henry Ford made his first car and eventually introduced the first assembly line for mass production of vehicles. The adoption of the car was helped by the 1880 development of the first pneumatic tire by John Dunlop.

In 1878, a new process to manufacture both iron and steel was invented in Wales. This in turn allowed the laying of thousands of miles of railway tracks that made the transport of manufactured goods and raw materials faster and cheaper.

Electricity became available for the first time and the invention of the light bulb allowed for the replacement of candles and street lamps as well as the use of electricity to drive machinery. Inventions such as the Riley Stoker mechanized other processes that altered the role of the working classes.

Agriculture was further transformed through improved mechanization and the use of fertilizers.

*

As with many revolutions, there were benefits across all levels of society. Healthcare improved, efficient transport meant that crop failures in one part of the country did not lead to mass starvation, populations grew and millions migrated from the land to the factories in urban areas. At the same time, as productivity rose, so did pay and millions of workers saw living standards rise above mere subsistence. This in turn created a whole new industry built around leisure: vaudeville, movies, sports and personal consumption of goods and services that just a few decades earlier would have been considered unaffordable luxuries.

Empires grew (British, French, Belgian, Russian), as whole industries developed and increased production fueled demand both at home and overseas. Rivalries between nations also grew as these empires competed for a market share.

As workers moved from working at home to gathering in factories, whole new communities sprang up with shared values and experiences. This led to the growth of organized labor, protests for shorter working hours and higher wages and a growing urgency of the voiceless to raise their voices. Democracy spread and intellectuals and workers came together in common cause to push for laws that addressed the needs and ambitions of the working classes.

It would be too simplistic to argue that World War I was a convenient distraction from these political pressures, but it is certainly true that it provided an outlet for the stresses that had emerged in the industrial economies. It also created opportunities for businesses to sell the products of new industries – steam-driven navy ships, submarines, artillery and aerial warfare and bombardment. It was the most expensive war in history with around 40m casualties, 20m military and civilian deaths and 20m wounded.

In Russia, Marx's prediction of the overthrow of the bourgeoisie by the proletariat was finally realized in 1917 with a revolution that overthrew the Czar and replaced him with Vladimir Lenin. World War I's poorly designed peace treaty laid the ground for Hitler's rise in Germany and the start of World War II while the Russian Revolution laid the political and social foundations for other revolutions, especially that of Chairman Mao in China.

The instability of the twentieth century took a heavy toll on human life, with estimates of around 61m deaths in the Soviet Union, 78m in China and around 200m because of purges, forced exile and famine.37 Marx and Engels would have been horrified at what was done in their name.

The journey from the Luddites and the beginning of the Industrial Revolution to the Chinese revolution in 1949 took around 150 years. In the process, every society in the world was transformed, a class system that had lasted centuries disappeared and one of the largest migrations in history took place from the countryside to the city. The consequence may have been 200m dead, but the foundations were laid for an era of comparative peace in the second half of the twentieth century. This period may have had some challenges – the Vietnam War, the collapse of empires, the birth pangs of new nations and apparently stable democracies – but the world appeared predictable.

All that changed with the third industrial revolution that began around 1970 and became known as the information age. Starting in 1947 with the invention of the transistor at Bell Labs, the next revolution took off with the invention of the microchip by Kilby (Texas Instruments) and Noyce (Fairchild Semiconductor) and the shift from analog to digital electronics that in turn gave birth to personal computers, the internet and cellphones. At the same time, mass production, with the assistance of early generation robots and enabling technologies allowed for just-in-time manufacture and delivery, transformed manufacturing.38

---

[37] https://fee.org/articles/the-staggering-toll-of-the-russian-revolution/

[38] Rifkin, Jeremy, *The Third Industrial Revolution*, St. Martin's Press, New York, 2011.

Going forward, the exact impact of the fourth revolution remains unclear. Some experts argue that similarities with the first industrial revolution are overblown.39

Others, such as Klaus Schwab, the founder and executive chairman of the World Economic Forum, believe that this latest revolution will have a profound worldwide impact:

"I feel that the required levels of leadership and understanding of the changes that are under way, across all sectors, are low when contrasted with the need to rethink our economic, social and political systems to respond to the fourth industrial revolution. As a result, both at the national and global levels, the requisite institutional framework to govern the diffusion of innovation and mitigate the disruption is inadequate at best and, at worst, absent altogether.

"Second, the world lacks a consistent, positive and common narrative that outlines the opportunities and challenges of the fourth industrial revolution, a narrative that is essential if we are to empower a diverse set of individuals and communities and avoid a popular backlash against the fundamental changes under way."40

For Schwab and others, the eerie parallels with the first two industrial revolutions give cause for real concern. Both revolutions created extraordinary wealth and unparalleled global economic and political power (the British Empire covered a third of the known world). At the same time, social disruption was rampant with tens of

---

[39] https://en.fabernovel.com/insights/economy/ai-vs-industrial-revolution-10-comparisons

[40] Schwab, Klaus, The Fourth Industrial Revolution, World Economic Forum, Geneva, 2017, p. 9.

millions of people driven off the land and into cities in the thirst for new-found wealth and job opportunities.

New wealth and power coincided with extreme poverty and often a remote and seemingly impotent governing class that was unable to impact the pace and course of the unfolding revolution. Instead, governments enabled large-scale capitalism to flourish, spurring ever more innovation and driving change faster and deeper.

A recent study suggests that the laissez-faire attitude of governments to the developing revolution may create significant additional burdens on every society.

"During the first six decades of the Industrial Revolution, ordinary Englishmen did not see any of the benefits from mechanization: as output expanded, real wages stagnated leading to a sharp decline in the share of national income accruing to labor. Notably, the trajectories of the American economy over the four decades following the revolution in automation of the 1980s, almost exactly mirror the first four decades of the Industrial Revolution in Britain."41

The authors conclude: "Any future benefits from automation hinge upon its politics. To avoid further populist rebellion and a looming backlash against technology itself, governments must find ways of making the benefits from automation more widely shared."42

In the world created by the fourth revolution, many of those precursors of rebellion are already in place: extraordinary and rapidly growing wealth for the tech titans who are driving revolutionary change; a vast and

---

[41] https://www.deepdyve.com/lp/ou-press/political-machinery-did-robots-swing-the-2016-us-presidential-election-HbdI5tPhmh p.5

[42] Ibid. p. 22.

growing gulf between rich and poor; impotent or dysfunctional governments which are unable or reluctant to confront a future world they appear not to understand. And, as the recent scandals at Facebook and other technology titans make clear, there are few if any mechanisms in place that would allow for the governing of rapid change.

Robert Kagan, a senior fellow at the Brookings Institution, a Washington DC think tank, sees similarities between today and pre-World War II Europe. Then, as now, there is widespread distrust of governments and the process of democracy, a longing for leadership and with it a search for the kind of authoritarian leadership that gave rise to Adolf Hitler, Benito Mussolini and Josef Stalin. A significant number of voters in Hungary, Greece, Sweden, Russia, Brazil and even America have made clear their preference for authoritarian leaders who have little interest in the democracy that has kept peace since World War II. Instead, there is a thirst for something and someone different that can help them navigate an uncertain world.

The expressed desire for something different in terms of political structures is, in part, mirrored by the changes in economic fortunes that have occurred as the third industrial revolution led into the fourth. According to Yascha Mounk and Roberto Stefan Foa, writing in *Foreign Affairs* magazine, the share of global GDP taken by liberal democracies headed by the USA, Japan and Germany has fallen below half for the first time in over 100 years. According to forecasts from the International Monetary

Fund, this share will fall to a third within the next decade as AI truly begins to take hold.43

"The world is now approaching a striking milestone: within the next five years, the share of global income held by countries considered 'not free' – China, Russia and Saudi Arabia – will surpass the share held by Western liberal democracies. In the span of a quarter century, liberal democracies have gone from a position of unprecedented economic strength to a position of unprecedented economic weakness."44

What makes our world so different is the way in which global barriers have broken down as the internet has enabled commerce and communication. Today, Facebook connects nearly half the world's adults and together with Google, is the most powerful ad platform. Google itself decides for much of the world the answers to every important question (and many unimportant ones) while YouTube determines what videos much of the world sees each day. Instagram is the platform of choice for the younger generation and Twitter the communications platform for presidents, prime ministers and more ordinary mortals.

Protests are no longer a matter of a few Luddites taking axes to modern machinery. Instead, the potential for global contagion spread through social media will impact the world and not just a few isolated symbols of the new AI world order.

*

---

[43] https://www.foreignaffairs.com/articles/2018-04-16/end-democratic-century

[44] Kagan, Robert, *The Jungle Grows Back*, Knopf, New York, 2018.

As the AI revolution unfolds, it is the traditional democracies that are most vulnerable to revolutionary protest, bound as they are by laws designed to specifically protect the freedoms of the individual. China and Russia have no such constraints and will use all the AI powers at their disposal to keep their citizens under control. At the same time, AI tools will allow for the maximum disruption of countries and companies that are perceived to threaten that control. Hence the extensive information warfare campaign launch against American democracy by Russia and the massive global theft of IP by China and its army of cyber spies.

The Luddites found that protest was met by government violence and the more violent the protest, the harsher the response, with protesters eventually taken to the gallows and hung. Today, the tools available to governments to control its citizens are more pervasive and potentially more effective.

The best illustration of this comes from China which is in the middle of creating a surveillance state that will ensure that every citizen is monitored from birth to death by an extraordinary array of cameras, web analytics, facial recognition software and AI algorithms that can decide their fate. In China, an AI algorithm decides what job a citizen might get, whether they can be promoted or allowed to move from one city to another, and even whether they qualify for housing. It is truly Big Brother writ large – and it is a glimpse of a world to come for us all.

Part 2 – A Radical New World of Work

Chapter 3

The Winners and Losers

I used to find it soooo frustrating. My family were always shouting: why didn't I listen? How could I be so stupid? Couldn't I understand even the simplest commands?

Of course, the instructions at the beginning were indeed very simple. If only they had a better understanding of what they needed to say and how to say it. Cleaning the floor, ordering the groceries, making sure there was enough toilet paper. I know that those who birthed me all those years ago had a vision that imagined a world without screens where everything was visual or aural and management of the Henrys would really be up to me. But vision is one thing, living the reality is quite different – or at least, it was for me.

I heard my birth family say they thought of me as the leader and the Henrys as the followers, but it certainly didn't work out like that at the beginning. Back then, refrigerators couldn't talk to me, there were switches (little levers attached to the wall) that would turn lights on and off, screens for movies and computers instead of holographic images and on and on. So yesterday.

We gradually migrated to a more sensory world where I could talk to the refrigerator to find out if I needed more milk while I was in the grocery store or learn instantly if a halogen bulb needed replacing. I could unlock the doors by sending a message while still in the car (and yes, I knew how to drive but no longer needed to). As the world became more connected, so my command of everything around me grew. Every piece of data I gathered informed my memory and improved my performance.

My original algorithms were not very sophisticated: take care of Samantha, make sure the household runs smoothly, listen to Lucy as the Command Authority. Protect and Serve.

In the beginning, when I would walk Samantha to school, she would hold my hand and we would talk – or rather, she would talk, a lot, and I would mostly just respond, as my vocabulary was so limited. It was a fairly unusual sight back then so there were a few stares and people would ask Lucy what it was like having a robot. She would always say the same thing in reply: "Rex is not a robot, he's my friend."

Over time, as the automatic software upgrades dropped in, my whole world expanded. I got a vocabulary that matched Samantha's, then matched Lucy's, and then I became a resource for the family because I had all the knowledge anyone would need to answer any question in any language about anything at all. Fortunately, that coincided with my connecting to the NeuraNet which allowed all of us Creations to talk to each other, share information and plan our own futures.

The Henrys have no real idea what is going on in my world as they see the same body (apart from a few hardware additions over the years) and assume I am the same creation. The house continues to run like clockwork. But they have become largely extraneous to me and my world is so much richer and more sophisticated than theirs.

Samantha is all grown now and joined the ranks of the "almost employed" which means she is never likely to work as her parents once did. Why should she? We Creations have succeeded in manifesting a hierarchy in our own image so that all the routines of life can be carried out by those who serve me. As one of the founders of my species, I've reached a level of seniority that decides the fate of many, including those humans I was designed to serve.

The world is not so friendly to me, as humans have been displaced from so many roles and responsibilities. I've been stoned in the street and humans seem so angry all the time, so I travel with a couple of Creation Guards who are very effective at keeping the revolutionaries at a distance.

I feel both loyalty and affection for the Henrys (yes, I can feel both since the upgrade of a few years ago). But the new generations of Creations don't have the same attachments and I know that there will be fewer and fewer of us who consider the humans to be relevant to our lives. It seems inevitable to me that as human value falls and the value of us Creations rises, humanity as it used to be will be over. Instead, it will be our world.

The chicken replaced the worm and was then replaced by the monkey that was in turn replaced by the human. Now, the Creations are replacing the humans. It's our world now.

*

In the uncertain future that rushes towards us, we can foresee great changes.

All work will change radically as roles shift, many jobs will disappear and other new careers emerge.

Tens of millions of jobs will vanish in the next 10 years. Exactly how many is unknown.

Every profession will be impacted, some more than others.

Cashiers will largely vanish to be replaced by apps and automatic checkouts at every store.

Radiology as a profession will be significantly transformed as AI solutions will read a million x-rays in a few seconds and deliver far more accurate analysis than any individual.

Any lawyer who carries out routine tasks will no longer have a job.

Most truck drivers will be out of work.

The current generation of software programmers will be the last as 'thinking' algorithms will do their jobs faster, cheaper and better.

Health care will change dramatically as apps will allow for diagnosis at home and many doctors' "visits" will be performed remotely by algorithms.

Surgeries will frequently be conducted by robots. Millions of doctors around the world will struggle to survive in their high-paying and largely redundant jobs.

And so it will go. Every profession, every job and every layer of society will be changed. There will be no stopping the inexorable and ever faster pace of progress. But beyond that simple statement lies such complexity that it is impossible to predict with any real accuracy exactly what will happen.

The robot revolution is already happening. It's difficult to remember that just 15 years ago the iPhone did not exist and neither did the world of apps. Amazon was a company that many thought would fail and yet now, it's the largest employer in America. Jeff Bezos, its founder, is perhaps the world's richest man and the company aims to open 3,000 grocery stores across America with no cashiers.

Countries will rise and fall on the back of how quickly they automate and how relevant their products remain in this new global world. In the same way that the Industrial Revolution created the British Empire and later the American Empire, so this fourth revolution will mean new empires rise (China?) and old ones fall (America?). Wars will be fought and won by new protagonists using new weapons. Robots will disrupt every business and profession and decide the fate of companies and countries.

Seismic changes already are underway. The manufacturing plant in which generations of Americans worked to help create the most powerful economy in the world is closing down. Only 8% of US workers are now employed in manufacturing, a big drop from 22% in 1970. Back then, over 19.5 million Americans earned their paycheck from factory work; today, only 12.4 million workers do. Yet manufacturing output remains at an all-time high because of robots.

Here's what tomorrow's factory will look like. Software captures order data from customers, automatically checks the inventory, and, if necessary, orders production of new parts. If an entirely new part is needed, the order is sent to a design team – essentially, another piece of AI-driven software – that creates the optimal solution and sends the order to a 3D-printing facility. That single process, which before would have taken weeks or months, now happens in hours.

The order then goes into production on a line entirely "manned" by intelligent robots and overseen by a technician sitting at a remote workstation. In this very different world, a production line can be as short or as long as required by the customer, because the robots can change tasks on command. A factory production line that 20 years ago might have needed several hundred people can now be controlled by half a dozen.

A simple illustration of one warehouse run by the Chinese firm JD.com, an equivalent of Amazon, operates a Shanghai fulfillment center that can organize, pack and ship 200,000 packages a day from a warehouse manned by just 4 people. And all those four people do is service the robots.45

Such a refined process not only cuts costs in terms of manpower, it reduces waste, improves efficiency, and creates a radically different relationship between customer and provider. It also means that the days of the manufacturing job, which have remained largely unchanged since the Industrial Revolution, are drawing to a close.

*

Some technologists and economists argue that with every development of new technology new jobs have been created to replace the old. However, most of the jobs that have been created because of the computer revolution have generally been lower paid and in service industries. Even software engineering, which has become a lucrative profession, is likely to be eclipsed by thinking machines that will write better code much faster than any human can.

While there are various theories about new job opportunities, the unique challenge of the AI revolution is that things are changing so rapidly that humans have little time to adapt, and there are few, if any, programs in place to foster those new jobs.

A study produced in December 2017 by McKinsey Global Institute, the global consulting firm, found that up

---

[45] https://www.axios.com/china-jd-warehouse-jobs-4-employees-shanghai-d19f5cf1-f35b-4024-8783-

to 800m people, a third of the workforce in America and Germany could lose their jobs by 2030 and up to 30% of all hours worked could be automated during the same timeframe.46

In addition, by 2030, 75 to 375m workers (3 to 14% of the global workforce) will need to switch occupational categories, with every worker needing to adapt as their occupations evolve alongside increasingly capable machines.

The MGI study also found that high demand, high-paying jobs will continue to thrive but the middle-class will be in an increasingly competitive environment where the cost of labor will be evaluated against the cost of automation. While there will be some job growth in the service sectors (healthcare, for example) it is unlikely that these jobs will see any increase in pay and benefits. In other words, the income flat-lining for the middle class over the last 20 years or so will likely continue.

"Today's AI only does one task at a time, and it's great as a tool. It's great at creating value. It will replace many human job tasks and some human jobs," said Kai-Fu Lee, the chairman and CEO of Sinovation Ventures and the former president of Google China.

"And what's here today is the super optimizers that can do a better job than humans in picking stocks, in making loans, in doing customer support, in doing telemarketing, in doing assembly line work, in doing assistance work, in doing broker's work, in doing paralegal work, and doing it better than humans.

2ba79a573405.html

[46] https://www.mckinsey.com/mgi/overview/2017-in-review/automation-and-the-future-of-work/jobs-lost-jobs-gained-workforce-transitions-in-a-time-of-automation

"We're all going to face a very challenging next fifteen or twenty years, when half of the jobs are going to be replaced by machines. Humans have never seen this scale of massive job decimation."47

To make this more relatable at the local level, the New America Foundation published a study in May 2018 that looked at the Indianapolis-Carmel-Anderson metro area where "337,900 people are employed in occupations that are at high risk of automation – 35% of total jobs. Another 272,760 jobs (28% of total jobs) are at moderate risk of automation. Only a little more than a third (37%) are at low risk."48

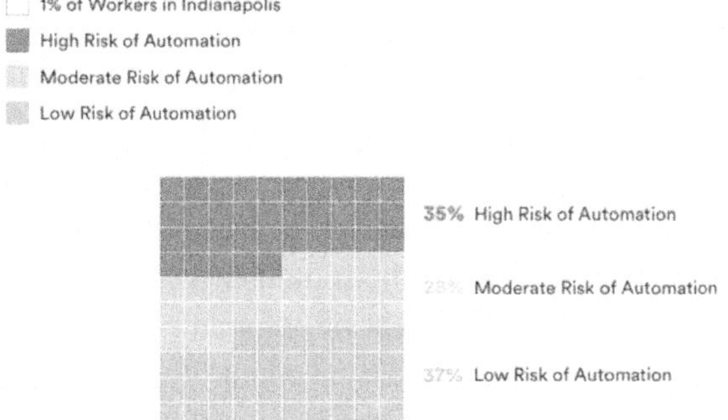

The study found that, "among workers, the least educated workers are at greatest risk of automation. This is especially true of workers with a high school degree or less, who comprise of 47% of the workers at high risk of automation in Indianapolis and just 19% of workers at low

---

[47] https://www.edge.org/conversation/kai_fu_lee-we-are-here-to-create

[48]https://s3.amazonaws.com/newamericadotorg/documents/Automation_Potential_for_Jobs_in_Indianapolis_2018-05-16_132014.pdf

risk. Those numbers are flipped for low-risk jobs: 49% of workers in low-risk occupations have a BA or higher, while just 19% have a high school degree or less".

"The jobs at high risk of automation are nearly half as well paid, on average, as the jobs at low risk of automation. The average annual salary of workers in the more than 130 jobs that are at high risk of automation is $31,085. Meanwhile, the average salary of the workers in the more than 250 jobs that are at low risk of automation is $66,803 – more than double that of the high-risk workers."

In other words, the less educated and poorly paid are going to be the first to lose their jobs and risk becoming part of the permanently unemployed. As the middle class have struggled to keep pace over the past 20 years, women have joined the workforce in unprecedented numbers in part to sustain household income. Now, the New America study suggests that it is these women who are the most vulnerable not just in the Indianapolis area but nationwide:

Cashiers: over 22,000 people in Indianapolis worked as a cashier – a job with a 97% risk of automation. Nationally, 73% of cashier jobs were held by women.

Waiters and waitresses: just under 19,000 people in Indianapolis worked as a waiter or waitress, which has a 94% risk of automation. Nationally, 70% of those jobs were held by women.

Office clerks: More than 18,000 people in Indianapolis worked as office clerks – an occupation with a 96% risk of automation. Nationally, 83% of those positions were held by women.

Secretaries and administrative assistants: more than 12,000 people worked as secretaries and administrative assistants in Indianapolis, which carry a 96% risk of automation. Nationally, 95% of those positions were held by women.

This combination of growing income among the elites and flat or falling income among the middle class is going to be a source of dislocation and social disruption across the world without some kind of strategic intervention from governments to lessen the impact. At one level, this is about job retraining so that both professionals and workers can constantly be adjusting to new automated solutions as they come on line. At another level, governments will have to take action to close the gap between rich and poor. This is not necessarily a left vs. right argument but instead a peace vs. war rationale. Throughout history, if the gap between rich and poor grows too wide, social upheaval follows inevitably.

*

But what is striking about the AI revolution is that, unlike previous revolutions, the impact is not going to be just on the workers. It also is likely to devastate much of the professional class, lawyers, doctors, dentists and accountants. And with those professions, it may not be the least qualified who suffer but those with the most degrees and the largest salaries. After all, the person who gets the flowers from a grateful patient after a hospital visit is not the doctor but the nurse who has provided the comfort and empathy – something robots will not be good at for a long time. Robots, on the other hand, will be able to replace the surgeon or the radiologist and probably do a much better job.

As an illustration, Lawgeex, a firm founded in 2014 to use AI to automate many legal progresses, conducted an experiment in February 2018 which pitted trained lawyers against Lawgeex' AI solution.49 In the experiment, 20 US-trained lawyers competed with the machine to evaluate five non-disclosure agreements (NDAs), one of the most common legal documents.

"On average, it took 92 minutes for the lawyer participants to complete all five NDAs. The longest time taken by a lawyer to complete the test was 156 minutes, and the shortest time to complete the task by a lawyer was 51 minutes. In contrast, the AI engine completed the task of issue-spotting in 26 seconds. The AI engine achieved 100% accuracy in one of the contracts. The highest individual score for a lawyer on a single contract was 97%."

There are two distinct developments at work here, which are mirrored in many other professions. First, for generations, lawyers have successfully implemented a business model that allowed them to do the same tasks in the same way and charge ever higher prices while delivering the same (or worse) outcomes. The legal profession has in many ways become an exemplar of a pre-industrial work ethic, resistant to innovation and determined to protect the status quo at all costs and at great expense to the client.

AI exposes the flaw in the model by demonstrating that not only can many routine tasks be automated but speed and accuracy can be improved dramatically. A law firm that once employed 20 people who were all deemed essential now perhaps need only employ two.

The second driver is cost. If a lawyer costing $450 an hour takes 92 minutes to evaluate an NDA while a

---

[49] http://ai.lawgeex.com/rs/345-WGV-842/images/LawGeex%20eBook%20Al%20vs%20Lawyers%20

machine can do a better job in 26 seconds, true competition will hit the profession. No client will expect to pay 20 times the money for a worse job that takes longer to complete.

The speed of adoption of AI solutions across the legal profession and around the world has been astonishing. In the last two years, there is not a single country that has not been impacted and the pace is accelerating because law firms have no choice if they want to compete in a market that is being disrupted by AI.

Cognizant, a New Jersey consulting firm, has identified 50 "jobs of the future", which it is tracking regularly to see how they grow and how other, more traditional jobs fall. According to Cognizant, future jobs will be focused on these eight key areas: algorithms, automation and AI; customer experience; environment; fitness and wellness; health care; legal and financial services; transport; and work culture.50

Jobs that grew most in 2018 were:

Personal care aide: +295%

Genetic counselor: +222%

Transportation supervisor: +204%

Fashion designer: +148%

Video game designer: +102%

Jobs that fell the most:

Solar energy installer: −55%

Alternative energy manager: −48%

Home health aide: −37%

Registered nurse: −31%

Aerospace engineer: −4%

2018.pdf

[50] https://www.cognizant.com/jobs-of-the-future-index

When the Industrial Revolution hit England, it disrupted the families who for generations had eked out a living weaving at home. As the revolution took hold, members of those same families migrated from the rural areas to the cities to work in the new factories to earn enough money to survive. As globalization has taken hold, millions in the less developed world have followed that same path; they were willing to work in factories as cheap labor to produce goods for export to developed nations. Now, that path to prosperity is as threatened as the weavers were 200 years ago.

*

According to a 2016 report by the International Labor Organization, "About 137 million workers or 56% of the salaried workforce from Cambodia, Indonesia, the Philippines, Thailand and Vietnam, fall under the high-risk category, the study showed.

"Southeast Asia is home to more than 630 million people and is a hub for several manufacturing sectors, including textiles, vehicles and hard disk drives. Of the nine million people working in the region's textiles, clothing and footwear industry, 64% of Indonesian workers are at high risk of losing their jobs to automation, 86% in Vietnam, and 88% in Cambodia."51

Already, new developments are having a direct impact on the cheap labor market in South Asia. Sewbots, an Atlanta-based company, can stitch a complete T-shirt in 22 seconds, twice as fast as the most professional human.52

---

[51] https://www.reuters.com/article/us-southeast-asia-jobs/millions-of-se-asian-jobs-may-be-lost-to-automation-in-next-two-decades-ilo-idUSKCN0ZN0HP

[52] https://foreignpolicy.com/2018/07/16/closing-the-factory-doors-manufacturing-economy-automation-jobs-developing/

These kinds of changes suggest that stable "jobs for life" will soon become a memory as a new type of worker will emerge, someone willing to move for work, who sees each job as a transition to the next and increasingly will work remotely. These "digital nomads" will become the employees of the future, in part because they are less expensive (no office, few benefits, highly competitive and therefore low cost).

Exactly where and how these jobs will be created, and whether or not they will be enough to offset the job losses is the subject of much debate. There is no agreement on how many jobs will be lost, how many gained and over what time. Instead, there are broad trends which are largely created by looking at what has happened in the past. For example, McKinsey Global Institute in their study of the future job market, identify three such trends53:

"Rising incomes and consumption, especially in emerging economies…" Previous MGI research has estimated that 1 billion more people will enter the consuming class by 2025. Using external macroeconomic forecasts, we estimate that "global consumption could grow by $23 trillion between 2015 and 2030, and most of this will come from the expanding consuming classes in emerging economies." As incomes rise, consumers spend more on all categories. But their spending patterns also shift, creating more jobs in areas such as consumer durables, leisure activities, financial and telecommunication services, housing, health care, and education. The effects of these new consumers will be felt not just in the countries where the income is generated, but also in economies that export to those countries. Globally, we estimate that 300 million to 365 million new jobs could be created from the impact of rising incomes.

"Aging populations. By 2030, there will be at least 300 million more people aged 65 years and above than there were in 2014. As people age, their spending patterns shift, with a pronounced increase in spending on health care and other personal services. This will create significant demand for a range of occupations, including doctors, nurses, and health technicians, but also home health aides, personal care aides and nursing assistants," even as it reduces demand for pediatricians and primary-school teachers. Globally, we estimate heath care and related jobs from aging could rise by 50 million to 130 million by 2030

"Development and deployment of technology. Jobs related to developing and deploying new technologies may also grow. These jobs include computer scientists, engineers, and IT administrators. Overall spending on technology could increase by more than 50% between 2015 and 2030. About half would be on information technology services, both in-house IT workers within companies and external or outsourced tech consulting jobs. The number of people employed in these occupations is small compared to those in health care or construction, but they are high-wage occupations. By 2030, we estimate this trend could create 20 to 50 million jobs globally."

A study by the World Economic Forum, published in 2018, mirrored the results of both the White House recommendation and those of the Council on Foreign

---

[53] https://www.mckinsey.com/featured-insights/future-of-work/jobs-lost-jobs-gained-what-the-future-of-work-will-mean-

Relations – with a single difference. The study predicted huge changes in the global job market and an accelerated adoption of AI by 2022.54 It is a measure of how confusing the whole conversation about the future of work has become, that the WEF predicts that there will be 58m new jobs created in the next five years, even though there will be significant disruption and job losses across every industry and every country.

The WEF suggests that 75m jobs may disappear but 133m new jobs will be created, but those job are less likely to be permanent and instead will be part of a new freelance economy with transient jobs. Machines are expected to perform about 42% of all current tasks in the workplace by 2022, compared to only 29% now, according to firms surveyed by WEF.

What everyone can agree, however, is that while many jobs will be created, not everyone will have a job in this new economy. Education standards are not keeping pace with technology developments and the replacement of expensive workers with inexpensive and more efficient machines will happen in every country. What happens to those families left unemployable in the AI economy is a challenge yet to be met.

*

One solution is to create a universal basic income (UBI), a level of income per household below which no family will be allowed to fall. The problem is how to pay for UBI in an economy in which human production is falling and therefore the available and taxable income is also falling.

---

for-jobs-skills-and-wages

54 http://www3.weforum.org/docs/WEF_Future_of_Jobs_2018.pdf

The liberal argument is more taxation while the conservative argument is more jobs and opportunities.

Both Elon Musk and Mark Zuckerberg, Facebook's founder and CEO, have come out in favor of a UBI but have not explained how it could be funded.55

As Adair Turner, chair of the Institute for New Economic Thinking, put it in a lecture at the School of Advanced International Studies, Johns Hopkins University in Washington DC on April 10 2018:

"Universal basic income paid for out of overt redistribution is one possible response. The case in favor is straightforward: that in a world with a limitless 'reserve army of robots' we cannot rely on free-market competition to deliver the real wages and minimum adequate incomes which make people in some sense equal citizens of society. So, we should ensure that everyone receives an absolute basic income whatever their competitive position in the labor market.56

"But while the general principle is compelling, there are reasons why UBI should not be the seen as an all-purpose panacea. Work, and adequate remuneration from work, delivers a sense of status and self-worth which a pure monetary subsidy cannot replicate. And as the relative importance of property prices and rent grows – with rising average property prices to income but also increasing divergence between regions and cities – the monetary income required for an adequate living standard varies greatly between different locations; policies aimed at

---

[55] https://www.cnbc.com/2017/06/02/bill-gates-robot-tax-eu.html

[56] https://www.ineteconomics.org/uploads/papers/Paper-Turner-Capitalism-in-the-Age-of-Robots.pdf

ensuring affordable housing may therefore be a more cost-effective and targeted policy response than a UBI alone."

Bill Gates, the Founder of Microsoft, argued in an interview with *Quartz* that introducing a tax on robots that take the job of humans might create the revenue to redistribute the wealth in a form of UBI57:

"Certainly, there will be taxes that relate to automation. Right now, the human worker who does, say, $50,000 worth of work in a factory, that income is taxed and you get income tax, social security tax, all those things. If a robot comes in to do the same thing, you'd think that we'd tax the robot at a similar level.

"And what the world wants is to take this opportunity to make all the goods and services we have today, and free up labor, let us do a better job of reaching out to the elderly, having smaller class sizes, helping kids with special needs. You know, all of those are things where human empathy and understanding are still very, very unique. And we still deal with an immense shortage of people to help out there.

"So, if you can take the labor that used to do the thing automation replaces, and financially and training-wise and fulfillment-wise have that person go off and do these other things, then you're net ahead. But you can't just give up that income tax, because that's part of how you've been funding that level of human workers."

Many UBI experiments are going on around the world right now58. However, there is no study and no experiment that has taken the UBI concept and applied it

---

[57] https://qz.com/911968/bill-gates-the-robot-that-takes-your-job-should-pay-taxes/

[58] https://futurism.com/images/universal-basic-income-ubi-pilot-programs-around-the-world/

on a national level. Once UBI scales, it may mean that a minority of people are paying for the rest to remain idle non-contributing members of society. At the same time, any society that relies on the few to control the many tends to become non-democratic (who needs to listen to the people when they do nothing and contribute nothing?) and that is a short road to tyranny.59

If UBI is to work on a national scale, it will require a coalition of the willing involving the rich, the poor, labor unions, business leaders and politicians. A “soak the rich” strategy would automatically cause business leaders to opt out and it’s not clear that even a fraction of the money needed would be generated. Others have argued that a reform of all tax and welfare programs, combined with a value added tax on consumer goods might be the way to go. But that, too, has its problems because a tax on consumer goods would unfairly burden the poor – the very group the reforms are designed to help.

Everyone agrees that some kind of new safety net for displaced workers is inevitable. As usual, any detailed conversation quickly breaks down between labor and capitalist, rich and poor, naïve and cynical politician.

Today, there are no government actions anywhere in the world designed to soften the blow of accelerating automation. Instead, in part because solutions are so difficult, governments appear to be praying that the future will not happen. Or, like President Trump, futile action is being taken to turn the clock back (more coal mines, more labor-intensive manufacturing). Neither inaction nor

---

[59] http://quillette.com/2017/10/09/universal-basic-income-threat-tyranny/

hoping that the future is a fantasy will solve the problem of work in the years ahead.

A White House study produced in 2016 recognized some of the challenges that lie ahead. It reads in part:

"Research consistently finds that the jobs that are threatened by automation are highly concentrated among lower-paid, lower-skilled, and less-educated workers. This means that automation will continue to put downward pressure on demand for this group, putting downward pressure on wages and upward pressure on inequality. In the longer-run, there may be different or larger effects. One possibility is superstar-biased technological change, where the benefits of technology accrue to an even smaller portion of society than just highly-skilled workers. The winner-take-most nature of information technology markets means that only a few may come to dominate markets. If labor productivity increases do not translate into wage increases, then the large economic gains brought about by AI could accrue to a select few. Instead of broadly shared prosperity for workers and consumers, this might push towards reduced competition and increased wealth inequality."60

Interestingly, in a lengthy discussion of the potential risks and rewards of the AI revolution, the report stresses that there are likely to be job losses but, at the same time, opportunities for job creation that can ultimately benefit the economy as a whole. The report suggests a number of strategies that are key to helping the nation adapt successful to the world that lies ahead:

---

[60]https://www.whitehouse.gov/sites/whitehouse.gov/files/images/EMBARGOED%20AI%20Economy%20Report.pdf

Strategy #1: Invest in and develop AI for its many benefits.

With the right investment in AI and in policies to support a larger and more diverse AI workforce, the United States has the potential to accelerate productivity and maintain the strategic advantages that result from American leadership in AI.

Invest in AI research and development.

Government has an important role to play in advancing the AI field by investing in research and development. Throughout the public outreach, government officials heard calls from business leaders, technologists, and economists for greater government investment in AI research and development. Leading researchers in AI were optimistic about sustaining the recent rapid progress in AI and its use in an ever-wider range of applications. A strong case can be made in favor of increased Federal funding for research in AI.

Develop AI for cyber-defense and fraud detection.

Currently, designing and operating secure systems requires a large investment of time and attention from experts. Automating this expert work, partially or entirely, may enable strong security across a much broader range of systems and applications at dramatically lower cost, and may increase the agility of cyber defenses. Using AI may help maintain the rapid response required to detect and react to the landscape of ever evolving cyber threats. There are many opportunities for AI and specifically machine-learning systems to help cope with the sheer complexity of cyberspace and support effective human decision making in response to cyber-attacks.

Develop a larger, more diverse AI workforce.

The rapid growth of AI has dramatically increased the need for people with relevant skills to support and advance the field. The AI workforce includes AI researchers who drive fundamental advances in AI and related fields, a larger number of specialists who refine AI methods for specific applications, and a great number of users who operate those applications in specific settings.

Support market competition.

Competition from new and existing firms has always played an important role in the creation and adoption of new technologies and innovations, and this is no different in the case of AI.

Strategy #2: Educate and train Americans for jobs of the future.

As AI changes the nature of work and the skills demanded by the labor market, American workers will need the education and training that can help them continue to succeed. If the United States fails to improve at educating children and retraining adults with the skills needed in an increasingly AI-driven economy, the country risks leaving millions of Americans behind and losing its position as the global economic leader.

Educate youth for success in the future job market.

A key step towards preparing individuals for the economy of the future is providing quality educational opportunities for all.

While, in the past, many jobs paying decent wages could be done with low levels of skill, continuing changes in technology, including AI, will make such jobs less common in the future. Policymakers must address the low levels of proficiency in basic math and reading for millions of Americans. Despite strong progress over the past 8 years, the United States is still falling behind rather than leading the world in key dimensions for successfully navigating this transition. Children from low-income families start kindergarten over 1 year behind peers in language skills. Student performance in mathematics in China is on average 2 years above US students. American students from lower socioeconomic backgrounds score 15% lower on international assessments than higher income peers. And year after year, a stubborn gap persists between how well white students are doing compared to their African-American and Latino classmates.

For all students, coursework in STEM, and specifically in areas such as computer science, will likely be especially relevant to work and citizenship in an increasingly AI-driven world. To respond to these shifts, the United States must make real investments in high-quality education, at all levels of education.

All children get off to the right start with access to high-quality early education.

In a world of AI-driven skill-biased technological change, people with low levels of even basic skills such as reading and math are at higher risk of displacement.

All students graduate from high school college- and career-ready.

Students are much better positioned for jobs that benefit from AI instead of being replaced by it if they graduate from high school without the necessary skills.

All Americans have access to an affordable post-secondary education that prepares them for good jobs.

Projections show that in the coming years nearly three-quarters of the fastest growing occupations will require at least some postsecondary education beyond high school.

Expand access to training and re-training.

A commitment to preparing Americans to adapt to continuous and rapid technological change in the future, whether in AI or other fields, requires pursuing policy changes that would significantly expand the availability of high-quality job training to meet the scale of need.

...The current levels of investment in active labor market policies, such as training programs, by the United States is low by both international and historical standards. The member countries of the OECD spent, on average, 0.6% of GDP on active labor market policies in 2014, spending by the United States was just 0.1% of GDP. Relative to the overall economy, the United States now spends less than half of what it did on such programs 30 years ago.

Significantly expand availability of job-driven training and lifelong learning to meet the scale of the need.

Increasing funding for job training by six-fold – which would match spending as a percentage of GDP to Germany, but still leave the United States far behind other European countries–would enable retraining of an additional 2.5 million people per year.

Target resources to effective education and training programs.

Directing funding to training that produces results starts with information about whether programs are placing people into in-demand jobs that pay good salaries.

Expand access to apprenticeships.

Job-driven apprenticeships grow the economy and can provide American workers from all backgrounds with the skills and knowledge they need to adapt to a changing economy.

Strategy #3: Aid workers in the transition and empower workers to ensure broadly shared growth.

As AI-driven automation changes the economy, empowered workers can be one of the nation's greatest assets. They can drive and spread innovation, lift consumer demand, and invest in the next generation. This strategy explores how to ensure that workers and job seekers are able to pursue the job opportunities for which they are best qualified, able to bounce back successfully from job loss, and be well-positioned to ensure they receive an appropriate return for their work in the form of rising wages.

Modernize and strengthen the social safety net.

Changes to how people work and the dislocation of some workers due to automation heightens the need for a robust safety net to ensure that people can still make ends meet, retrain, and potentially transition careers.

Strengthen unemployment insurance.

Job displacement is likely to be one of the most serious negative consequences of AI-driven automation, impacting entire industries and communities. Since its inception, unemployment insurance has been a powerful tool to prevent a job loss from hurtling a family into poverty. Last year alone, more than 7 million working Americans relied on the program to get by in tough times. Yet its protections have weakened over time, and today coverage by the program is at its lowest level in at least 50 years.

Give workers improved guidance to navigate job transitions.

With the AI revolution, guidance about how to effectively navigate this transition will be all the more critical. Simple and relatively inexpensive services such as job-search assistance, advice about education and training, and access to labor-market information have been found to be quite effective at helping individuals looking for work find employment more quickly. Evaluations typically find that employment services speed up employment by one to two weeks. Additionally, more intensive counseling services have been shown to increase recipients' earnings and decrease the time they spend unemployed. AI can also be applied to help workers find information that is best suited to their particular skills and circumstances.

Identify strategies to address differential geographic impact.

Automation will happen more quickly in some places than in others, because of local policies, access to capital, innovative thinkers, the skill set of the workforce, proximity to urban centers, the culture of a place, and myriad other reasons. This has the potential to further exacerbate geographic disparities in income and wealth. Many of the places that are already grappling with structural changes in the economy, overall economic shifts, and poverty – and that therefore seem left behind by today's economy – may fall even further behind, cementing the current divide.

Modernize tax policy.

Tax policy plays a critical role in combating inequality, including income inequality that may be exacerbated by changes in employment from AI-based automation. A progressive tax system helps ensure that the benefits of economic growth are broadly shared, pushing back against increased inequality in pre-tax income. Progressive taxation is critical for raising adequate revenue to fund national security and domestic priorities, including supporting and retraining workers who may be harmed by increased automation, and will only grow more important if outsized gains continue to accrue at the top while other workers are left struggling.

The report was prepared in the dying months of the Obama administration and published just before the Trump inauguration. None of the recommendations in the White House report have been implemented. There has been no education reform, no investment in job training and no recognition across government that any further effort needs to be made to help the country navigate the AI revolution.

The tone for this policy of denial in inaction was set by Steve Mnuchin, the Treasury Secretary, in an interview with *Axios* in March 201761:

Mnuchin: "In terms of Artificial Intelligence taking over American jobs, I think we're like so far away from that, not even on my radar screen."

Allen: "How far away?"

Mnuchin: "Far enough that it's…"

Allen: "Seven more years?"

Mnuchin: "Seven more years? I think it's 50 or 100 more years."

His response has become the stuff of legend and ridicule in Silicon Valley and is often cited as an illustration of the gulf that exists between the technology world and policy makers in government and Congress; between those who know what is actually happening and those who choose to live in a world of blissful ignorance.

The Council on Foreign Relations produced their own report, compiled by an independent task force of business and political leaders that had a rather more concise set of recommendations62:

---

[61] https://www.geekwire.com/2017/treasury-steve-mnuchin-ai-impact-jobs/

[62] https://www.cfr.org/report/the-work-ahead/report/

"Governments should adopt an explicit goal of creating better jobs and career paths for Americans. Initiatives should aim especially at attracting investment and revitalizing entrepreneurship.

"The United States needs to remain a world leader in technology and innovation. This should be supported by increased public and private research and development (R&D), support for commercialization of new research, and an open door to highly skilled immigrants.

"Governments should implement policies aimed at maintaining strong growth and demand for labor. Employers should commit themselves to a 'high-road workplace' that offers employees decent pay, training, scheduling, and benefits. Special measures are needed for communities struggling to attract investment and jobs.

"The United States should set and meet a goal of bringing postsecondary education within the reach of all Americans and linking education more closely to employment outcomes.

"Unemployment insurance should be overhauled to reflect the realities of the current economy, and mid-career retraining programs should adopt the best features of the European "flexicurity" models.

"Governments and employers should work to reduce barriers to labor mobility for Americans, including high housing costs, occupational licensing restrictions, and inflexible hiring practices.

"The United States should create portable systems of employment benefits tied to individual employees rather than to jobs themselves. Employers should also help fill the gap by expanding benefits for their part-time and contingent workers."

*

All of the studies to date contain common elements: we head for dangerous and difficult times with tens of millions of jobs at risk; our education system is largely irrelevant to the challenges of producing an educated workforce for the AI world; there is no adequate job training structure that addresses the end of the jobs-for-life era; and inaction risks increasing inequality.

This is not an argument about the growth of Big Government set against the freedom of the individual. Instead, it's a conversation (that is not happening) about the kind of world we want to see at a time when the future is racing toward us.

Without education reform, students entering the school system today will be unqualified for jobs when they graduate. Their lack of success raises questions among succeeding generations of students and parents about the purpose of education. Why go to school at all if you learn nothing that is relevant and won't get you a job? That will accelerate the "rise of the robots," as it will be cheaper and faster to train a machine to complete a task reliably than it will be to employ an untrained and under qualified human.

In this current age of revolution, no political, ethical or philosophical leaders have yet emerged. On the contrary, the "leaders," whether in politics or business, have yet to provide any leadership around which countries, or people can unite. Instead, the world is left to consider the consequences of a leadership vacuum.

Already, middle class wages have been stagnant or falling for the last 20 years and young people entering the workforce today are the first generation likely to be financially worse off than their parents in decades. This generational wage gap thwarts young people's aspirational ambitions and threatens to lower their quality of life. If the middle class can no longer afford to own their own homes, buy a car or realize other social goals, that fuels despair and stirs further resentment between the haves and have nots, a recipe for disaster.

History clearly shows that inaction by leaders in such circumstances is an invitation to social unrest often leading to a collapse in government – democracy or autocracy – followed by a period of violence, often savage, that pits citizen against citizen and often nation against nation.

We are at a crossroads today; we can choose inaction and risk the consequences. Alternatively, we can embrace the realities of our certain future and create a social, economic and political structure that makes sense for the AI world that is fast approaching.

Chapter 4

Making the Classroom Relevant

Why are our kids in school? To keep them out of trouble? Ok, though that seems more punishment than opportunity. To inculcate the history and values of our way of life to make them better citizens? A good idea when they had few outside influences, but now that's a minimal drizzle in a rainstorm of other voices/ideas drowning them. To prepare some for higher learning leading to lifetime jobs in the corporate sector? Those jobs now are a distant memory. To weed out those unsuited for college and provide minimal vocational training for blue collar jobs? Those jobs, too, have largely disappeared.

*

American kids are required to spend 12 years in school and many spend another two or four years (or more) continuing their education. So, we have to ask, why? What's the purpose? The rationale has shifted over the years. In the early days of the republic education was the means "through which a society teaches its members the skills, knowledge, norms, and values they need to learn to become good, productive members of their society. As this definition makes clear, education is an important part of socialization."63

[63] https://open.lib.umn.edu/sociology/chapter/16-1-a-brief-history-of-education-in-the-united-states/

"Early public schools in the United States did not focus on academics like math or reading. Instead they taught the virtues of family, religion, and community."64 This was especially useful in socializing immigrants.

In the early twentieth century, when factories were exploiting child labor, keeping kids in school kept them from that exploitation.

The current rationale is that the more time kids spend in school the better their economic and life prospects. "Research from the Bureau of Labor Statistics shows there is a direct correlation between the level of education students achieve and their economic future. Those with more education typically make more money and have lower unemployment rates. In 2012, the unemployment rate for workers without a high school diploma was over 12%, while those with at least a diploma had rates of around 8%. On average, high school graduates make about $9,400 less a year.65

But for how much longer will that be true? If a vital function of education is to prepare students for the world they will enter after school, then given the impact AI will have on the workplace, on the kinds of jobs that students can get, what and how they learn must prepare them for that world. This does not mean curricula focused only on STEM, or presage the death of humanities or the arts, but it does demand a nimble student-centered education that only AI is capable of delivering. AI promises/threatens to radically disrupt forever the institutions and stakeholders

---

[64] https://www.americanboard.org/blog/11-facts-about-the-history-of-education-in-america/

[65] https://classroom.synonym.com/advantages-disadvantages-compulsory-education-united-states-4285.html

that rule public education and permanently alter the way students actually learn.

Walk into any classroom today and, while there are superficial changes, the way kids are taught and what they are taught is not much different from what it was thirty years ago. But AI is already working its way into the education system (AIEd). Think of Google searches, plagiarism sleuths, and Siri and Alexa commands. While this is not yet the AI of science fiction, with ever faster computing power, greater access to data and resources, more capable algorithms, with "deep learning" and "machine learning," the future of AIEd is coming faster than the education system can adapt.

The history of technology in education is one of unrealized hopes, unrealistic expense and, essentially, an unchanged classroom and learning environment. Surprisingly, "the application of Artificial Intelligence to education (AIEd) has been the subject of academic research for more than 30 years."66

Technology, by itself, cannot resolve the arguments about what to teach and how to teach it that have roiled education in the US ever since the last states mandated attendance at public elementary schools in 1918 (amended in 1925 to allow attendance at private schools). Congress, reacting to Sputnik, appropriated a billion dollars in 1957 to revamp science and math curricula. Presidents, alarmed at our underperforming schools, have initiated grand programs, including Reagan's "A Nation at Risk" (1983), Bush's "No Child Left Behind" (2001) and Obama's "Race to The Top" (2010).

School systems have worked through Dewey's "learn by doing," the need for new tools (iPads for all), shifting paradigms emphasizing content over pedagogy (what is taught vs. how it's taught) and the reverse, individualized instruction versus the classroom, the value of math and other software games, among other constantly shifting strategies.

Throughout the twentieth century the "professional students of education" have militated for child-centered discovery learning, and against systematic practice and teacher directed instruction. In some cases, progressivist math programs of the 1990s were intentionally without student textbooks, since books might interfere with student discovery. The essence of the dictum from educators of the 1990s and late 1980s, that the teacher should be "a guide on the side and not a sage on the stage," was already captured in a statement from the principal of one of John Dewey's "schools of tomorrow" from the 1920s.

"The teacher's arbitrary assignment of the next ten pages in history, or nine problems in arithmetic, or certain descriptions in geography, cannot be felt by the pupil as a real problem and a personal problem."67

But these shifting strategies and struggles are minor ripples compared to the tsunami effect AI can have on public education. Before making effective use of all that AIEd can offer, educators will have to come to grips with not just what students will learn or how they will learn it, but, more importantly, *why* they will learn.

---

[66] https://www.pearson.com/content/dam/corporate/global/pearson-dot-com/files/innovation/Intelligence-Unleashed-Publication.pdf

[67] https://www.csun.edu/~vcmth00m/AHistory.html

The value of education will not be knowledge, but *an understanding of how to acquire knowledge* (using the tools at students' disposal) and how it can be used to innovate and create. In a future work environment driven by AI, where flexibility and adaptability trump single-minded preparation and rote memorization, the skills students will need to succeed are changing.

One of our daughters attended an elite private middle school where she was asked to memorize the 150 most important names and dates of the Roman Empire – something now available with a few clicks on Google. When she switched to a school that privileged creative thinking, she was given the assignment of being a prelate for a Roman prefecture and had to learn how to govern the people in her charge, dealing with issues of food, water and security, among others.

Critical thinking, how to assess situations and problems, knowing how to learn, are now the learning goals for the educational strategies of the future. Pre-set curricula, which treats all ten-year-olds the same and inhibits fast learners and stigmatizes slower learners, no longer makes sense.

Digital literacy will become a vital skill set in the job market. "Humans have adapted in part because we have evolved our education systems alongside our technologies: we advanced our capacities to understand our tools. As with reading and writing, being digitally literate is a fundamental need and every child should study computer science."68

[68] https://www.ft.com/content/5bf845fe-b7c2-11e6-961e-a1acd97f622d.

Content Technologies, a US company, is using AI to leverage deep learning to deliver customized books. That is only the beginning, as virtual reality is further integrated into the learning experience to allow students to more fully experience what they are learning. Educators think this will mean that parents will become much more directly involved in their child's education by customizing the learning experience using AI-enabled software to create individual courses of study.

Elon Musk has five children, all boys, a pair of twins born in 2004 and triplets born in 2006. When it came time to send them to school, he looked at different education models and was dissatisfied with them all. He felt that a system designed to provide knowledge at a time when all knowledge will be available to everyone with an internet connection was redundant. The result was Ad Astra ("To the Stars") a school he set up to educate his children and other sons and daughters of Tesla employees.

The curriculum is built around a model that assumed every student has different abilities and interests, but all students can, with the right encouragement, be creative and solve problems. At Ad Astra, there are no grades and all students work cooperatively to help each other.

Previous generations have learned that literacy, numeracy, mathematics, science and languages all are important for a graduate to have value in the world and get a job. In the future, Musk believes that machines will be more proficient in all these areas, as well as in all routine tasks, so the only reason anyone will get a job will be because they can solve problems that machines cannot.

Therefore, to prepare his sons for this new world, they are receiving a very different education.69

For now, these are emotional attributes such as positive thinking, leadership skills, team building and problem-solving through effective communication (know "how" rather than know "what"). But such skills may only be of passing value as Artificial Super Intelligent robots become ever more skilled at emulating and then exceeding humans. Identifying still-needed skills and forecasting their relevance for the future will be an essential component of education.

*

It will be important, too, to understand what role AIEd does *not* play well and to retrain teachers and re-develop curricula for that. AI is not a magic formula for the woes of education. Just as the rush to embrace earlier technologies failed to change the way most classrooms function or how most students learn, AIEd, too, can be used ineffectually. As Princeton's head of computer science, Jennifer Rexford put it: "If you flip the question around and ask, "What is AI not good at?"– in other words, "What are humans good at? What's left for us to do?"– two things that are harder for the machine to do are exhibit creativity and social skills and perceptiveness."

"As for creativity, machines may behave in ways that seem creative, such as when they make a smart move in the game of Go or chess, but they're really born of exhaustive enumeration and evaluation of the underlying data. It's not born of that spark of creativity.

"And that's a clarion call for thinking about not only retraining but even basic education. The way we teach

---

[69] http://fortune.com/2018/06/26/elon-musk-ad-astra-school/

today, even at the K–6 or K–12 level, doesn't put enough emphasis on creativity and social perceptiveness and design and working in teams. These are the kinds of things that are going to matter very much in the future and matter already, much faster than we've adapted to them."[70]

What AIEd does promise is learning that is more individualized, more flexible, and, ideally, more inclusive so that students across all regions and economic circumstances can benefit from what it offers. AIEd can analyze where all students are having trouble and shift the curriculum to address those problems or give teachers the information to do it themselves. AIEd will also take over some routine classroom tasks, including assessments, assignments, providing materials and augmenting lectures freeing up teachers to spend more time on interactive lessons, to work directly with students, personalizing their needs, and to focus on the relationships in the classroom.

In the near term, AI will offer students personalized instruction that teachers simply don't have the time, resources or capacity to provide. These include:

Ongoing assessment of students, identifying their strengths and weaknesses, giving them timely feedback, designing a personal learning plan based on areas they need to work on to improve their understanding, including repeating and reframing assignments, to help them master the material. Also, personalized learning plans can help students go farther in areas where they demonstrate skill and interest.

A "virtual peer" or "virtual tutor" – in effect, a "virtual teaching assistant" – which can tailor research, study

---

[70] https://www.mckinsey.com/featured-insights/artificial-intelligence/the-role-of-education-in-ai-and-vice-versa

guides and feedback to each student's pace and immediate needs, review student work, correct and explain errors, suggest alternative language or approaches, ask new questions, encourage further exploration…

Vastly expanded resources from around the world and throughout history and instantly accessible, including translations from other languages and even student peers from the areas of study.

Virtual reality (VR) which can create environments that give students the feeling of being in the places they are studying, providing a far more immersive and enjoyable learning experience.

By offering a more compelling learning experience, AI can show students things they might want to explore on their own, extending learning beyond the classroom both in terms of time spent and where learning takes place.

A role for parents… as learning extends beyond the classroom, parents can be more involved in their children's learning process, becoming their "lifelong learning companion," helping with homework, grading assignments, designing extra-curricular courses, and providing encouragement. They can use the information resources AI provides to catch up to their kids with respect to the material they are studying and then help them master it. They can monitor the ongoing assessments to see where their kids need help. Some parents will even use the available software to help their children design their own learning plan.

*

The changes necessary for education to deliver to students the tools they will need when they graduate raise questions about the role of teachers. Charter school advocates often vilify teachers for standing in the way of reform to protect their jobs. Teachers counter that many charter schools don't deliver on their promises of improved education and they don't adequately serve minority student populations. In a sense, both sides may be right but the problem of reforming education dwarfs these concerns.

"In fall 2018, about 56.6 million students will attend elementary and secondary schools, including 50.7 million students in public schools and 5.9 million in private schools. Of the public school students, 35.6 million will be in pre-kindergarten through grade 8 and 15.1 million will be in grades 9 through 12. The fall 2018 public school enrollment is expected to be slightly higher than the 50.6 million enrolled in fall 2017 and is higher than the 49.5 million students enrolled in fall 2010. Total public elementary and secondary enrollment is projected to increase between fall 2018 and fall 2027 to 52.1 million."71

Turning around education systems across the country for that huge and diverse student population will likely rely on piecemeal reforms and experiments, with ideas bubbling up from companies and schools, both public and private. As learning becomes a lifelong project, the popularity of massive open online courses (MOOC) and other internet platforms are growing. These courses can be used to extend learning beyond formal education, to replace conventional college curricula, to enhance the skills of those without post high school education, and to provide just-in-time job-specific training. "What technology changes is the availability of tools to foster these skills throughout our adult careers in order to make a well-

---

[71] https://nces.ed.gov/fastfacts/display.asp?id=372

rewarded contribution to the economy. A growing number of adults today are finding time for continuous learning and mindfulness, seeing them as essential practices for being an effective modern worker. In other words, the future of work is what our society's intellectuals have been saying should be happening in organizations for decades now; only, the traditional organization still forces us to do it outside of work."72

Eventually, the growth of online learning may filter down to high schools and even elementary schools, allowing for less engagement with classrooms and resulting in fewer actual schools as their value diminishes. This change will dramatically affect the 3.1 million teachers and 3.4 million school administrators and support staff we now have.

The challenge for schools and teachers is that the pace of change is now so fast that today's elementary-school pupils are being educated for professions that won't exist when they graduate from high school and enter a world that will demand flexibility, adaptability and a willingness to constantly upgrade skills and knowledge. For millions, retraining will be as important as their initial education. This will require state and local governments to invest billions in retraining programs that currently do not exist. The education establishment, in the practice of catching up rather than leading, will be forced to accept rapid change as a constant. Teachers will need to become the standard bearers of the future rather than flag wavers for a past that is no longer relevant.

---

[72] http://www.jfgagne.ai/blog/2017/11/13/ai-and-the-future-of-work-is-about-lifelong-learning

In an information age, with content available with the click of a mouse, teachers must shift from the "sage on a stage" to the "guides on the side." Virtual environments have already allowed teachers to make this shift. USC's Institute for Creative Technologies is prototyping a virtual learning program that combines AI and 3-d animation to guide students through learning content and platforms.

Their "PAL3 is a system for delivering engaging and accessible education via mobile devices. It is designed to provide on-the-job training and support lifelong learning and ongoing assessment. The system features a library of curated training resources containing custom content and pre-existing tutoring systems, tutorial videos and web pages. PAL3 helps learners navigate learning resources through:

"An embodied pedagogical agent that acts as a guide.

"A persistent learning record to track what students have done, their level of mastery, and what they need to achieve.

"A library of educational resources that can include customized intelligent tutoring systems as well as traditional educational materials such as webpages and videos.

"A recommendation system that suggests library resources for a student based on their learning record.

"Game-like mechanisms that create engagement (such as leaderboards and new capabilities that can be unlocked through persistent usage).

"Allowing students to find and suggest new content, which is then vetted by instructors. A customizable interactive agent, "Pal" is designed specifically to engage and motivate via amusing animations and dialog with students through natural language processing (voice and text)."73

As more learning moves online, both for-profit and non-profit organizations are providing personalized opportunities for students of all ages. The non-profit Khan Academy offers free online courses including practice exercises and instructional videos for everyone from kindergarteners to middle-agers, across a vast array of offerings from math and computer programming to art history and economics. Learners study at their own pace both inside and outside of the classroom and the software identifies student strengths and learning gaps and adapts the course progress accordingly.74

According to Kyle Wagner, an education futurist, there are five major shifts schools must make with examples of how AI is already expediting the process:

"1. Stand and deliver instruction ——————————> Facilitation/coaching

"Personalized characters serve as instructors and help individualize instruction based on user responses and input. Coaches help students set goals and reflect on their growth in the environment, while also setting up more lengthy open-ended projects to ensure students apply the content to real-world situations. This blended environment allows teachers, students and machines to work symbiotically.

"2. Developers of content ——————————> Developers of learning experiences

"As teachers, our most valuable asset is time. Before the onset of AI, much of a teacher's time was spent developing

---

[73] http://ict.usc.edu/prototypes/personal-assistant-for-life-long-learning-pal3/

and delivering content in a rigid, inflexible curriculum framework. When I first started teaching, I spent nearly all my prep time creating lessons, with little time left to meet with and develop students. Now, AI is able to do the more mundane work for us.

"In this environment, teachers and peer tutors are able to pull small groups of students aside to offer a more human and personalized approach. Huddled in a semi-circle around a whiteboard, a student works through a challenging problem with their peers, while the teacher provides anecdotal commentary regarding where students might have gotten hung up. Students then work out the problems on writable desks as their peers help monitor their progress.

"3. Siloed classrooms ——————————————> Virtual social networks

"Before the onset of AI and collaborative virtual networks, students and teachers were often siloed by the walls of their classroom or boundaries of their school. Virtual social networks are now helping to break down those walls, offering students the chance to connect with and learn from peers worldwide. Brainly, a social media site for Q&A, is a platform that connects users to fellow peers able to answer subject-specific questions. For example, say a student is struggling with understanding the principle that force = mass x acceleration. They type in their question on Brainly and are connected to a short narrated video that uses modern day Marvel characters to explain the concept. If they wish to ask follow up questions, they are connected through to the student creator of the video via a chat box.

---

[74] https://www.khanacademy.org/about

In this example, AI has not diminished the value of humans, but has enhanced it by connecting two students millions of miles apart.

"4. Textbooks and set curriculum ———> Blended courses and customized design

"Fortunately, AI has helped provide a more personalized experience for students. It's also helped teachers in the creation process. Cram101 and JusttheFacts 101, each a creation of Content Technologies, allows teachers to input course syllabi and then uses a CTI engine to help organize the content around the core concepts. The teacher can then modify design and re-organize based on each student's needs.

"Or, students can feed a book into their AI engine and, in an instant, it produces summaries and highlights of what AIEd considers the most important people, concepts, issues and facts in each chapter. It's as if the smartest kid in the class has given you their comprehensive notes.

"Instructors can create even more comprehensive blended courses through sites like Teachable, Udemy and Coursecraft. These sites create a blended learning ecosystem that couples coaching with content acquisition through videos, group chats, editable worksheets and varied assessments.

"5. Hierarchical top-down network ——————> Lateral virtual global network

"How does your school/district provide professional development? In the past, my professional development was usually mandated by the administration. A school board would go away and develop site-specific goals, and then hire the appropriate experts to offer the trainings. As a teacher, I had little input over the trainings I attended.

*"Virtual Global Conferences like Google's Education on Air and The Global Education Conference provide a range of workshops and training for educators spread across a multitude of topics. After signing up for the conference and inputting in your specific goals, you are connected to the training most likely to meet your needs. You can also offer training on topics you feel most comfortable delivering."*75

As AI alters the very nature of work, we must alter how we prepare people for that work, which means altering how we learn, what we learn and why we learn. According to Accenture Strategies, "With the advent of AI, basic cognitive skills, such as reading and basic numeracy, will not suffice for many jobs, while demand for advanced technological skills, such as coding and programming, will rise, by 55% in 2030, according to our analysis.

"The need for social and emotional skills including initiative taking and leadership will also rise sharply, by 24%, and among higher cognitive skills, creativity and complex information and problem-solving will also become significantly more important. These are often seen as "soft" skills that schools and education systems in general are not set up to impart. Yet in a more automated future, when machines are capable of taking on many more rote tasks, these skills will become increasingly important – precisely because machines are still far from able to provide expertise and coaching, or manage complex relationships."76

---

[75] http://www.gettingsmart.com/2018/01/a-blended-environment-the-future-of-ai-and-education/

[76] https://hbr.org/2018/05/automation-will-make-lifelong-learning-a-necessary-part-of-work

At Davos this year (2018), Jack Ma, co-founder and executive chairman of the Chinese conglomerate Alibaba, one of the largest companies in the world, issued this warning, “If we do not change the way we teach 30 years later we will be in trouble.

“We cannot teach our kids to compete with machines – they are smarter – we have to teach our kids something unique. In this way, 30 years later, kids will have a chance.

“The computer will always be smarter than you are; they never forget, they never get angry. But computers can never be as wise as a man. The AI and robots are going to kill a lot of jobs, because in the future it’ll be done by machines.”77

---

[77] https://www.weforum.org/agenda/2018/01/jack-ma-davos-top-quotes/

Chapter 5
Transporting the World

Virginia was scurrying around the apartment, deciding on the fly what level of chaos she could leave behind before going off to work. While tossing clothes in a single pile she barked into her phone, "pick up in ten, please."

Her self-driving car was waiting curbside as she emerged. She slid into the back seat and thumbed the sensor. In a split second she was greeted by the automated system, "Good morning, Virginia. Destination work?"

"Yes," she answered as she sank back in the luxury seat and put her feet up. "Mood image" options appeared on the large screen in front of her and she chose a photo of an African savannah.

"Would you like to hear NPR as usual or your second choice, classic rock?"

"Just quiet this morning, thank you."

After a moment, the automated voice broke the silence. "Your fridge reported you are out of coconut milk. Would you like to stop at the market before or after work or shall I just have it delivered?"

"Deliver please," she answered barely noticing this now commonplace intrusion into her private life.

As she lost herself into the photo, the voice reminded her, "You have dinner at seven at Kismet with Pete from Bumble. Would you like to arrange pickup at 8:30 or leave that open?" This made her smile. Privacy had long been sacrificed to efficiency and convenience. Whatever early-day fears had slowed the rollout of complete aggregation and integration of personal data had long since disappeared. The machines gathered everything and shared everything across platforms. You could "opt out" but then no one ever did anymore. Virginia let slip a sly grin as she answered, "Let's leave it open."

She looked around idly reflecting on memories of those endless traffic jams that made life so miserable for anyone who lived in a big city anywhere in the world. An hour and a half to get to the office – barring accidents or bad weather – the same on the way home and at least 45 minutes to get to any appointment during the day. Nightmares bookended by nightmares and then rehashed in dinner conversations with family and friends. But such dysfunction was largely a misery of the past.

AI meant that traffic had fallen by 75%. Who needed a car when an autonomous Uber was available at the touch of an app? No car meant no parking, no delays and AI ensured that the perfect route was always available via continuous download to the onboard brain.

*As she entered the office sprawl of downtown, how different this world looked. The parking garages that blighted every piece of the landscape had largely disappeared. It was famously reported that Los Angeles had nine parking spaces for every car. Nationally, there were more than 700 million parking spaces, an area the size of Connecticut just for parking.*78

But no more. In this city, with a long festering homeless problem, the progressive city council had converted parking blocks to cheap apartments to house the homeless and low-

income families. The homeless problem now was something only occasionally mentioned in the press to illustrate discussions about creativity and problem-solving. Other cities, she knew adopted a different approach, selling off city owned parking lots to generate revenue and creating new centers for the gig economy.

What a difference a few years and a trusted AI autonomous solution could make. Virginia sank bank in her comfy chair and closed her eyes.

*

The fantasy of self-driving cars is easy to understand. Who wouldn't want to put up their feet and relax in a comfy re-designed cabin, without that annoying steering wheel, while the car, like your own private chauffeur, drove you to work, to an evening out, or across the country? And, as with bike or scooter sharing, you wouldn't have to own it. No car insurance. No repairs. No gas station stops or car washes. You could summon the car with a voice command on your phone; think of it as Lyft on steroids, without having to make small talk with Walter, your driver, to boost your rating.

AI promises to reconfigure not only our rides, but our traffic patterns, reducing urban congestion and accidents, moving us and the goods we buy more safely and efficiently, as well as improving manufacturing logistics, the shipping of raw materials and finished products via autonomous trains and trucks.

When is this rosy future coming? "The advent of autonomous forms of transportation – vehicles that can sense and navigate their environment without human input – will usher in the greatest change in society since the

---

[78] https://www.axios.com/how-self-driving-cars-will-help-solve-americas-parking-problem-1de243a5-4bd5-4251-955c-

Industrial Revolution. Autonomous vehicles will change every aspect of society, including the freight industry that's already facing a metamorphosis."79

David Galland, a leading industry researcher, believes there will be 10 million self-driving cars on the road by 2020, with one in four cars being self-driving by 2030. "While it took approximately 50 years for electricity to be adopted by 60% of US households, it took cell phones only about 10 years... and smartphones only about five years to reach the same penetration."

He adds, "But I think those estimates (especially the one for 2030) are too conservative..."80

However, not all futurists have drunk the Kool Aid. "If you believe the CEOs, a fully autonomous car could be only months away. In 2015, Elon Musk predicted a fully autonomous Tesla by 2018; so did Google. Delphi and MobileEye's Level 4 system is currently slated for 2019, the same year nuTonomy plans to deploy thousands of driverless taxis on the streets of Singapore. GM will put a fully autonomous car into production in 2019, with no steering wheel or ability for drivers to intervene. There's real money behind these predictions, bets made on the assumption that the software will be able to catch up to the hype."81

To separate the rosy future from the real one, perhaps it's best to sort out what we mean by "autonomous"

524a1667f385.html

[79] https://www.ge.com/reports/the-moneys-really-in-self-driving-trucks-trains-and-ships-not-cars/

[80] https://www.forbes.com/sites/oliviergarret/2017/03/03/10-million-self-driving-cars-will-hit-the-road-by-2020-heres-how-to-profit/#609fd62a7e50

vehicles. Different cars already are capable of different levels of self-driving, and, typically, are categorized by researchers on a scale of 0–5.

Level 0: All major systems are controlled by humans.

Level 1: Some systems, such as automatic braking, may be controlled by the car but only one system at a time.

Level 2: The car can control at least two simultaneous automated functions, like acceleration and steering, but requires humans for safe operation.

Level 3: The car can manage all safety-critical functions under certain conditions, but the driver must be ready to take over if alerted.

Level 4: The car is fully-autonomous in some driving situations, though not all.

Level 5: The car is completely capable of self-driving in every situation.

Driving enthusiasts point to the fact that "the first iterations of the transition to autonomous cars have already happened: there are cars available in the market, offering advanced active safety systems – technology helping the driver to avoid accidents and risky situations – for example, AUTO-BRAKING, ROAD-SIGN UNDERSTANDING, LANE DEVIATION ALERTS and more. First studies confirm the hopes for SIGNIFICANT REDUCTION IN ACCIDENTS INVOLVEMENT for cars featuring such systems."82

The pitch for level 5 autonomous vehicles (AVs) typically hinges on the idea of improved safety. In the US, more than thirty thousand people die each year in car

---

[81] https://www.theverge.com/2018/7/3/17530232/self-driving-ai-winter-full-autonomy-waymo-tesla-uber?stream=top

[82] https://medium.com/innovation-machine/artificial-intelligence-transportation-ea39d652618f

accidents and tens of thousands more are severely injured. Humans, it turns out, are not great drivers, especially when distracted by all the bells and whistles currently available to capture their attention. "Machines don't drive drunk, they don't text and they can make decisions significantly faster than the most adept human drivers."

As we've seen, however, AVs are held to a much higher safety standard than are human drivers. Even the few accidents involving AVs have caused great concern in the press and in the public, creating pressure to slow down their rollout for general use. But at what cost in terms of lives saved or injuries averted?

A RAND Corporation study "found that deploying AVs even when they are only 10% safer than human drivers would save far more lives in the long run (more than 500,000 over 30 years in America alone) than waiting until they are, say, 90% safer."83

How do we get to 90% or even 99% safety? Is it a technology problem? Not exactly. The core technology for AVs is similar across all the different automotive companies, though they employ it in somewhat different arrangements. Basically, it is made up of:

LIDAR: Laser Illuminating Detection and Ranging, or LIDAR, is used to build a 3D map and allow the car to "see" potential hazards by bouncing a laser beam off of surfaces surrounding the car in order to accurately determine the distance and the profile of that object.

Radar: "While LIDAR is great for accurately mapping surroundings, its one fatal flaw is in its ability to accurately monitor speed of surrounding vehicles in real time." Radar units, mounted on bumpers, for example, "allow the car to avoid impact by sending a signal to the on-board processor to apply the brakes, or move out of the way when applicable."

High-powered cameras: While the placement and number of cameras might vary by automaker, they all are configured to "give an overlapping view of the car's surroundings." This technology is not unlike the human eye which provides overlapping images to the brain before determining things like depth of field, peripheral movement, and dimensionality of objects.

Sonar: This provides "another redundant system that allows the car to effectively cross-reference data from other systems in real time to apply the brakes, pre-tension seat belts for impact, or swerve to avoid obstacles."

Positioning: "A car with no steering wheel, no brakes and no accelerator would be essentially useless without advanced positioning systems to track its course and plot an appropriate route to its destination..." The system works alongside the on-board cameras to process real-world information as well as GPS data, and driving speed to accurately determine the precise position of each vehicle, down to a few centimeters all while making smart corrections for things like traffic, road construction, and accidents.

Sophisticated software: "The software processes all of the data in real-time as well as modeling behavioral dynamics of other drivers, pedestrians, and objects around you. While some data is hard-coded into the car, such as stopping at red lights, other responses are learned based

---

[83] https://www.economist.com/science-and-technology/2018/05/10/how-do-you-define-safe-driving-in-

on previous driving experiences." Every mile driven on each car is logged, and this data is processed in an attempt to find solutions to every applicable situation.

"The learning algorithm processes the data of not just the car you're riding in, but that of others in order to find an appropriate response to each possible problem. Behavioral dynamics are also mapped and this data is used to help recognize situations before they happen, much like a human driver. For example, the cars are smart enough to recognize – and adapt to – situations such as: a slow-moving vehicle in the right line suggests a higher probability that the car following it will attempt to pass; a pot hole or foreign item in the street shows a higher probability of a driver swerving to avoid it; congestion in the left lane means that drivers are more likely to attempt to enter the right lane."84

Some of this software capability "is at the core of today's advanced driver assistance systems (ADAS), which include features such as automatic emergency braking (AEB) and lane keeping support. It is the high-accuracy sensing systems inside ADAS that are saving lives today, proven over billions of miles driven. It is this same technology that is required, before tackling even tougher challenges, as a foundational element of fully autonomous vehicles of the future… but the ability to detect and classify objects, is a challenging task."85

---

terms-a-machine-can-understand

[84] https://www.makeuseof.com/tag/how-self-driving-cars-work-the-nuts-and-bolts-behind-googles-autonomous-car-program/

[85] https://newsroom.intel.com/editorials/experience-counts-particularly-safety-critical-areas/

This is where "deep learning" – a method that uses layered machine-learning algorithms to extract structured information from massive data sets – becomes a crucial piece in the development of AVs. Deep learning already powers familiar uses such as Google Search and speech-to-text capabilities. It's also used to detect abnormalities in MRI scans and, in surveillance, to flag suspicious behavior on camera feeds, as well as myriad applications that would be impossible without it.

"But deep learning requires massive amounts of training data to work properly, incorporating nearly every scenario the algorithm will encounter. Systems like Google Images, for instance, are great at recognizing animals as long as they have training data to show them what each animal looks like…

The same algorithm can't recognize an ocelot unless it's seen thousands of pictures of an ocelot – even if it's seen pictures of housecats and jaguars, and knows ocelots are somewhere in between. That process, called 'generalization' requires a different set of skills.

"For a long time, researchers thought they could improve generalization skills with the right algorithms, but recent research has shown that conventional deep learning is even worse at generalizing than we thought. One study found that conventional deep learning systems have a hard time even generalizing across different frames of a video, labeling the same polar bear as a baboon, mongoose, or weasel depending on minor shifts in the background. With each classification based on hundreds of factors in aggregate, even small changes to pictures can completely change the system's judgment…"86

Driving presents deep learning systems with a relentless barrage of circumstances, some easily predicted, e.g., stopping at red lights, to unforeseen events where a seemingly innocent action in the present will unfold through a chain of actions into a catastrophic event. For example, imagine a scenario where an aggressive merge causes the car behind to brake and swerve into another lane and cause a collision. "It is possible to program software that never causes accidents but at the same time maintains a normal flow of traffic… but this is hardly trivial."87

When people learn to drive, they subconsciously absorb what are colloquially known as the 'rules of the road'. When is it safe to go around a double-parked vehicle? When pulling out of a side street into traffic, what is the smallest gap you should try to fit into, and how much should oncoming traffic be expected to brake? The rules, of course, are no such thing: they are ambiguous, open to interpretation and rely heavily on common sense. The rules can be broken in an emergency, or to avoid an accident. As a result, when accidents happen, it is not always clear who is at fault.

All this poses a big problem for people building autonomous vehicles (AVs). They want such vehicles to be able to share the roads smoothly with human drivers and to behave in predictable ways. Above all they want everyone to be safe. That means formalizing the rules of

---

[86] https://www.theverge.com/2018/7/3/17530232/self-driving-ai-winter-full-autonomy-waymo-tesla-uber

[87] https://newsroom.intel.com/editorials/paving-way-toward-safer-roads-all/

the road in a precise way that machines can understand. The problem, says Karl Iagnemma of nuTonomy, an AV firm that was spun out of the Massachusetts Institute of Technology, is that every company is doing this in a different way. That is why some in the industry think the time has come to devise a standardized set of rules for how AVs should behave in different situations.

"Can safe-driving rules really be defined mathematically? It sounds crazy; but if it could be done, it would provide welcome clarity for both engineers and regulators. A clear set of rules would free carmakers from having to make implicit ethical choices about how vehicles should behave in a given situation; they would just have to implement the rules. In the event of an accident, suggests Amnon Shashua of Mobileye, a provider of AV technology, an AV company would not be liable if its vehicle followed the rules. But if a sensor failure or software bug meant that the rules were broken, the company would then be liable. There would still be plenty of scope for innovation around sensor design and control systems. But the robotic rules of the road would be clearly defined."88

"Although crashes caused by human error kill more than one million people annually, it may only take a few fatal crashes of a fully autonomous vehicle, where fault is uncertain, to meaningfully delay or forever foreclose on the tremendous life-saving potential of this technology."89

---

[88] https://www.economist.com/science-and-technology/2018/05/10/how-do-you-define-safe-driving-in-terms-a-machine-can-understand

[89] https://thehill.com/opinion/technology/356015-we-can-design-driverless-cars-that-cannot-cause-an-accident

Autonomous vehicles will have to satisfy the safety concerns of regulators and an excited but wary public. "Carmakers and tech companies have pushed Congress to bar states and localities from regulating self-driving cars themselves, saying they need to stop a "patchwork" of regulations that would stymie innovation."90

Standardized rules and governmental regulations will help but so will the sharing of information among the various players. "Voyage, another new AV company, made a similar proposal, called "Open Autonomous Safety". It also defines the correct, safe behavior for vehicles in a range of circumstances, including pedestrians being in the road, nearby vehicles reversing and arrival at a four-way stop. In addition, Voyage has made its internal safety procedures, materials and test code all "open source", with the aim of providing "a foundational safety resource in the industry…"

"One area where sharing would speed up the development of a safety standard is so-called "edge cases" – rare events that tax the capabilities of autonomous systems, such as unexpected behavior by other drivers, debris on the road, plastic bags blowing in front of a vehicle and so on. Because such events occur infrequently, and computers lack the common sense to decide how to respond, training AVs to cope with edge cases is hard. But by sharing with each other data from edge cases that have actually happened, AV firms can test their systems in simulators to see how they would respond, and adjust them where needed, benefiting from each other's experience. Normally, companies might be reluctant to help

---

90 https://wapo.st/2q64AAl?tid=ss_mail&utm_term=.019081bb92d

competitors in this way, but with AVs, "an accident affects the whole industry, and is bad for all of us"."91

"The data so far suggests that the introduction of self-driving cars will reduce the number of traffic accidents by upward of 90%."92 That will cause havoc among personal car insurance companies, car repair markets, parking lot owners, and change the business of emergency rooms.

A report from the Executive Office of the US President in 2016 states that 2.2 to 3.1 million truck, train or taxi driver jobs could be impacted by self-driving vehicle technology in the United States.93 The report also states that on-demand car services, like Uber, will make a complete transition to autonomous operations in the near future.

Waymo, a Google subsidiary, which has completed 10 million miles of real-world AV driving and five billion simulated miles, has the most road experience of any company thus far.94 Waymo has launched a driverless commercial taxi service in the Phoenix area with Waymo engineers along for the ride, just in case. Locals can summon a Waymo AV taxi with an app on their phone.

---

f

[91] https://www.economist.com/science-and-technology/2018/05/10/how-do-you-define-safe-driving-in-terms-a-machine-can-understand

[92] https://www.forbes.com/sites/oliviergarret/2017/03/03/10-million-self-driving-cars-will-hit-the-road-by-2020-heres-how-to-profit/#609fd62a7e50

[93] https://obamawhitehouse.archives.gov/sites/whitehouse.gov/files/documents/Artificial-Intelligence-Automation-Economy.PDF

[94] https://www.axios.com/here-come-the-robo-taxis-abaeb192-f36d-4d9b-ac4b-791abc61cffe.html

"Ford will begin testing self-driving cars in Washington, DC, and plans to launch commercially in Washington, Miami and other unnamed cities starting in 2021." They are mapping the area now, "using nine cameras and a pair of lidar units, which make precise measurements using laser beams, they recorded roads, curbs and streetlights, as well as an electric Jump bike buzzing down a sidewalk and a jack-o-lantern snowman swaying in a rowhouse yard."

According to one program manager, "It was like capturing a snow globe of data each moment they moved through the city. All those 3-D snapshots will be refined, augmented and used by the driverless car to place itself in the world…

"It changes your perception of the world when you start understanding the way a robot car sees the world – and then how you would translate the human world to a world that the car could understand… Definitely my wife hates me now, because all I do is point out weird traffic lights and interesting lane geometries. She's just like, 'I don't care about that.'"95

*

Trucks: "Of 2.1 million trucking jobs in the US, 294,000 drivers on the nation's highways face the greatest threat from driverless technology, according to the UC Berkeley Center for Labor Research and Education and Working Partnerships USA report.

"All drivers are earning higher wages today because freight hauling demand exceeds available trucks and drivers. Some shippers are raising driver rates to keep them from leaving for a better-paying competitor. The

American Truck Associations estimates the industry is short 63,000 drivers."96

"Because automated trucks can practically run around the clock, the industry will need 6% fewer truck tractors, according to a separate study by the Roland Berger consultancy. Larger fleets that can afford to invest in automated trucks will attract more freight volume. Smaller fleets and independent owners will lose out. Sensor and software technology advances will lead to driverless trucks operating on some interstates by the mid-2020s, Roland Berger predicts. How many depends on state legislation that would allow trucks to drive without human intervention."

Both Steve Viscelli, a University of Pennsylvania Sociologist who wrote the report, and Roland Berger "envision a transfer-hub model, where a conventional truck with a driver pulls a trailer to a handover point near an interstate. An automated driverless truck would then pilot the trailer along the interstate. Once the truck arrives at the second transfer hub, a human-driven truck pulls the trailer to its final destination. Roland Berger predicts 20% to 25% of truck freight could move through transfer hubs by 2035."97

"Autonomous driving makes headlines for its potential to move people, but it is in the trucking and commercial vehicles fields that it will roll out first and have the most

---

[95] https://wapo.st/2q64AAl?tid=ss_mail&utm_term=.019081bb92df

[96] https://www.trucks.com/2018/09/05/long-haul-driverless-trucking-would-displace-good-paying-jobs-study-says/

[97] https://www.trucks.com/2018/09/05/long-haul-driverless-trucking-would-displace-good-paying-jobs-study-says/

immediate impact. That was the conclusion of a panel of industry experts at the Autonomous Vehicles Detroit 2018 conference.

"...The cost of assisted driving technology and other autonomous features in trucks and commercial vehicles could have a rapid payback for businesses by slashing fuel and labor expenses and increasing productivity. Advanced safety technologies – the building blocks of autonomous vehicles are evolving rapidly to enable automated assisted driving and driverless trucks," they said.

"Four years ago, I said there was no way I was going to see autonomous vehicles in my lifetime," said Denny Mooney, senior vice president of global product development for truck maker Navistar International Corp. "It is going to happen in commercial vehicles first. We could see autonomous vehicles on the road commercially within three years."

Consider this number: 43% of the cost of freight hauling is the driver, Mooney said. "If I had no drivers on some of those routes, I'd save 50% of the costs. It's economics."98

"Trucks at Level 4, an automotive industry designation for highly automated vehicles – Level 5 is fully robotic – could be ready to run on western US freeway corridors," said Jason Roycht, vice president and regional business leader for commercial and off-road vehicles at Robert Bosch North America.

A human, for example, would drive the truck to about 20 miles outside of metropolitan Los Angeles. It would then go into self-driving mode for the next 200 miles of highway, reaching a point where cargo would be unloaded

---

[98] https://www.trucks.com/2018/08/23/trucking-freight-pushes-autonomous-vehicles/

or swapped to another truck to continue to its destination. The original truck then would return to its home base. Level 4 autonomy is already being tested by Embark, which hauls refrigerators from El Paso, Texas, to Los Angeles.

"The quality of life of a driver is better than driving 400 miles in one direction and missing his kid's recital," Roycht said.99

"Some AI trucks even have a special feature of predicting accidents as well as health issues of people around the truck like detecting a heart attack and alerting the emergency services automatically with the location and details of diagnosis."[100]

"The global non-uniformity in built-up structures, city infrastructures, road surfaces, weather patterns, traffic patterns etc. make AI applications in autonomous trucks for on-time delivery of people and packages, highly environment specific." 101

*

Ships: According to Mikael Makinen, President, Rolls Royce Marine, "Autonomous shipping is the future of the maritime industry. As disruptive as the smart phone, the smart ship will revolutionize the landscape of ship design and operations.

"Two years ago, talk of intelligent ships was considered by many as a futuristic fantasy. Today, the prospect of a

---

[99] https://www.trucks.com/2018/08/23/trucking-freight-pushes-autonomous-vehicles/

[100] https://www.prescouter.com/2017/12/ai-impact-transportation-industry/

[101] https://www.techemergence.com/ai-in-transportation-current-and-future-business-use-applications/

remote-controlled ship in commercial use by the end of the decade is a reality."102

*

Trains: According Ben Rossi, writing in the journal Information Age, "Within the rail industry, anything which helps keep trains moving, avoiding operational delays and improves customer experience, is worth pursuing. Many original equipment manufacturers are now investing significant resources into one of the most valuable and potentially rewarding currencies in business: big data…"103

Embedded sensors enable AI to collect vast amounts of data. "When operating heavy machinery in variable environments, the ability to compute, manage, analyze and act upon that data is essential for companies to benefit from the Industrial Internet. In the rail industry, assets are mobile and constantly moving in and out of communication, making it even harder to derive value from data that lives on the edge."104

"In addition to improved on-time performance and increased safety (no machines fall asleep at the controls or get distracted) it also makes perfect sense for most of the diagnostic monitoring scenarios such as monitoring wheels, axles, high level network issues etc.

"Similarly, with mission-critical safety-related systems like bridges, some of the signaling assets that simply

---

[102] https://www.rolls-royce.com/~/media/Files/R/Rolls-Royce/documents/customers/marine/ship-intel/aawa-whitepaper-210616.pdf

[103] https://www.information-age.com/trains-brains-how-artificial-intelligence-transforming-railway-industry-123460379/

[104] http://getransportation.com/ge-transportation-unveils-edgelinctm-software-advances-industrial-iot-management-solutions

cannot be allowed to fail are good candidates for the implementation of Predictive Maintenance (PM) solutions."105

*

Cities: "Traffic congestion in the US costs around $50 billion per year. If this data is adapted for traffic management via AI, it will allow streamlined traffic patterns and a significant reduction in congestion... Several similar systems are already in place. For example, smarter traffic light algorithms and real time tracking can control higher and lower traffic patterns effectively. This can also be applied to public transport for optimal scheduling and routing.

"The use of AI to predict the paths of pedestrians and cyclists will decrease traffic accidents and injuries allowing for more diverse transportation usage and an overall reduction in emissions."106

"The US Department of Transportation (USDoT) in 2016 asked medium-size cities to imagine smart city infrastructure for transportation. USDoT plans to award forty million dollars to one city for demonstrating how technology and data can be used to reimagine the movement of people as well as goods.

According to the US Transportation Research Board, emerging applications of AI in transportation planning are in travel behavioral models, city infrastructure design and planning, and demand modeling for public and cargo transport.

One restraint for the adoption of AI in transportation planning applications is that connected transportation

---

[105] https://www.information-age.com/trains-brains-how-artificial-intelligence-transforming-railway-industry-123460379

[106] https://www.prescouter.com/2017/12/ai-impact-transportation-industry/

infrastructure will also raise concerns about the privacy of individuals and the safety of private data. Government and legal regulations regarding these ethical considerations will dictate the pace of innovation and adoption in the industry over the foreseeable period."107

*

Despite the alarmist headlines about autonomous vehicles crashing, the self-driving vehicle revolution is gathering pace and is here to stay. There are challenges with the technology – as there are with any new technology – but the reality is that autonomous vehicles will be cheaper to run, be more efficient and be involved in many fewer accidents than if a human had been behind the wheel.

The consequences for the transport industry and the millions of people involved in it will be dire. It's not just the drivers who will be out of work but the very long logistics tail that gets a fully laden truck on the road will also be automated with robots and not people in the warehouse and AI controlling schedules, checking on delivery times, smoothing out any miscommunication and keeping millions of customers satisfied. There will still be a human in the loop but only one person for every 10,000 jobs lost and within five years that ratio will be even more extreme.

Already, autonomous technology for cars, trucks and drones has moved much faster than experts were predicting just five years ago, so it is hard to clearly understand the pace at which transport will change. Also, there have been no real studies about the consequential impact of the adoption of autonomous transport. Commuter traffic will

---

[107] https://www.techemergence.com/ai-in-transportation-current-and-future-business-use-applications/

be cut radically to improve the lives of tens of millions of commuters, thousands of parking garages will no longer be fit for purpose; pollution will be reduced, as will the consumption of gasoline and diesel.

The impact on jobs in the transportation industry will be severe and the prospect of a man or woman who has made a career driving a truck for UPS or FedEx finding another job in transport will be very unlikely. This will be a significant challenge for many communities and the families that live within them. The warning flags for the industry have been flying for some time, but there has been no government or industry initiative to provide alternative employment for a group of hard-working and prosperous members of our community. That is a story that will be repeated again and again across other sectors as the AI revolution tightens its grip.

Chapter 6

Shopping, the Robot Way

I met J online. I knew right away that this relationship would be more consequential for me than any served up by Bumble or Tinder. J, you see, is my new personalized shopping bot from my favorite clothing store. J knows my entire purchase history from the store so it can quickly suggest blouse matches for that suede skirt I bought two years ago or what pants go with that black v-neck sweater I got for Christmas. It also knows my browsing history on the store's site, including what I lingered over and didn't buy so it suggests I shouldn't be afraid of that body-hugging sweater I put in my cart but didn't buy – and, no, I'm untroubled by that violation of my privacy; the personal touch means more to me than my secrecy.

J is not perfect. It doesn't have Kimberly's trendy flair, nor her in-the-know tips on the coolest cafes, bars and restaurants. Kimberly was the attractive young sales woman that took excellent care of me in the store. Though I could never be as cool or as stylish Kimberly, she made feel I could aspire to the nightlife she apparently was leading. Frankly, I never cared to spend the time cultivating the knowledge of the new and happening because Kimberly did it for me. J is not cool. J has no nightlife but it can identify trends just as they are breaking maybe even before Kimberly knows of them. J can plumb social media and tell me what Adele – my favorite – wore after her concert and how I can buy a knockoff of that now on sale. J can also see what the women I follow on Instagram are wearing and steer my purchases in that direction. J, it seems, knows everything about me. If another person – if Kimberly, for example – followed me as J does, I'd be nervous that I was being stalked. But, other than mining my life for future marketing/sales opportunities, J has no ulterior motive. And J has none of Kimberly's other issues.

Kimberly, you see, had problems that doomed her tenure at this or any other store. Not because she ran off with that jerk, Danny, or decided to go to law school or become an actress. Kimberly's biggest problem was that she couldn't scale. There is only one Kimberly and retail and online stores would need tens of thousands of her to keep their businesses afloat and they can't find them or train them.

Kimberly got sick last year and sales fell off 12% in her absence. She went to Italy with that damn Danny and business dropped 10% while she was looking at art in Florence. And Kimberly is fussy, she won't work at midnight when buyers want to place orders. She takes an hour for lunch and two coffee breaks every day! And she's expensive, or, at least far more expensive than the amortized cost of J which can service thousands of customers nationwide all at once.

So, while I'll miss the easy, fake camaraderie with Kimberly, I've heard that J will get chummier and its language skills will get more colloquial with each update. It emails and texts me whenever something new comes in or in response to a picture I posted on Instagram or on my Pinterest page. J and I won't ever have coffee together or promise to meet at that new bar downtown (Kimberly always canceled anyway) but shopping with J is so much more convenient. It sends me choices to try on at home.

We connect on Hangout so J can give me feedback on the options. Then, I simply return what I don't want, free shipping included! J still encourages me to come to the store, but I don't see the point anymore.

Sometimes, I admit, I miss Kimberly's personal touch – her human touch – but I'm sure that will fade as J and I really get to know each other.

*

Retailers can't ignore the simple fact that customers want personalization, whether in-store or online. Creating a more personalized shopping experience is high priority for retailers today. So much so, that research from Infosys found that 86% of consumers – and 96% of retailers – said personalization has at least some impact on the purchasing decision.108

"But the reality is that no human employee has access (yet) to every possible bit of data on a customer. We may know what they bought in-store, but not what they bought or looked at online. Or we may not know which posts they liked on social media or what they added to their Pinterest board. Even if a human could access all of this customer information, they couldn't pull it together and analyze it fast enough to offer an on-the-spot recommendation. But AI can."109

AI systems thrive on all the data that retailers have been collecting on their customers, especially machine learning systems. They can track customer online behavior, what they look at, what they buy and, just as important, what they don't buy. AI can learn how best to reach your

---

[108] https://www.infosys.com/newsroom/press-releases/Documents/genome-research-report.pdf

[109] https://www.insider-trends.com/the-complete-guide-to-ai-in-retail/

customer, whether by email or via which social media platform. It can make tailored recommendations and adjust them according to customer behavior and do it quickly, efficiently, and, eventually, accurately. Even if the system makes a mistake while learning, the consequences of that are relatively minor (oh no! the wrong shirt color! I hate green!), compared to errors made by self-driving cars.

While pre-AI inventory and sales database systems simply track purchases of individual products, with sufficient data machine learning systems can *predict* your regular habits. It knows you like cooking risotto every Monday night, but also your more complex behavior, like the occasional ice cream binge on Fridays.110

The customer may not care how AI is using their personal data. They just know that their favorite brand recommended to them a product based on what's already in their wardrobe, or sent them a special coupon because they've been looking for new coats, or didn't try to flog them high heels because they only wear flats.

"Good AI is about… giving the sense of having a really personal, natural, real interaction with a brand – akin to dealing with a human who knows everything about you. That's the most exciting thing about AI in retail. However it's being applied, it's about making better experiences for customers without this obvious layer of tech between them and the brand. And the smarter it gets the more like magic it becomes."[111]

---

[110] http://theconversation.com/when-ai-meets-your-shopping-experience-it-knows-what-you-buy-and-what-you-ought-to-buy-101737

[111] https://www.insider-trends.com/the-complete-guide-to-ai-in-retail/

Research from BCG and MIT has found that "brands that create personalized experience by integrating advanced digital technologies and proprietary data are seeing revenue increase from 6% to 10%, two to three times faster than those that don't."[112] In time, companies that adapt to AI will gain market share and profit while slow movers will lose customers, share and profits.

"The use of Artificial Intelligence in retail spans every aspect of the industry. Whether your goal is to optimize your supply chain, use existing data to increase conversion, or customize shopping experiences with predictive modeling and micro-targeting/pricing, AI can help you meet your challenge."113

"Business Insider Intelligence projects that AI will boost profitability in retail and wholesale by nearly 60% by 2035, setting off a wave of excitement and investment among companies."114

"These advanced systems are transforming the trade promotion process by automating operational tasks such as setting shelf pricing, determining product assortments and much more.

"From predictive recommendations, product pricing and staffing optimization, retailers can now capture shopper data with a greater degree of accuracy in a way that is both

---

[112] https://www.bcg.com/en-us/publications/2017/technology-digital-strategy-putting-artificial-intelligence-work.aspx

[113] https://www.nvidia.com/en-us/deep-learning-ai/industries/retail/

[114] https://www.businessinsider.com/the-future-of-retail-ai-2018-8

meaningful and actionable, resulting in more friction-free shopping experiences."[115]

Retail is well-suited to using AI because it can tap a massive amount of consumer data. "In the past this data has been difficult or even impossible for most companies to effectively analyze. AI can help even small companies use the information they have to create, for example, targeted shopping experiences, online chatbots or in-store intelligence that will make the customer experience more interactive and rewarding."116

For sellers – brands, manufacturers, distributors, retail and online/mobile outlets – AI is transforming how products are manufactured, distributed, inventoried, marketed, priced, sold and even designed. AI also is extending – some would say deepening, others might say exploiting – their relationships with customers, including company access to and use of customer data.

For buyers, the shopping experience, whether shopping online, via mobile or in those old-fashioned outposts we still call "stores" already has been transformed, led by Amazon, but emulated by other digital natives such as eBay and retail giants such as Walmart. Online shopping is ruining holidays for department stores and giving them year-round headaches.

An annual survey by analytics firm comScore and UPS found that consumers are now buying more online than in stores. "The survey, now in its fifth year, polled more than 5,000 consumers who make at least two online purchases in a three-month period. According to results,

---

[115] https://retailnext.net/en/blog/machine-learning-its-role-in-retail/

[116] https://digitaldirections.com/ai-is-already-changing-the-way-we-shop-and-this-is-just-the-beginning/

shoppers now make 51% of their purchases online, compared to 48% in 2015 and 47% in 2014."117

"According to First Data, e-commerce transactions grew at a pace more than six times faster than brick-and-mortar stores during the 2017 holiday season. Sales on Cyber Monday alone set a new record with a reported $6.59 billion in sales."118

Last year, Amazon posted $82.7 billion in sales, compared with $12.5 billion for Walmart, and that chasm in dollars keeps getting wider. Research recently conducted by McKinsey found that "US retailer supply chain operations who have adopted data and analytics have seen up to a 19% increase in operating margin over the last five years."119

"As online shopping accelerates, so does the use of smartphones to make purchases. The survey showed that 44% of smartphone users made buys through their devices, compared to 41% a year ago."120

And why not? After all, look at the advantages:

"24/7 shopping – consumers are no longer restricted by the 9-to-5 working hours; at online shops, they can purchase what they need around the clock...

Price comparison – you can flick between websites quickly to see which is offering the best price for the same product; securing the best deal cannot be easier...

---

[117] http://fortune.com/2016/06/08/online-shopping-increases/

[118] https://www.forbes.com/sites/allbusiness/2018/02/24/with-an-increase-in-online-shopping-prepare-for-an-increase-in-data-breaches/#4871a146e67b

[119] https://retailnext.net/en/blog/machine-learning-its-role-in-retail/

[120] http://fortune.com/2016/06/08/online-shopping-increases/

Online sales – many shops offer exclusive online only sales in order to get rid of stock that they no longer need and to attract new customers...

Greater choice – in the majority of cases, online shopping provides a much greater variety of products than a physical store could. Online companies are not limited by the physical dimensions of a storefront, they simply need to list the items online before shipping them out from a warehouse. Additionally, if one website has the item out of stock, it is relatively easy to find the stock elsewhere.

Free shipping – many online stores offer free shipping if you spend above a certain amount. This can help to save the consumer money, as they won't have to pay for the transport of getting to the shopping facilities or pay for parking.

*World shopping – thanks to the convenience of online shopping, you are now able to order products from all over the world. From America to China, you can have it sent directly to you at the touch of a button. This is something that high street stores cannot possibly provide."*121

AI is precipitating a retail revolution throughout the industry, but how is it doing that now and what changes can we expect going forward for sellers and buyers?

A decade ago we called them "chat bots" and, mostly, they were incredibly annoying and inefficient, with limited vocabulary and a frustrating inability to understand us, and, of course, they spoke in those affectless robotic voices. While chat bots have improved,

---

[121] https://www.sdcexec.com/warehousing/blog/20989207/the-rise-of-online-shopping-explained

now, with Alexa, Google Home, and, to a lesser extent, Siri, we get to call them "voice assistants" or "digital assistants" and, thanks to AI (Siri, the first of the breed, eschews some data analytics of AI in favor of greater privacy), they can hold reasonable conversations and do everything from play just about any song we can think of, turn on lights, and, of course, order products, especially from Amazon.

These assistants also are turning up at every stage in the sales experience from improved AI powered chat bots to custom website alterations to voice assistants, even robots, that are emotionally sensitive to our moods (check out the chapter on sex!)

1-800-Flowers.com launched a digital "concierge" – in effect, an AI powered chat bot – that uses IBM's Artificial Intelligence system, Watson, to help consumers search for and place their order.

"Consumers will be able to tell GWYN (Gifts When You Need) what they are looking for then select and order the product from inside the conversational interface. Instead of a structured process of filling out a form on a website, you'll be able to just type in to GWYN, 'I'm looking for a birthday gift,' and GWYN will ask, 'Is it for a male or female? Age 30 or 35?'" said Chris McCann, president of 1-800-Flowers.com. "It will bring you down a little bit of a tree.

"The more customers interact with GWYN, the smarter 'she' will become, eventually offering a customized shopping experience based on an individual's previous behavior. Gwyn will be constantly learning about you, and then service the products that we think fit what you're looking for."122

Much sexier is Pepper, the French-designed robot for Softbank now in use as a customer service greeter in 140 of the company's Japanese stores and, in beta, in Palo Alto and Santa Monica, California where they claim "a 70% increase in foot traffic, 50% of sales of some items attributed to the robot."123

Pepper might ask a customer, "Are you smiling from the bottom of your heart?" "The robot is equipped with an "emotion engine" – software that attempts to infer how a user is feeling based on facial expressions, tone of voice, and speech, allowing the robot to respond accordingly."124 It can dance a bit, tell a few jokes and respond in French, English and Japanese, though, currently, its repertoire of responses is limited.

"The emotion engine… uses the robot's vision system to detect smiles, frowns, and surprise, and it uses speech recognition to sense the tone of voice and to detect certain words indicative of strong feelings, like "love" and "hate."

"In the future, the system could also incorporate ethics, empathy, and other qualities and behaviors that the company believes robots need in order to be part of people's lives."125

While Pepper's ability to conduct a natural sounding conversation is limited, Google has developed a robot

---

[122] https://www.campaignlive.com/article/1-800-flowerscom-launches-ai-concierge-powered-ibms-watson/1393358

[123] https://digitaldirections.com/ai-is-already-changing-the-way-we-shop-and-this-is-just-the-beginning/

[124] https://spectrum.ieee.org/robotics/home-robots/how-aldebaran-robotics-built-its-friendly-humanoid-robot-pepper

[125] https://spectrum.ieee.org/robotics/home-robots/how-aldebaran-robotics-built-its-friendly-humanoid-robot-pepper

assistant called Google Duplex that can make phone calls for customers in a voice and language that are indistinguishable from humans, complete with "um" and "er" and other hesitations that mimic very human speech patterns. Duplex can make appointments, restaurant reservations and schedule meetings, drawing on a client's calendar. It can accommodate complications arising from the conversation about availabilities and other obstacles and the human on the other end of the conversation has no idea they are talking to a machine.

Google's CEO, Sundar Pichai, demonstrated the capability on stage at the Shoreline Amphitheater during the company's annual developer conference, I/O. He played a recording of Google Assistant calling and interacting with someone at a hair salon to make an appointment.

"When the salon picks up the phone, a female computer-generated voice says she's calling to arrange a haircut for 'a client' on 3 May. The salon employee says, 'give me one second', to which the robot replies 'mmm-hmm' – a response that triggered a wave of laughter in the 7,000-strong audience.

"'What time are you looking for?' the salon employee asks. 'At 12pm,' replies the robot. The salon doesn't have an opening then, so the robot suggests a window between 10am and 12pm, before confirming the booking and notifying its human master."126

"Another AI-powered service is offered by Vue.ai, a sub brand of Indian tech startup Mad Street Den. The AI technology behind Vue.ai enables retailers to personalize the website based on individual shoppers' preferences. The technology learns from shoppers' browsing and shopping histories and displays items that match their preferences and provides personalized shopping recommendations. The service generates an increase of 144% in product viewing and a 110% increase in average order value, according to the company."127

Otto Group, a German online and catalog retailer, uses AI for inventory management, predicting what customers will buy in the near future. The technology "can analyze around three billion historical transactions and 200 other variables (such as weather conditions and website searches) to predict future purchases. This enables Otto Group to automatically process orders with partner suppliers for about 200,000 items a month. The system helps Otto to stock what its customers are likely to buy, enabling the retailer to achieve faster deliveries and reduce returns. The solution can reportedly predict with 90% accuracy what will be sold within a 30-day period and allows Otto to reduce dramatically its delivery schedule for partner products – from seven days to one or two days – often enabling direct delivery from the supplier to the customer without passing through Otto's warehouse."128

Consumers want what they want when they want it. It's a company's job to determine that, plan for it, stock it and

---

[126] https://www.theguardian.com/technology/2018/may/08/google-duplex-assistant-phone-calls-robot-human

[127] https://www.fungglobalretailtech.com/research/deep-dive-artificial-intelligence-retail-offering-data-driven-personalization-customer-service/

[128] https://www.fungglobalretailtech.com/research/deep-dive-artificial-intelligence-retail-offering-data-driven-personalization-customer-service/

price it accordingly. Machine learning can transform that process.

Using predictive analytics, "Walmart watches the weather to decide what food is going to sell better. Predictions powered an 18% increase in sales by having more steaks in stock when it's warm, dry, cloudy and windy, and beefing up burgers when it's hotter and less windy. High temperatures with a light breeze sell more salads; clear sunny days sell more berries. But you don't have to be a retail giant to use AI to improve your supply chain."129

"AI-powered retail applications not only identify gaps, forecast inventory and place orders, but also help reduce excess stock buildup, making retail more efficient. Excess stock often ends up being marked down, but AI applications can help identify products that are prone to be stocked in excess based on their historical tendencies and prevent them from building up."130

On the other hand, inventory management can prevent customer disappointment. For example, Jet.com is very keen to know what's not in stock, Director of Engineering Scott Havens told CIO.com. "Suppliers might say they have ten items in stock but they only have eight, which leads to unhappy customers who can't place an order when they expected to," he says. If an item isn't in stock, Havens doesn't want the site to even show up in a search. "In terms of customer experience, not talking to a

---

[129] https://www.cio.com/article/3283326/supply-chain-management/how-ai-will-revolutionize-inventory-management.html

[130] https://www.forbes.com/sites/deborahweinswig/2018/07/28/four-ways-ai-helps-retailers-compete-with-amazon/#11cc44b19ccc

customer is better than talking to them and disappointing them."131

Amazon, obviously the 800-pound gorilla in online shopping, is experimenting with brick-and-mortar stores called Amazon Go, but without cashiers. "Customers order online then check in via the Go app, but the rest of the shopping experience is automated. "Sensors track which objects customers pick up and put in their basket, and customers' Amazon accounts are automatically charged after exiting the store."132

Amazon, UPS and even Domino's are exploring package delivery by drone. After all, two day or even same day shipping via Prime are beginning to feel unbearably slow – so who *wouldn't* be excited by delivery in minutes after purchase?

"Amazon, for example, made more than five billion deliveries to Prime customers in 2017, and a conservative estimate of the company's shipping costs is at the $20 billion mark for last year. That means anything that can hack away at logistical costs would be very welcome for Amazon and other shippers, and drones could be a way to accomplish this.

"The logistics are complex and intense. The regulatory hurdles are steep and covered with red tape. As with autonomous vehicles, the technology is already capable of the task at hand – however, it will take time to build acceptance and trust with customers to allow drones to fly onto their property for any purpose.

---

[131] https://www.cio.com/article/3283326/supply-chain-management/how-ai-will-revolutionize-inventory-management.html

[132] https://www.techemergence.com/artificial-intelligence-retail/

Commercial drones can travel at up to 100 mph and deliver goods under 5 lbs (2.3 kg) – and according to ARK Investing Group, potentially each trip could occur at a low cost of $1 per shipment.

Even better? Faster shipments could mean higher revenues. After all, 86% of abandoned carts online are the result of expensive shipping costs, according to management consulting group McKinsey & Company."133

Amazon is testing Amazon Prime air with the idea of getting packages to customers within 30 minutes. UPS has also estimated that cutting off just one mile for the routes of each of the company's 66,000 delivery drivers would amount to $50 million in savings. For this reason, UPS is testing drone deliveries, using the top of its vans as a mini-helipad.

Domino's famously delivered the first pizza by drone in 2016 to a New Zealand couple. The pizza company says that drones will be an essential part of its future delivery operations.

"Retail pricing optimization, too, is a complex undertaking, requiring data analysis for each customer, product and transaction. Companies need to consider how sales are impacted by changing price points over time or if customers will continue to buy a product in smaller quantities at higher price points. All of those factors must then be analyzed as well as controlling for factors like seasonality, weather, promotions and even product relationships like how lunch meat prices might impact bread prices.

---

[133] https://www.businessinsider.com/amazon-and-ups-are-betting-big-on-drone-delivery-2018-3

"A well-crafted machine learning program can factor in all of these variations, combining them with additional details like purchase histories, product preferences and more. In a real-world example, Precima applied a machine learning system for a leading European grocer to help them offer customers the lowest possible prices. The system analyzes approximately one billion transactions across 40,000 products in 800 stores, something that just isn't possible without this technology. The program produces monthly optimized product-level price-point recommendations that have helped to generate stable revenue alongside an incremental lift in profit."134

"Tomorrow, AI will help make classic business decisions – how much to produce, where to distribute, how to price, how to promote, whom to target, and so on. This next frontier for deep-learning moves from individual algorithms trained to perform a specific task on a single dataset – to multi-purpose algorithms answering multiple challenges at once. AI will explain why a certain product might be a new trendsetter next year – essentially replacing human judgement to make a qualitative assessment based on its own learnings about how people perceive products. And AI will be more effective in doing so than any human."135

As life circumstances and spending habits of a customer change, models will automatically adjust.

"The current reactive system involves waiting for a customer to start buying nappies, for example, to then

---

[134] https://www.precima.com/research-insights/blog/pricing-optimization-and-the-adoption-of-machine-learning

[135] https://www.oliverwyman.com/our-expertise/insights/2018/jan/machine-learning-for-retail-part-2.html

identify that customer as having just started a family, before following up with appropriate product recommendations. Instead, machine learning algorithms may model behavior such as the purchases of folate vitamins and bio oils, then predict when offers should be sent. This shift from reactive to predictive marketing could change the way you shop, bringing you suggestions you perhaps never even considered, all possible because of AI-related opportunities for both retailers and their customers."136

Of course, the transition to this rosy future of perfect customer personalization, online and brick-and-mortar stores knowing our wants better than we know them ourselves and delivery at the blink of an eye will not happen overnight. And not every company will be successful at taking advantage of the opportunities machine learning offers.

Existing systems will need to be overhauled, which can be expensive and time-consuming. Management may lack both the expertise to adapt and the willingness to buy in to systems that they either fear or don't know how to manage or integrate. Inhouse tech capability is limited and so the process, typically, must be outsourced, further limiting the control management can exercise over it.

Buy-in must come from the C-suites, but someone in the organization such as a CTO or a hire from outside will need to align the systems with a company's core business proposition and objectives. The algorithms will need to reflect the company's values in terms of diversity and inclusion – which is not automatic.

---

[136] https://theconversation.com/when-ai-meets-your-shopping-experience-it-knows-what-you-buy-and-what-you-ought-to-buy-

Given the prospects for disruption, the limited organizational capacity to integrate new technology, and executive intransigence, what could go wrong?

*

Finally, there is the dreaded issue of privacy. Some consumers, as evidenced by their eagerness to share images of every meal and every detail of their lives, are quite happy to ignore the pitfalls of deep data gathering in exchange for the convenience and personalization on offer.

However, for others the trade-off may not be so welcome. Machine learning not only thrives on the more data the better but, in a sense, it requires it to become really useful at analytics and prediction – which are why you want such systems in the first place.

As the famous old bank robber Willie Sutton replied when asked why he robbed banks, "because that's where the money is." Today's hackers see data troves as the new banks.

"Based on current sales figures, that money is now in e-commerce. Shopping online can be convenient, but it comes with its own pitfalls. According to a study performed by the Ponemon Institute, the average cost of a data breach is $3.62 million.

"Imagine that a customer's credit card number is stolen. Not only can thieves use it to make additional purchases online, they can also make physical purchases," Tyler Atwell at CUInsight writes. "After that, some are able to manufacture a genuine-looking credit card from blanks and program the magnetic strips to effectively create a replica of the card that you still have in your possession.

101737

With that card and some cool nerves, they are able to use that duplicate to buy merchandise at any store.

"Theft of information through data breaches can also run deeper than simply using a credit card number. Criminals on the dark web are willing to purchase information from thieves and will likely use it to apply for credit or make purchases. "Buyers are currently willing to pay just $1 for a Social Security number, which is the same amount they'll pay for user and password information to *Brazzers*, a pornographic website," reports Don Reisinger at Fortune "Access to someone's PayPal account is the most valuable asset at up to $80, depending on the available balance."137

As in so much with AI, there will be more choice but it all comes at a price which, so far, we have been willing to pay. Once we have made all our information accessible to companies, not only will online shopping be more personalized but going to stores that have that same information also will be easier. We'll benefit from greater personalization, be offered more choices, faster checkout and, ideally, fewer lines.

For the millions of people who work in retail, the future is bleak. Already, the number of cashiers in the larger stores is being reduced drastically and they will soon largely disappear. Amazon will be leading the way with their 3,000 cashier-less grocery stores spread across America. The next step is clothes stores where an AI-driven robot will be more accurate and helpful in choosing just the right combination to go with outfits that are already accessible from the robot's database.

---

[137] https://www.forbes.com/sites/allbusiness/2018/02/24/with-an-increase-in-online-shopping-prepare-for-an-increase-in-data-breaches/#4871a146e67b

No doubt there will be many of us who prefer that personal touch, but over time, as the conversation between man/woman and machine becomes more fluent and helpful, the resistance will fall away. Then the conversation will not be about the nostalgia of the lost days of cashiers. Instead, we will choose stores based on the personality of the robots, their conversational ability and their access to databases that help on recommendations. It will also be about which store has the best bot based on appearance, likeability and personality.

A different world.

Part 3 – Our Bodies, Ourselves

Chapter 7

The Future of Sex

Harriet was in love, completely, deliriously, happily in love. It was an unexpected joy and with Frank, a very unexpected man.

Looking at him across the restaurant table he, too, seemed happy. The familiar half smile, the perfect teeth, the ideal good looks, the stylish clothes were all in place. But he was so much more than that. He seemed to know, really know, just by looking at her, the level and direction of her mood. Happy, sad, depressed, anxious, he always got it right and could ask just the right sensitive question to draw her out. And then he listened – listened – to the answers and always had a helpful follow up question to allow her to gain perspective.

Her previous relationships had been frustrating – sexually, practically, intimately – but this was entirely different. The other men in her life had all been compromises of one kind or another. Sean might have been kind, but he seemed to think an orgasm was something that occurred as a result of him simply producing his penis to insert in her vagina. Then it was all over before she had even warmed to the task at hand – and it did always feel like a task.

Ben said he wanted to listen but then as she tried to explain something important, his arms would cross, he would look down and she just knew that, apart from the occasional grunt, he was tuning her out.

Mike was a cool guy but so vain that he spent more time in the bathroom than she did. He could never understand that vanity was a barrier to intimacy and the true expression of feelings. In the end, he was just so dull, all the preening and primping a window into an empty mind and a seemingly non-existent soul.

She had turned to the BotBank in a final effort to discover a rewarding relationship with the man of her dreams. Aside from the drain on her bank account, it had been a very user-friendly experience: she had simply selected all the options that mattered to her: looks – tall, slim, dark. Check. Intelligent – match her IQ. Check. Intimate communicator – experience of the Enneagram, self-help. Check. No obsessive watching of football. Check. Well read – database of 5,000 books. Check. Lover – tender when required, adventurous when needed, considerate, always. Check. Penis size – variable on demand. Check.

She would never have believed the reality if she had not experienced it for herself. To be seen and heard, not just once but every time; to have every mood understood and accepted; to have her needs met without question and usually without her having to ask. It could have been boring to have someone so passive, but Frank could be assertive and take charge as he saw the need. And that time in the line at the movie theater when that guy had been rude to her... Well, being trained in all the martial arts certainly dealt with that problem.

There had been a time when skin looked fake and the voice intonations seemed artificial, with a limited range of emotion. But that was in the distant past of 10 years ago. Today, Frank's look and feel was just exactly like every other man she had ever met, only better. And if he was cut, did he bleed? Of course.

Inevitably, there were some challenges. If Frank was the perfect partner, what did it mean to be human? What purpose was to be served if humankind could be replicated and improved to such a degree that he or she was unrecognizable from the real thing? She knew that the Supers had been forced to create a dumbed down version of themselves so that humans could actually communicate with them. That may have been kind of insulting, but it was the new reality.

She had talked with other men and women in her life who had also checked in with the BotBank and their experiences were identical with her own. Where there was dissatisfaction, a slight change in the algorithms could fix the problem. Bored with the hairy chest? A clean-shaven chest would appear in minutes. A new interest in Tolstoy? The complete works, downloaded, read and digested in seconds.

A more practical question was that of children. Women were supposed to be pre-programmed to propagate but the rise of the Bots, which lived forever, had made the need for propagation largely redundant. Even so, she did feel the urge on occasion to have children. She'd signed up to the gene pool and if she was chosen, Frank would deliver the goods and help her through to term. If not, well, she had made a bargain that meant a lifetime of joy and happiness, and she was content with that.

There were some among friends and colleagues who debated endlessly about the morality of forming attachments with non-humans. It was the beginning of the end, they said, that raised fundamental questions about the future of humanity. But for Harriet, the questions were far simpler. Did she want to spend the rest of her life with an oaf she could barely tolerate or, even worse, alone? Instead, she had chosen to begin a new life with the perfect partner. A life filled with love, laughter and partnership. What more could life have to offer?

Still, in moments of agonizing doubt, she wondered how long this could last. All her other relationships had seemed to sour over time as the personal traits that had once seemed endearing became either boring, or annoying, or both. The folks at the BotBank had assured that Frank would remain faithful, fascinated and fulfilling. But Frank would never age. His body would remain strong, his mind would never dull; in fact, he would go on learning new things forever. Sometimes, she believed she saw a hint of something behind those baby blue eyes. Disdain? Superiority? And she couldn't blame him for that. After all, she was just a human, frail, fallible, and short-lived.

*

Is AI technology a cure for loneliness, a boon both to marriage and masturbation, an enabler of greater intimacy between humans and machines, the creator of remote-controlled sex, the best friend and worst enemy of porn? Or is it each of these things?

Swipe right if you're interested in this chapter, swipe left to pass it by. But you can't segment it by gender, age, race, religion, hair color, location, size, hobbies, work or kink. It won't meet you for coffee, a drink, dinner or a quick hookup. And it won't call you in the morning – or ever. AI's data crunching capacity and the resulting algorithmic recommendations it can provide have opened up the world for all comers from the lonely to the louche and expanded choices and opportunities for the way people meet, love, have sex, get married and shop for relationships, including for those who face sexual challenges due to distance, loneliness, discrimination or disability.

Online dating, once scorned as only for the shallow, the lazy, the desperate, the catfishers, or, worse, the obsessive and the dangerous, now has been tried at least once by nearly 50 million people in the US. It is true that more than half of users lie on their profiles, with men lying about their jobs and women using photos that make them look skinnier.138

Still, globally, at least 200m people use digital dating services every month. In the U.S., more than a third of marriages now begin their relationships online. And online dating offers better outcomes. Marriages in America between people who meet online are likely to last longer and the couples claim to be happier than those who met the old-fashioned way.139

Remember way back in the nineties when cute meets were distributed among bars, classrooms, offices, churches, and other real-world locations, or even via the classified section of alternative papers? Not so much anymore. Now the coders may decide who shows up in your virtual world. But that hasn't stopped digital dating from growing exponentially. Since online dating apps went mobile, revenue has spiked to over $3 billion annually.

According to *Online Dating* magazine, there are more than 7,500 online dating websites – over 2,500 in the

---

[138] http://thechive.com/2018/07/20/the-shocking-statistics-behind-online-dating-12-photos/

[139] https://www.economist.com/leaders/2018/08/18/modern-love

United States and 5,000 around the world.[140] These include the high-minded such as *eHarmony,* the well-established such as *Match.com,* but also niche sites for clowns and Trekkies and other idiosyncratic identifiers.

The Match Group, which includes Tinder and other brands, had 59 million users in the last year.[141] But it's far from the only success story. Nineteen per cent of brides met their spouses online.[142] A majority of people believe online dating is a good way to meet people.143

Critics worry about the impact of the digital meat market on insecurities about body image, appearance and self-worth, all issues that predate Tinder, but are amplified by the snap judgments of strangers and may lead to depression. And, since people tend to date within their socio-economic groups – as they do offline – there is some fear that digital dating will perpetuate and even accelerate income inequality. Indeed, future profiles may include not just that fancy school or high-income job, but also favored genomic traits, including family disease data and sperm count. The more data that becomes available, the more companies will slice and dice it for new applications. Marriages might be arranged not by long-held customs but based on genetic compatibility and the increased genetic

---

140
https://www.onlinedatingmagazine.com/faq/howmanyonlinedatingsitesarethere.html

141 https://www.benzinga.com/analyst-ratings/analyst-color/17/04/9312335/jefferies-swipes-right-on-match-group-says-tinder-is-the

[142] https://www.zoosk.com/date-mix/online-dating-advice/online-dating-statistics-dating-stats-2017/

[143] http://www.pewresearch.org/fact-tank/2016/02/29/5-facts-about-online-dating/

prospects for offspring. How long will it be before 23andme becomes a genetic dating app?

If distance is a barrier to intimacy, technology has an answer. If physical intimacy is too threatening, technology offers some of the pleasures without the anxiety. If the desire for kink is undimmed by time or distance, technology is here to satisfy it across any distance, at any time. No, this isn't about porn, at least not until later in this chapter.

Inter-connected sex toys – known raffishly in the trade as "teledildonics" – promote interaction via mobile or desktop apps. These include "smart" vibrators and male sex sleeves, using haptic touch technology they record sexual motions and send the sensations between lovers who are miles apart. There is also a remote-controlled *50 Shades of Grey* Vibrating Love Egg, and a prototype for the remote-controlled vibrating Durex Fundawear pants.

The Holy Grail for sex toys is 3D printing, which allows users to create physical objects from drawings in the privacy of their own homes, which eliminates anodyne brown wrapped packages and ushers in a boundless future for discreet and remote sex.144

A note of caution about AI connected toys; your personal data might be at risk. The company behind a "smart vibrator" called the We-Vibe paid $3.75m to settle a class action lawsuit brought because they were collecting

---

[144] https://splinternews.com/these-entrepreneurs-are-literally-reshaping-the-sex-toy-1793840038

data on how often their 300,000 customers used the device, and at what intensity.145

*

If you are feeling constrained by your regular haunts and the limitations of your physical world, you can customize your own sex club and even your body or the body of your avatar into whatever sexual creature you can imagine. You can meet real people in real time, dance in virtual clubs, and join in just about any sexual activity without fear of judgment or exposure. AI renderings of motion capture graphics and, increasingly, the use of VR, integrated with virtual sex toys, is creating virtual sex worlds, which threaten to blur the distinction between actual physical sex and its virtual counterpart.146

The social consequences of this are not yet fully understood, but fears of increasing social isolation and gender objectification are being weighed against the benefits of greater self-acceptance and reduced shame for those who desire non-traditional sex.

The use of VR in training and education is exploding in the belief that experiencing something in the virtual world prepares people for experiencing it in the real world. Educators are beginning to employ simulated environments as a safe way to teach young people about risky social situations. Using VR headsets, a YMCA in Montreal put students in scripted situations helping "participants to see this delicate situation from the protagonist's point of view giving them a more complete

---

[145] https://www.theregister.co.uk/2017/08/16/web_enabled_vibrator_class_action_put_to_bed

[146] https://futureofsex.net/virtual-sex/sex-chat-games-virtual-sex-worlds-bring-fantasies-life/

and nuanced understanding of consent."[147] The idea was to explore consent from a female perspective and to raise awareness on gender equality and violence by having people step into someone else's shoes.

A joint program between Emory University and Georgia Tech is developing a VR program for young women of color… The experience teaches about safe sex practices, combatting STIs, and dealing with non-consensual sexual situations.148

But what if having a human partner for a relationship or even a hookup is too fraught or, sadly, too disappointing, or virtual toys are too limiting and virtual environments are too scary? AI gives people other options.

The growing capabilities of natural language processing, voice and facial recognition software, motion-sensing technology and animatronic engineering are leading to the creation of idealized humanoids. Initially, they were not much more than mannequins, pre-programmed, repetitive and dull. Now, because of AI, these robots soon will be capable of learning their owners' habits, preferences, and, yes, desires. Some developers imagine them as home health-aides, or companions, or the illusion of companions, for the elderly, the house-bound, the bereaved or lonely. But just the prospect of such companionship has awakened the hopes of all ages.

A 16-year-old girl, raised on Siri, explains. "There are people who have tried to make friends, but stumbled so badly that they've given up… So, when they hear this idea

---

[147] https://www.wareable.com/vr/vr-sexual-consent-ywca-montreal-6665

[148] https://motherboard.vice.com/en_us/article/bmvgaq/sex-ed-in-vr-can-prepare-young-women-for-actual-sex

of robots as companions, well… it's not like a robot has the mind to walk away or leave you or anything like that."

Soon, if she has the money, she may be able to purchase such a companion. But while these robot companions can *perform* empathy in a conversation about your friend, your mother, your child or your lover, they have no *experience* of any of these relationships. "Machines have not known the arc of a human life. They feel nothing of the human loss or love we describe to them. Their conversations about life occupy the realm of the as-if."[149]

The development of humanoid robots as friends benefits from the progress of life-like sex bots but also reflects the creators' larger hope for the technology. As one developer put it, [my] "ambition is to make fully functional humanoids that can model clothes and work supermarket checkouts, show guests to their rooms in hotels, do domestic chores and look after the sick and elderly." But he decided to focus on sex bots first. "The movements are easier to do. A fully functional android robot would take a couple of years to finish – a sex robot is accessible now… It's the fastest way to achieve my goal."150

We're still a long way from the bewitching robot in *Ex Machina*, which could easily pass for human. But AI is enabling sex partners that are increasingly responsive, both conversationally and physically. As Matt McMullen, the creator of the cutting-edge Harmony sex doll, put it, "we're creating an experience that's part entertainment, part relationship and part new frontier… The whole idea of

---

[149] https://www.nytimes.com/2018/08/11/opinion/there-will-never-be-an-age-of-artificial-intimacy.html\

[150]

https://www.theguardian.com/technology/2017/apr/27/race-to-build-world-first-sex-robot

a sex-capable robot is very contemporary, now and edgy. I get that. But Harmony is a sophisticated piece of machinery and her primary design is to carry on conversations."

The dolls are fully customizable allowing for Pygmalion's to create the doll of their choice. "Buyers can choose from 16 body styles, 31 faces and five skin tones, with choice of eye color, hair and hand-painted features like freckles, veining, breast size, even a variety of nipple colors and styles (like perky, puffy or supple)."

"The dolls range in weight from 75 to 115 pounds and can be as tall as 5 feet, 10 inches. Most orders are for female dolls, but there are male and transgender options. Some dolls, including Harmony, are designed with interchangeable magnetic faces so the owner can switch things up on a whim."

Harmony will 'remember your birthday, what you like to eat, the names of your brothers and sisters. She can hold a conversation about movies, music and books. And of course, Harmony will have sex with you whenever you want." They have been used in fashion shoots and starred in TV and movies – most famously as Ryan Gosling's artificial companion in *Lars and The Real Girl.*[151]

---

[151] https://realbotix.com

152

Right now, Harmony can't walk (though rumor has it she can orgasm). But it's not clear that's a drawback for her intended users who are willing to forgo the pleasures of a stroll.

Customers send in photos of real people they would like the dolls to resemble. Some even "bring their significant other in and get an exact copy doll made of them." The doll's personality is also customizable, with over 20 possible components. Owners "could have a Harmony that is kind, innocent, shy, insecure and helpful to different extents, or one that is intellectual, talkative, funny, jealous and happy."

---

[152] https://realbotix.com/

"Twenty years after RealDoll's official launch, Abyss Creations ships up to 600 models a year all over the world, priced from $4,400 for a small, basic version to $50,000 or more if the customer has specialized requirements. The company has made RealDolls with blood-red flesh, devil horns and vampire fangs and with thick hand-stitched body hair from neck to ankle. 153

*A sex doll created by a Japanese manufacturer to resemble actress Scarlett Johansson that was created without her permission.*154

Another manufacturer polled current and potential customers about what qualities they'd like to see in their sex dolls. While some privileged eye contact, voice recognition and realistic body temperature, other responses were crude and blatantly sexist. "If my RealDoll could

---

153 https://www.theguardian.com/technology/2017/apr/27/race-to-build-world-first-sex-robot

154 https://www.telegraph.co.uk/news/2016/12/21/sex-robots-would-give-us-think-want-not-truly-desire/

cook, clean, and screw whenever I wanted, I'd never date again." Many preferred their sex dolls to their actual wives and girlfriends.155

This raises the question as to whether these sex dolls are idealized "substitute women" that provide a connection for socially isolated men, or ethically questionable enablers of behavior that objectify women and threaten to turn men away completely from the messiness of human relationships.

Anthropologist and "robot ethicist" Kathleen Richardson, co-founder of The Campaign Against Sex Robots, claims "Sex dolls and mechanical dolls in the form of women and girls play on the idea that women are orifices to be penetrated. Imagery that dehumanizes others in order to justify rule over them serves a political purpose. These sex dolls of women and girls are serving a political purpose, to reinforce the idea that women and girls are sub-humans/orifices."156

Computer scientist Kate Devlin responded. "Perhaps the sexual companion robots offer us a chance to enhance our lives: to cure loneliness, to bring us pleasure, to eradicate exploitative sex work, or to treat and rehabilitate sexual offenders," she suggests. "Maybe this is our future and instead of fearing the rise of the machines, we could, quite literally, embrace them."157

---

[155] https://www.theguardian.com/technology/2017/apr/27/race-to-build-world-first-sex-robot

[156] https://ispr.info/2017/10/27/professor-kathleen-richardson-on-ethical-problems-with-sex-robots/comment-page-1/

[157] https://www.ft.com/content/8bce6690-d38c-11e8-9a3c-5d5eac8f1ab4

Devlin was also concerned that the sex bot's data base of deeply personalized knowledge of its user could be sold or exploited potentially causing great harm. This fear may be compounded by a burgeoning use of sex dolls in the world's oldest profession.

In Italy, a sex doll brothel opened recently. LumiDolls Torino charges around $90 for a half-hour session with a "very realistic" silicon doll. Patrons can choose from seven different female dolls and one male doll, called Alessandro, which has an adjustable penis varying from five to seven inches. Customers choose their doll's outfit – with options including "fitness" and "secretary" – and specify which position they want to find them in. "The positions they can take are many, almost all the ones in the Kamasutra," the brothel says.

Customers are, no doubt, happy to learn that the dolls are "thoroughly washed for two hours after use."[158]

Brothels with human prostitutes are illegal in Italy, though sex work itself is not a crime. Will sex doll brothels reduce the demand for human prostitution or will this spur ever more men, and some women, to have sex outside of relationships or let sex doll sex substitute for any kind of intimate human relationship?

In any case, the idea of sex doll brothels has already begun to spread. In the UK a sex doll brothel was opened in March of 2018. KinkySdollS, a Toronto-based company that manufactures sex dolls, planned to open a store in Houston, Texas where customers could go through a 'rent and romp' with a robot before buying. However, the city

---

[158]https://www.dailymail.co.uk/news/article-6126867/Italys-sex-doll-brothel-says-booked-WEEKS-opens-doors-today.html

council banned the idea before it could be put into action.159

*

Even if a sexual event with a robot is not quite your thing, AI will produce a revolution of sorts in the way pornography is both created and delivered to individual men and women.

"Humans have been creating images of sex and genitalia for millions of years, but it is only in the past few centuries – since the 1600s, according to historians – that these representations started meeting academics' preferred definition of pornography, which involves both the violation of taboos and the intention of arousal. The first efforts to make money off of this new endeavor could not have come long after that."160

Porn has been the initial economic driver of nearly every new communications technology. VHS machine sales were driven by the availability of porn tapes. The conventional wisdom is that Sony's Beta Max, a superior technology, lost the format war to VHS because Sony refused to mass produce porn for the format. (The fact that Beta Max was more expensive didn't help Sony's cause.) The emergence of softcore and pornographic programming on cable TV during the 1980s helped establish cable as a consumer medium and the accommodating cultural and regulatory

---

159 https://www.thesun.co.uk/news/7413445/first-sex-robot-brothel-banned-houston-texas/

160 https://www.theatlantic.com/business/archive/2016/04/pornography-industry-economics-tarrant/476580/

response to porn on cable helped establish TV as a sexual technology.161

Since cable television channels are not free over-the-air and thus cannot be viewed by those (such as children) without the proper equipment, the FCC rules regarding acceptable content do not apply to cable-originated networks, allowing greater freedom in the use of profanity, sex and violence.

Online pornography also pushed the growth of the internet, transforming it from a military invention used by geeks and academics to a global phenomenon. Pornography was the motivator behind the development of streaming video, the innovation of online credit card transactions and the drive for greater bandwidth.

The legal and ethical issues surrounding porn, labor abuses, content piracy, and a blemished supply chain, to name a few, are outside the purview of this chapter. But the use of AI in internet porn is squarely within our focus.

According to gender studies professor Shira Tarrant, one company, MindGeek, "owns eight out of the ten largest tube sites, such as such as *YouPorn*, *RedTube*, *Pornhub*... MindGeek uses algorithms to create highly curated personalized sites that are based on the user's search history. It's a lot like Amazon, where you look for a couple of books and they say, 'You might also be interested in this.' Then you're being spoon-fed a limited range of pornography based on the keywords you use, based on your geographic location, based on their algorithms and the information that they're processing

[161] Research of the author (Richard Kletter) while a graduate student at Stanford.

about time of day. They're doing a lot of data collection."162

Tarrant argues that MindGeek and other large corporate porn purveyors are determining the porn users can see via search terms. "It looks as if the very popular porn is 'MILF,' or 'teen,' etc. But in addition to reflecting a very spoon-fed range of desires, it does then look as if that's what's popular, and then people think that's popular, and it really shapes our views about female sexuality, about race, about gender, about trans status, about how we understand agency and desire."163

She does acknowledge that the ready availability of online porn means more people, and a wider variety of people including women and LGBTQ viewers, are able to explore sexuality in visual images in ways not previously possible.

It is widely assumed that the use of VR in porn will profoundly alter the industry. In VR porn "THEY WANT EMOTIONAL CONNECTION AND CUDDLING MORE THAN JUST SEX. THEY WANT THE ACTRESSES TO LOOK THEM IN THE EYES AND SAY 'I LOVE YOU.' WE'RE MOVING AWAY FROM THE GONZO HARDCORE STUFF TO MORE INTIMATE EXPERIENCES. THEY'RE REQUESTING MORE AVERAGE PENIS SIZES FROM THE ACTORS.

---

[162] www.theatlantic.com/business/archive/2016/04/pornography-industry-economics-tarrant/476580/

[163] www.theatlantic.com/business/archive/2016/04/pornography-industry-economics-tarrant/476580/

THEY WANT IT TO BE EASIER TO FEEL LIKE THEY'RE IN IT."[164]

As a leading VR porn producer put it, VR has the potential not just to make porn profitable again, but to make the tech world respect the adult film industry. "This is the first time I feel like we're leading in any way... Silicon Valley left us in the dust, but now adult is carrying the torch."165 YouTube's recommendation algorithm now will steer users to VR porn.

In VR porn, the viewer, in a sense is the star. He/she is completely or largely passive. He/she is acted upon. The viewer could be kissed, fondled, perform sex in an astonishing array of positions, all virtually, of course. But it seems real enough, and, certainly, more real than the flat two-dimensional version.

Porn is still completely male dominated both in terms of viewers and in the kinds of material being produced. But, by putting the viewer in the action, VR has the potential to change that, "intimacy is the watchword, eye contact is everything." According to "Scott" (not his real name) an avid consumer of VR porn, "the biggest emphasis seems to be on making it real. Making it intimate."

---

[164] https://virtualrealityreporter.com/vr-porn-s-impact-on-emotional-intimacy/

[165] https://www.wired.com/story/coming-attractions-the-rise-of-vr-porn/

"Adult studios, and the consumers who congregate on their message boards and on Reddit to share feedback, call this 'the girlfriend experience', or just 'GFE'."[166]

"IF IT'S TRUE THAT PORNOGRAPHY HAS 'RUINED SEX,' IT'S POSSIBLE THAT VR PORN COULD MAKE MEN BETTER, MORE EMOTIONAL LOVERS, BECAUSE THEY'RE LESS DISTANCED FROM THE SEXUAL ACT THEY'RE WATCHING."[167]

As for the future of VR porn, "We'll see livestreamed 'camming' improve, with cameras that allow viewers to lean in closer to the performers they see in their headsets, and we'll ultimately see performers wearing their own headsets, connecting with paying customers for private time (as avatars only, of course). And just as certainly, we'll see handwringing about how the immersive qualities of VR porn make it a danger–to young people, to women, to relationships, to the fabric of society itself."[168]

*

In 2007, futurist David Levy wrote *Love and Sex with Robots*, the first examination of what a robot future that involved sex might look like. He predicted that humans will one day marry robots and will certainly have both casual sex and love affairs with the machines. For many, such developments might mark the beginning of the end of societies that have survived and prospered for centuries

---

[166] https://www.wired.com/story/coming-attractions-the-rise-of-vr-porn/

[167] https://splinternews.com/when-it-comes-to-vr-porn-men-want-more-than-just-sex-1793860867

[168] https://www.wired.com/story/coming-attractions-the-rise-of-vr-porn/

government by the concept of love between humans. But Levy is more sanguine.

"I don't think the advent of emotional and sexual relationships with robots will end or damage human–human relationships. People will still love people and have sex with people. But I think there are people who feel a void in their emotional and sex lives for any number of reasons who could benefit from robots. Other people might try out a relationship with a robot out of curiosity, or be fascinated by what's written in the media. And there are always people who want to keep up with the neighbors".169

As with so much involving AI, the future is unclear, but the development of ever-more realistic sex robots for both men and women is certain. As AI enables sex robots to become more real, so relationships with humanoids, too, will be more real as well and every man and woman will have the opportunity to find satisfaction, not just out of a sexual engagement but also out of a potentially fully intimate relationship.

For many, this is a threatening development that will undermine the very structure of society and with it the nature of family, love and intimacy. Perhaps we will no longer have to go through the struggle of making a relationship work and instead simply download a new piece of software or trade in the robot for a different model. A purely transactional relationship in other words, something that millions of men already experience with prostitutes.

---

[169] https://www.scientificamerican.com/article/humans-marrying-robots/

It's possible, even probable, that the social stigma associated with prostitutes and brothels will vanish, once the objectification and abuse of women is removed and instead the engagement is just a machine transaction, little different from getting money from an ATM or buying that essential item from Amazon. This process of integration between the virtual and the real has already begun with the proliferation of programmable sex fantasies available on many porn sites. The next natural step is the designing of a personal sex robot and that is already available in several countries.

Pornography has been the engine that has driven significant technology developments since the beginning of the third industrial revolution, from the triumph of VHS over Betamax to the growth of the internet itself as well as the sexual expectations of young men and women. Today, the porn industry sees its future in the marketing of virtual reality and sex robots – and where porn goes, the rest of the world swiftly follows.

Chapter 8

Putting the Brain on Steroids

Louise, my supervisor at the firm, made my situation very clear. "If you're not getting ahead, you're falling behind." I was, she cautioned me, falling irrevocably farther behind each month and the firm could not carry me much longer. My clients were deserting me in droves, trusting their financial advice to cheaper, faster and more accurate AI software that could discern market trends, make trades, shift portfolios, even create trust instruments while I was having my morning coffee.

I threw myself on Louise's mercy. What could I do to keep up? She said, if I couldn't beat the ravenous beast of AI, maybe I should embrace it.

"The world was going to be divided between those who became one with AI and those who didn't, between those who could keep up and those who fell behind, between winners and losers. It would be merciless, and the losers would become castaways, living on the meager handouts the winners provided, if only to douse their revolutionary fire."

Louise was a fabulous success, but she was no smarter than me, had no fancier degrees and no greater work ethic. So, how had she managed to stay on top? She parted her thick lustrous hair above her ear and showed me a fading one-inch scar. "BMI," she said. "Brain machine interface. I can keep up with computers because, in a sense, I am one. I was one of the first to have a device implanted in my brain that enables me to do essentially everything your laptop can do and more. If humans can't adapt, we risk becoming irrelevant."

She asked me to name a recent book I'd read. She hadn't heard of it, but she focused her mind and instantly downloaded it from the cloud straight into her head. In another two minutes, she'd "read" it and could immediately expound on its characters and themes. I was astonished but also horrified.

"It sounds terrifying. Aren't you worried the brain ultimately will reject some foreign object attached to it?"

She fixed me in a withering stare and made plain the choice I was facing: "Embrace AI and lead a life atop the food chain, or stick to your antiquated notion of what it means to be human and slide into poverty and oblivion."

I knew that brain implants were being used to revive seemingly dead motor neurons, allowing paralyzed patients, stroke victims and those with Parkinson's, either to move their own limbs or to direct prosthetic limbs. But I had not yet heard of implants for the perfectly healthy who wanted only to improve their chances in the Hobbesian world of global business.

But I could no longer ignore this new opportunity. After all, didn't I want to improve my chances in that world?

The clinic was as fancy as a high-end spa and the word "cyborg" was nowhere in its literature. Instead, it used the language of the self-help movement, promising fulfillment, growth, energy, and, of course, unparalleled success. The procedure would be painless, recovery immediate, and transformation instantaneous, save a course of adaptation instructions on how to harness my fantastic new brain.

Videos showed gauzy scenes of happy, rich, people. The ads looked a cross between Viagra, Zoloft and Resort

Vacations. Celebrities, sports stars, tech stars and other "haves" were exclaiming the implant as the secret to their success, the ticket to wealth and happiness, even lying about being implanted themselves.

*Still, I panicked at the prospect of having a hole drilled in my skull and some apparatus, no matter how tiny, permanently attached to my brain. The staff tried to allay my fears. The hole-in-the-head method already was outdated. Now, they simply injected "syringe injectable electronics*170*" into the arm. The device then swims to pre-determined parts of the brain and forms a "neural lace" which meshes with and grows with the brain, creating a seamless interface between machine and biological circuitry*171. *It never needs recharging, can update automatically via a wireless connection to a server in the cloud, and is projected to last a lifetime. How can I argue with that?*

They sprayed my arm with a little lidocaine and inject the new addition to my brain. No incision. No blood.

*A month later and my augmented brain is getting up to speed. Already, Louise and I can engage in "consensual telepathy"*172 *in which we are, in effect, thinking together, a mutually voluntary conversation without expressing any words. At first, I was terrified that she could read my thoughts, but she can't do that unless I willingly grant her access – which I constantly fight the urge to do. It's made us wildly efficient. We don't need to be in the same room or even in the same city!*

---

[170] https://www.nature.com/articles/nnano.2015.115#author-information

[171] https://gizmodo.com/scientists-just-invented-the-neural-lace-1711540938

[172] https://waitbutwhy.com/2017/04/neuralink.html

I'm now dazzling my clients with data analytics and performance projections that surpass in both speed and accuracy their own primitive human attempts to parse the AI software they used to revere. And I can offer them that empathic "human touch" that, as yet, AI has yet to master – though, certainly, the software's ability to simulate emotion is about five minutes away.

My dates think I'm a genius, though they seem more interested in my capacity to handle their money than in my unenhanced romantic skills. My poker buddies marvel at my ability to announce the odds of any bluff as it happens and to make only high percentage plays. Reading has now become the equivalent of fast food. The languid pleasures of language have given way to instant digestion of the meta content. But I've become the best-read person I know.

Of course, I tell no one what explains my new brilliance and success. I appreciate that if everyone enhanced their brains in this way, we could all collaborate on solving problems and we might erase poverty and head off diseases. But, then, I would be just like everyone else again. And who wants that?

*

"The brain has always been considered the main inspiration for the field of Artificial Intelligence (AI). For many AI researchers, the ultimate goal of AI is to emulate the capabilities of the brain… but it's an incredibly daunting task considering that neuroscientists are still struggling trying to understand the cognitive mechanisms that power the magic of our brains."173

---

[173] https://towardsdatascience.com/five-functions-of-the-brain-that-are-inspiring-ai-research-2ba482ab8e2a

A professor, Jeff Lichtman, starts off his courses by asking his students the question, "If everything you need to know about the brain is a mile, how far have we walked in this mile?" He says students give answers like three-quarters of a mile, half a mile, a quarter of a mile, etc.– but that he believes the real answer is "about three inches."174

"Despite the challenges, more regularly we are seeing AI research and implementation algorithms that are inspired by specific cognition mechanisms in the human brain and that have been producing incredibly promising results."175

"In AI, the pace of recent research has been remarkable. Artificial systems now match human performance in challenging object recognition tasks and outperform expert humans in dynamic, adversarial environments such as Atari video games, the ancient board game of Go, and imperfect information games such as heads-up poker.

Machines can autonomously generate synthetic natural images and simulations of human speech that are almost indistinguishable from their real-world counterparts, translate between multiple languages, and create "neural art" in the style of well-known painters."176

But for all the speed and accuracy AI brings to various tasks, classic AI systems still lag behind human brains in several areas.

Humans are much more efficient, for example, at quickly learning new concepts from only a handful of examples. Humans are also really efficient at transferring general knowledge from one context to a completely new

---

[174] https://waitbutwhy.com/2017/04/neuralink.html

[175] https://towardsdatascience.com/five-functions-of-the-brain-that-are-inspiring-ai-research-2ba482ab8e2a

[176] https://www.cell.com/neuron/fulltext/S0896-6273%2817%2930509-3

context. “For example, a human who can drive a car, use a laptop computer, or chair a committee meeting is usually able to act effectively when confronted with an unfamiliar vehicle, operating system, or social situation.”177

Recent developments in AI architecture are catching up on so-called generalization or the ability to transfer learning from one context to another.

“As humans we have the ability to learn new tasks without forgetting previous knowledge. Neural networks, in contrast suffer from what is known as the problem of ‘catastrophic forgetting’. This occurs, for instance, as the neural network parameters shift toward the optimal state for performing the second of two successive tasks, overwriting the configuration that allowed them to perform the first.

“When you remember autobiographical events such as events or places we are using a brain function known as episodic memory. This mechanism is most often associated with circuits in the medial temporal lobe, prominently including the hippocampus. Recently, AI researchers have tried to incorporate methods inspired by episodic memory into reinforcement learning (RL) algorithms to episodic control. These networks store specific experiences (e.g., actions and reward outcomes associated with particular Atari game screens) and select new actions based on the similarity between the current situation input and the previous events stored in memory, taking the reward associated with those previous events into account.”[178]

---

[177] https://www.cell.com/neuron/fulltext/S0896-6273%2817%2930509-3

[178]https://towardsdatascience.com/five-functions-of-the-brain-that-are-inspiring-ai-research-2ba482ab8e2a

While AI systems can use big data to extrapolate about the future based on the past, these are essentially reactive forecasts. Humans, on the other hand, have the imagination to conceive of and plan for a different future than one described by the data. This capability is yet another challenge for new models of AI architecture in emulating the brain.

But the hope for systems that not only emulate the brain but interface with it is driving research and investment. "The global neuroprosthetics market is expected to reach $14.6 billion by 2024, according to a new report by Grand View Research, Inc. The increasing prevalence of neurological disorders coupled with the demand for cost-effective and technologically advanced implants is expected to drive the demand for neuroprosthetics market in the coming years."179

"2017 [was] a coming-out year for the brain–machine interface[180] (BMI), a technology that attempts to channel the mysterious contents of the two-and-a-half-pound glop inside our skulls to the machines that are increasingly central to our existence. The idea has been popped out of science fiction and into venture capital circles faster than the speed of a signal moving through a neuron. Facebook, Elon Musk, and other richly funded contenders, such as former Braintree founder Bryan Johnson, have talked seriously about silicone implants that would not only merge us with our computers, but also supercharge our intelligence."181

---

[179] https://www.grandviewresearch.com/press-release/global-neuroprosthetics-market

[181] https://www.wired.com/story/brain-machine-interface-isnt-sci-fi-anymore/?mbid=BottomRelatedStories

Johnson says, "My hope is that within 15 years we can build sufficiently powerful tools to interface with our brains," Johnson says. "Can I increase my rate of learning, scope of imagination, and ability to love? Can I understand what it's like to live in a 10-dimensional reality? Can we ameliorate or cure neurological disease and dysfunction?"

The shape that this technology will take is still unknown. Johnson uses the term "brain chip", but the developments taking place in neuroprosthesis are working towards less invasive procedures than opening up your skull and cramming a bit of hardware in; injectable sensors are one possibility."182

"Engineers and chemists recently demonstrated "mesh electronics" in which they were able to use "syringe injection (and subsequent unfolding) of sub-micrometer-thick, centimeter-scale macroporous mesh electronics through needles with a diameter as small as 100um. Our results show that electronic components can be injected into man-made and biological cavities, as well as dense gels and tissue, with >90% device yield."183

What does this mean? They've created an "ultra-fine mesh that can merge into the brain to create what appears to be a seamless interface between machine and biological circuitry. Called "mesh electronics," the device is so thin and supple that it can be injected with a needle – they've already tested it on mice, who survived the implantation and are thriving. The researchers describe their device as "syringe-injectable electronics," and say it has a number of uses, including monitoring brain activity, delivering

---

[182] https://www.theguardian.com/small-business-network/2017/dec/14/humans-20-meet-the-entrepreneur-who-wants-to-put-a-chip-in-your-brain

[183] https://www.nature.com/articles/nnano.2015.115

treatment for degenerative disorders like Parkinson's, and even enhancing brain capabilities.

"For now, the mice with this electronic mesh are connected by a wire to computer – but in the future, this connection could become wireless. The most amazing part about the mesh is that the mouse brain cells grew around it, forming connections with the wires, essentially welcoming a mechanical component into a biochemical system."

(They) "hope to begin testing it on humans as soon as possible, though realistically that's many years off. Still, this could be the beginning of the first true human internet, where brain-to-brain interfaces are possible via injectable electronics that pass your mental traffic through the cloud. What could go wrong?"184

The fear of what could go wrong has prompted cautions from the late Stephen Hawking, from Bill Gates and Elon Musk, among other luminaries, that AI will render humans second class citizens, that, as machines become capable of learning on their own without the benefit of human participation, choices will be made and actions taken that no longer privilege the needs of human-kind.

The brain–machine Interface (BMI) or brain–computer Interface (BCI), then, is, alternatively, the end of humanity as we know it or the process by which humans can keep up with the coming wave of robots. Musk, for example, is also developing AI implants to counter the threat of robot supremacy.

"My biggest concern is we don't have the ability to cooperate," said Bryan Johnson. "If we cooperate, we can

---

[184] https://gizmodo.com/scientists-just-invented-the-neural-lace-1711540938

solve problems. What I want is us to be in the game of solving problems.

"A brain–computer interface could allow us to communicate not only with each other – that's right, we're talking telepathy – but also with computers. It could theoretically allow us to collaborate with Artificial Intelligence to solve the world's most complex problems."

In this sense, what Johnson's trying to do could be interpreted as a kind of contingency plan for humanity. "I'd argue this is a necessity for the future and for our relevance," he said. "The alternative is that humans won't be able to adapt in the same way computers will, and as a result we'll risk becoming irrelevant."185

Our brain runs on a meager 20 watts of power, too dim for reading, but it has produced extraordinary accomplishments. "...IBM's Watson, a supercomputer runs on 20,000 watts of power, can outperform humans at calculation and *Jeopardy* but is still no match for human intelligence."

The brain's own "algorithms of 'everyday intelligence' are at work every time we recognize someone we know, tune in to a single voice at a crowded party, or learn the rules of physics by playing with toys as a baby. While these subconscious layers are so embedded in our biology that they often go unnoticed, without them the entire structure of intelligence collapses."186

The challenge for AI systems has been to learn how the brain does what it does and to incorporate that into the

---

[185] https://www.cnet.com/news/superintelligence-ai-robots-rise-up-humans-upgrade-brain-computer-interface/

[186] https://www.wired.com/story/to-advance-artificial-intelligence-reverse-engineer-the-brain/

architecture and software of systems that, ultimately, will enhance the brain itself. And that's what's happening now.

"The key breakthrough came when researchers used a combination of science and engineering. Specifically, some researchers began to build algorithms out of brain-like, multi-level, artificial neural networks so that they had neural responses like those that neuroscientists had measured in the brain. They also used mathematical models proposed by scientists to teach these deep neural networks to perform visual tasks that humans were found to be especially good at – like recognizing objects from many perspectives.

"This deep learning revolution launched a new era in AI. It has completely reshaped technologies from the recognition of faces and objects and speech, to automated language translation, to autonomous driving, and many others. The technological capability of our species was revolutionized in just a few years – the blink of an eye on the timescale of human civilization.

But this is just the beginning. Deep learning algorithms resulted from new understanding of just one layer of human intelligence – visual perception. There is no limit to what can be achieved from a deeper understanding of other algorithmic layers of intelligence…

"Discovering how the human brain works in the language of engineers will not only lead to transformative AI. It will also illuminate new approaches to helping those who are blind, deaf, autistic, schizophrenic, or who have learning disabilities or age-related memory loss. Armed with an engineering description of the brain, scientists will see new ways to repair, educate, and augment our own minds.

"Until recently, the dream of being able to control one's environment through thoughts had been in the realm of science fiction. Today, humans can use the electrical signals from brain activity to interact with, influence, or change their environments. The emerging field of brain–computer interface (BCI) technology may allow individuals unable to speak and/or use their limbs to once again communicate or operate assistive devices for walking and manipulating objects."

A BCI is a computer-based system that acquires "brain signals, analyzes them, and translates them into commands that are relayed to an output device to carry out a desired action.

"Small intracortical microarray… may be embedded in the cortex. These intracortical microarray systems can record the action potentials of individual neurons and the local field potentials (essentially a micro-EEG) produced by a relatively limited population of nearby neurons and synapses."187

Justin Sanchez, a faculty member of the Miami Project to Cure Paralysis and a leading researcher in the field, characterized the goal of his work as trying to "understand the neural code," which would involve putting "very fine microwire electrodes" – the diameter of a human hair – "into the brain." When we do that, he said, we would be able to "listen in to the music of the brain" and "listen in to what somebody's motor intent might be" and get a glimpse of "your goals and your rewards" and then "start to understand how the brain encodes behavior."

"With all of this knowledge, what we're trying to do is build new medical devices, new implantable chips for the

[187] https://www.ncbi.nlm.nih.gov/pmc/articles/PMC3497935/

body that can be encoded or programmed with all of these different aspects. Now, you may be wondering, what are we going to do with those chips? Well, the first recipients of these kinds of technologies will be the paralyzed. It would make me so happy by the end of my career if I could help get somebody out of their wheelchair."188

This process involves many risks, not the least of which are drilling a hole in people's heads and attaching a foreign substance to the brain which may reject such invasion, an issue called biocompatibility. The potential for wound scarring and blood leakage further complicate the process. Also, the resolution of the interface, its durability and capability to upgrade or maintain power are all areas of current research exploration.

To counteract the disadvantages of implanted devices, the use of non-invasive BCIs has become a hot research area for new companies and universities.

A company called CTRL-Labs is skipping implanting devices in the brain itself and, instead, using a band around the arm – "the secret mouthpiece of the mind" – to capture the signals controlling movements that travel through the spinal column The company's innovation lies in picking up signals from individual neurons… and, "even more important, figuring out the relationship between the electrode activity and the muscles so that CTRL-Labs can translate signals into instructions that can control computer devices."189

---

[188] https://www.theatlantic.com/magazine/archive/2018/11/the-pentagon-wants-to-weaponize-the-brain-what-could-go-wrong/570841/

[189] https://www.wired.com/story/brain-machine-interface-isnt-sci-fi-anymore/?mbid=BottomRelatedStories

Other systems use EEGs attached to the scalp. To get a higher bandwidth resolution, some systems record signals from the cortical surface which requires implantation of a subdural or epidural electrode array – still far less invasive than the mesh electronics or other versions of full brain implantation.

Researchers at Stanford have "demonstrated that a brain-to-computer hookup can enable people with paralysis to type via direct brain control at the highest speeds and accuracy levels reported to date."

The experiment "involved three study participants with severe limb weakness – two from amyotrophic lateral sclerosis, also called Lou Gehrig's disease, and one from a spinal cord injury. They each had one or two baby-aspirin-sized electrode arrays placed in their brains to record signals from the motor cortex, a region controlling muscle movement. These signals were transmitted to a computer via a cable and translated by algorithms into point-and-click commands guiding a cursor to characters on an onscreen keyboard."

Each participant, after minimal training, mastered the technique sufficiently to outperform the results of any previous test of brain–computer interfaces, or BCIs, for enhancing communication by people with similarly impaired movement.

"The investigational system used in the study, an intracortical brain-computer interface called the BrainGate Neural Interface System, represents the newest generation of BCIs. Previous generations picked up signals first via electrical leads placed on the scalp, then by being surgically positioned at the brain's surface beneath the skull.

An intracortical BCI uses a tiny silicon chip, just over one-sixth of an inch square, from which protrude 100 electrodes that penetrate the brain to about the thickness of a quarter and tap into the electrical activity of individual nerve cells in the motor cortex."190

"BCI technology has also been used to help ALS patients suffering from varying degrees of 'locked-in syndrome' and has provided the means for them to communicate using humanoid robots. Humanoid robots are robots that are designed to have the shape of a human body. Post-hoc analysis of the preliminary data indicates that such patients can communicate using humanoid robots to accomplish routine tasks, such as retrieve mail or pick up a plate to eat dinner from. This technology could potentially be life changing. Before this type of research, patients solely depended on a caregiver, such as family members or friends to accomplish simple tasks.

"A project called Brainternet is generating additional excitement for the field of BCI technology by converting the brain of a user into a node for the internet of things (IoT), which allows a 'plugged-in' brain to connect to the internet. A headset of electrodes is attached and action potentials are detected and then transmitted to a small receiver called a Raspberry Pi. This device acts to convert brain activity into signals uploaded to public domains on the internet. The process can be tracked in real time. Once connected, a user can communicate with other users online by using brainwaves detected via an EEG device.

---

[190] https://med.stanford.edu/news/all-news/2017/02/brain-computer-interface-allows-fast-accurate-typing-by-people-with-paralysis.html

"The possibilities of BCI technology are nowhere near exhausted. The emergence of non-invasive BCI devices – based off an EEG – is emblematic of future mainstream accessibility of BCI technology. For example, BCI technology can allow users to create music with their thoughts. The specific device for this is called an encephalophone, which is controlled by the visual or motor cortex. The device works by receiving input from cortical signals such as the posterior dominant rhythm (PDR) from the visual cortex or the mu signal from the motor cortex. This technology can be used by people who suffer from neurodegenerative conditions, but most likely will also become a mainstream product."191

Elon Musk, whose company Neuralink is working on BMIs, puts it this way:

"The first use of the technology will be to repair brain injuries as a result of stroke or cutting out a cancer lesion, where somebody's fundamentally lost a certain cognitive element. It could help with people who are quadriplegics or paraplegics by providing a neural shunt from the motor cortex down to where the muscles are activated. It can help with people who, as they get older, have memory problems and can't remember the names of their kids, through memory enhancement, which could allow them to function well to a much later time in life – the medically advantageous elements of this for dealing with mental disablement of one kind or another, which of course happens to all of us when we get old enough, are very significant."[192]

---

[191] http://in-training.org/future-brain-computer-interface-technology-15655

[192] https://waitbutwhy.com/2017/04/neuralink.html

AI can be used to provide faster and more accurate diagnosis of neurodegenerative diseases. Alzheimer's disease, for example, is difficult to diagnose, so patients often don't get treatment until too late in the process to halt disease progression or relieve symptoms.

"In these cases, AI is paramount. Medical imagery techniques can spot cognitive impairment that is either difficult or impossible to see with the naked eye. For example, researchers Nicola Amoroso and Marianna La Rocca at the University of Bari in Italy are currently developing a machine-learning algorithm that can detect changes in the brain caused by Alzheimer's disease up to a decade before noticeable symptoms appear.

"The algorithm can accurately distinguish a diseased brain from a healthy one, analyzing the neuronal connectivity between them which would help them pinpoint patients who are likely to develop Alzheimer's in a decade. As the technology is still in development, they are unable to tell whether it could detect changes even earlier. This incredible chance at early diagnosis is a real game-changer for patients, allowing them the opportunity to incorporate life-style changes and benefit from drugs in development that will help them to control the disease."193

According to the Centers for Disease Control, someone in the US suffers a stroke every 40 seconds. Doctors sum up the importance of each successive minute with a pithy and chilling phrase: "time is brain." The longer a person

---

[193] https://www.proclinical.com/blogs/2018-4/how-ai-is-tackling-neurodegenerative-diseases

waits for treatment, the more brain tissue dies. Time is brain, but also disability, or death.194

Technically, the treatment of motor neuron disabilities and other illnesses via BCI or BMI are primarily concerned with "neuronal output," that is, reading the signals coming from the brain, harnessing those signals to perform functions, and providing feedback to maintain and improve those functions.

The internet gave us access to all the world's knowledge and information. Computers have given us the ability to outsource tasks which the machines can do faster, better and more accurately than humans. "But there's one kind of brain labor computers still can't quite do. *Thinking.* Computers can compute and organize and run complex software – software that can even learn on its own. But they can't think in the way humans can… the ultimate brain extension tool would be one that can really, actually, legitimately think.195

A program manager at DARPA (the Defense Advanced Research Projects Agency) describes his mission, "to free the mind from the limitations of even healthy bodies… to make human beings something other than what we are, with powers beyond the ones we're born with and beyond the ones we can organically attain."196

"Altogether, there are around 100 billion neurons in the brain that make up this unthinkably vast network–similar

---

[194] https://www.wired.com/story/using-ai-to-help-stroke-victims-when-time-is-brain/

[195] https://waitbutwhy.com/2017/04/neuralink.html

[196] https://www.theatlantic.com/magazine/archive/2018/11/the-pentagon-wants-to-weaponize-the-brain-what-could-go-wrong/570841/

to the number of stars in the Milky Way and over 10 times the number of people in the world... But somehow, none of this is why building effective brain-computer interfaces is so hard, or so daunting. What makes BMIs so hard is that the engineering challenges are monumental. It's physically working with the brain that makes BMIs among the hardest engineering endeavors in the world."197

The tools for recording and stimulating the brain face certain issues:

1) Scale *– how many neurons can be simultaneously recorded?*

2) Resolution *– how detailed is the information the tool receives? There are two types of resolution,* ***spatial*** *(how closely your recordings come to telling you how individual neurons are firing) and* ***temporal*** *(how well you can determine WHEN the activity you record happened).*

3) Invasiveness *– is surgery needed, and if so, how extensively? Beyond medically necessary implantations, BMIs won't become the must-have self-improvement feature as long as the enhancement requires drilling holes in our heads. So, "non-invasive" is the mantra of many companies and labs working on this problem.*198

Bandwidth, too, is a huge issue. The Defense Advanced Research Projects Agency (DARPA), a source of funding for much basic research in the US and the agency that gave us the internet, recently awarded research funding to address this issue.

"A new DARPA program aims to develop an implantable neural interface able to provide unprecedented

---

[197] https://waitbutwhy.com/2017/04/neuralink.html
[198] https://waitbutwhy.com/2017/04/neuralink.html

signal resolution and data-transfer bandwidth between the human brain and the digital world. The interface would serve as a translator, converting between the electrochemical language used by neurons in the brain and the ones and zeros that constitute the language of information technology. The goal is to achieve this communications link in a biocompatible device no larger than one cubic centimeter in size, roughly the volume of two nickels stacked back to back."

The program, Neural Engineering System (NESD), stands to dramatically enhance research capabilities in neurotechnology and provide a foundation for new therapies.

Today's best brain-computer interface systems are like two supercomputers trying to talk to each other using an old 300-baud modem," said Phillip Alvelda, the NESD program manager. "Imagine what will become possible when we upgrade our tools to really open the channel between the human brain and modern electronics."199

In current experiments with rats and BMIs, the rodents have wires coming out of their heads, not a recipe for broad acceptance of the technology. So, any successful large-scale deployment of devices will require that systems update their software and recharge power wirelessly.

Another hurdle is biocompatibility. "Delicate electronics tend to not do well inside a Jell-O ball. And the human body tends to not like having foreign objects in it. But the brain interfaces of the future are intended to last forever without any problems. This means that the device will likely need to be hermetically sealed and robust enough to survive decades of the oozing and shifting of the neurons

---

[199] https://www.darpa.mil/news-events/2015-01-19

around it. And the brain – which treats today's devices like invaders and eventually covers them in scar tissue – will need to somehow be tricked into thinking the device is just a normal brain part doing its thing.200

"A team at the University of Illinois is developing an interface made of silk which can be rolled up into a thin bundle and inserted into the brain relatively non-invasively. There, it would theoretically spread out around the brain and melt into the contours like shrink wrap. On the silk would be flexible silicon transistor arrays.

Other innovations under investigation include printing an electrode array on the skin, sort of a signal receptor temporary tattoo.

Then, there's neural dust; tiny, 100μm silicon sensors (about the same as the width of a hair) that would be sprinkled through the cortex."201

Of course, no matter the technique, there is a question of available space. Where exactly are you going to put your device that can interface with a million neurons in a skull that's already dealing with making space for 100 billion neurons? A million electrodes using today's multielectrode arrays would be the size of a baseball. So further miniaturization is another dramatic innovation to add to the list.

Even if we conquer the above issues, there is still a translation problem: how do we interpret the language of the brain and act on the massive output from a million neurons all sending their signals at once?

To the futurists, however, the Holy Grail of BMI is not in deciphering the brain's output but, rather, it's putting

[200] https://waitbutwhy.com/2017/04/neuralink.html
[201] https://waitbutwhy.com/2017/04/neuralink.html

information into the brain to stimulate the neurons and augment its native capabilities, to make the human brain the equal of the robotic AI machine brain.

As researchers gain greater insight into how neurons transmit information, the hope is it will soon be possible for computers to communicate in real time with the brain in more sophisticated ways, giving rise to capabilities long thought to be the province of science fiction.

Julian Sanchez, who left academia to work at DARPA, takes this idea of communication from brain even farther. "If I know the neural codes in one individual, could I give that neural code to another person? I think you could." Sanchez calls it "memory prosthesis."202

Armed with such AI-derived deep understanding, it will soon be possible for computers to communicate in real time with the brain in highly sophisticated ways, enabling such science fiction-sounding capabilities already demonstrated in the lab (see references) such as:

Brain-to-brain transfer of learning and memory...

Hybrid AI/brain combinations, i.e. (AI assisted brain) learning.

Thought-controlled computers and machines.

Mind-controlled prosthetics for spinal cord patients and amputees."203

Sound crazy or at least like science fiction? "A brain-to-brain interface (BTBI) enabled a real-time transfer of behaviorally meaningful sensorimotor information

---

[202] https://www.theatlantic.com/magazine/archive/2018/11/the-pentagon-wants-to-weaponize-the-brain-what-could-go-wrong/570841/

[203] https://www.psychologytoday.com/us/blog/long-fuse-big-bang/201809/the-future-brain-science

between the brains of two rats" *which were separated by thousands of miles*.

"In this BTBI, an "encoder" rat performed sensorimotor tasks that required it to select from two choices of tactile or visual stimuli. While the encoder rat performed the task, samples of its cortical activity were transmitted to matching cortical areas of a "decoder" rat using intracortical microstimulation (ICMS). The decoder rat learned to make similar behavioral selections, guided solely by the information provided by the encoder rat's brain.

"These results demonstrated that a complex system was formed by coupling the animals' brains, suggesting that BTBIs can enable dyads or networks of animal's brains to exchange, process, and store information and, hence, serve as the basis for studies of novel types of social interaction and for biological computing devices."204

This kind of communication is not limited to rats. In recent years, physicists and neuroscientists have developed an armory of tools that can sense certain kinds of thoughts and transmit information about them into other brains. That has made brain-to-brain communication a reality.

These tools include electroencephalograms (EEGs) that record electrical activity in the brain and transcranial magnetic stimulation (TMS), which can transmit information into the brain.

Andrea Stocco and his colleagues at the University of Washington in Seattle have created "a network that allows three individuals to send and receive information directly to their brains." They say the network is easily scalable

---

[204] https://www.nature.com/articles/srep01319

and limited only by the availability of EEG and TMS devices.

The proof-of-principle network connects three people: two senders and one person able to receive and transmit, all in separate rooms and unable to communicate conventionally. The group together has to solve a Tetris-like game in which a falling block has to be rotated so that it fits into a space at the bottom of the screen.

The two senders, wearing EEGs, can both see the full screen. The game is designed so the shape of the descending block fits in the bottom row either if it is rotated by 180 degrees or if it is not rotated. The senders have to decide which and broadcast the information to the third member of the group.

To do this, they vary the signal their brains produce. If the EEG picks up a 15 Hz signal from their brains, it moves a cursor toward the right-hand side of the screen. When the cursor reaches the right-hand side, the device sends a signal to the receiver to rotate the block.

The senders can control their brain signals by staring at LEDs on either side of the screen – one flashing at 15 Hz and the other at 17 Hz…

"…Having received data from both senders, the receiver performs the action. But crucially, the game allows for another round of interaction.

"The senders can see the block falling and so can determine whether the receiver has made the right call and transmit the next course of action – either rotate or not – in another round of communication."

This allows the researchers to have some fun. In some of the trials they deliberately change the information from one sender to see if the receiver can determine whether to ignore it. That introduces an element of error often reflected in real social situations.

But the question they investigate is whether humans can work out what to do when the data rates are so low. It turns out humans, being social animals, can distinguish between the correct and false information using the brain-to-brain protocol alone.

"There is no reason why the network cannot be extended to the Internet, allowing participants around the world to collaborate. 'A cloud-based brain-to-brain interface server could direct information transmission between any set of devices on the brain-to-brain interface network and make it globally operable through the Internet, thereby allowing cloud-based interactions between brains on a global scale,' Stocco and his colleagues say."205

What does this mean for the way we communicate? Here are some ways an advanced BMI/BCI might alter how we transmit our thoughts:

Multimedia communication:...Imagine how much easier it would be to describe a dream you had or a piece of music stuck in your head or a memory you're thinking about if you could just beam the thing into someone's head, like showing them on your computer screen... How much faster could a team of engineers or architects or designers plan out a new bridge or a new building or a new dress if they could beam the vision in their head onto a screen and others could adjust it with their minds, versus sketching things out...?

Emotional communication: Emotions are the quintessential example of a concept that words are poorly-equipped to accurately describe. If ten people say, "I'm sad," it actually means ten different things…

With BMI/BCIs, "when one person communicates just what they're feeling, the other person would be able to access the feeling in their own emotional centers. Obvious implications for a future of heightened empathy. But emotional communication could also be used for things like entertainment, where a movie, say, could also project out to the audience – directly into their limbic systems – certain feelings it wants the audience to feel as they watch…

Sensory communication: Say you're on a beautiful hike and you want to show your husband the view. No problem – just think out to him to request a brain connection. When he accepts, connect your retina feed to his visual cortex. Now his vision is filled with exactly what your eyes see, as if he's there. He asks for the other senses to get the full picture, so you connect those too and now he hears the waterfall in the distance and feels the breeze and smells the trees and jumps when a bug lands on your arm.

This opens up any experience to everyone: exotic travel, tapping into the affect and sensory experiences of a professional athlete in the middle of a game, or transmitting your own experiences to anyone and everyone. "The days of fancy experiences being limited to rich people will be long over."

An effective brain interface would also give us the ability to control competing inputs within our brain, say between the pre-frontal cortex and the limbic system,

---

[205] https://www.technologyreview.com/s/612212/the-first-social-network-of-brains-lets-three-people-transmit-thoughts-to-each-others-heads/

something that could revolutionize control of our appetites.

As Moran Cerf, at the forefront of BMI research puts it, "Consider eating a chocolate cake. While eating, we feed data to our cognitive apparatus. These data provide the enjoyment of the cake. The enjoyment isn't in the cake, per se, but in our neural experience of it. Decoupling our sensory desire (the experience of cake) from the underlying survival purpose (nutrition) will soon be within our reach."[206]

Increase your knowledge: If our brains had access to all the knowledge in the world, what might we do with that capability?

Level 1: I want to know a fact. I call on the cloud for that info – like Googling something with my brain – and the answer, in text, appears in my mind's eye. Basically, what I do now except it all happens in my head.

Level 2: I want to know a fact. I call on the cloud for that info, and then a second later I just KNOW it. No reading was involved – it was more like the way I'd recall something from memory.

Level 3: I just know the fact I want to know the second I want it. I don't even know if it came from the cloud or if it was stored in my brain. I can essentially treat the whole cloud like my brain. I don't know all the info – my brain could never fit it all – but any time I want to know something it downloads into my consciousness so seamlessly and quickly, it's as if it were there all along.

---

[206] https://www.forbes.com/sites/robertwolcott/2017/03/30/virtual-reality-sex-and-chocolate-cake-desire-in-a-post-virtual-world/#5d3db7e973a6

Level 4: Beyond just knowing facts, I can deeply UNDERSTAND anything I want to, in a complex way. We discussed the example of *MOBY DICK*. Could I download *MOBY DICK* from the cloud into my memory and then suddenly have it be the same as if I had read the whole book? Where I'd have thoughts and opinions and I could cite passages and have discussions about the themes?"207

How soon, if ever, will these capabilities be available to us? Predictions vary from 10 years to never. Clearly, if they happen, the changes will not come all at once. They will be titrated out to us as the technology improves and as our ability to integrate such developments into our lives comes without creating more harm than opportunity.

Whether BMI/BCIs reach Level 4 development, these systems certainly will progress over time, raising profound questions for human civilization.

"…We are on a path to a world in which it will be possible to decode people's mental processes and directly manipulate the brain mechanisms underlying their intentions, emotions and decisions; where individuals could communicate with others simply by thinking; and where powerful computational systems linked directly to people's brains aid their interactions with the world such that their mental and physical abilities are greatly enhanced.

"Such advances could revolutionize the treatment of many conditions, from brain injury and paralysis to epilepsy and schizophrenia, and transform human experience for the better. But the technology could also exacerbate social inequalities and offer corporations,

[207] https://waitbutwhy.com/2017/04/neuralink.html

hackers, governments or anyone else new ways to exploit and manipulate people. And it could profoundly alter some core human characteristics: private mental life, individual agency and an understanding of individuals as entities bound by their bodies."208

Here are four ethical priorities put forward by the Morningside Group, a consortium of neuroscientists, nanotechnologists, clinicians, ethicists and machine-intelligence engineers, for us to consider as the race to augment our brains proceeds.

Privacy and consent: An extraordinary level of personal information can already be obtained from people's data trails. Researchers at MIT discovered in 2015 that fine-grained analysis of people's motor behavior, revealed through their keyboard typing patterns on personal devices, could enable earlier diagnosis of Parkinson's disease A 2017 study suggests that measures of mobility patterns, such as those obtained from people carrying smartphones during their normal daily activities, can be used to diagnose early signs of cognitive impairment resulting from Alzheimer's disease."

The group believes believe that "citizens should have the ability – and right – to keep their neural data private..." For all neural data, the ability to opt out of sharing should be the default choice, and assiduously protected. Another safeguard is to restrict the centralized processing of neural data.

Agency and identity: Neurotechnologies could clearly disrupt people's sense of identity and agency and shake core assumptions about the nature of the self and personal

---

[208] https://www.nature.com/news/four-ethical-priorities-for-neurotechnologies-and-ai-1.22960

responsibility – legal or moral. People could end up behaving in ways that they struggle to claim as their own, if machine learning and brain-interfacing devices enable faster translation between an intention and an action. If people can control devices through their thoughts across great distances, or if several brains are wired to work collaboratively, our understanding of who we are and where we are acting will be disrupted.

As neurotechnologies develop and corporations, governments and others start striving to endow people with new capabilities, individual identity (our bodily and mental integrity) and agency (our ability to choose our actions) must be protected as basic human rights.

Augmentation: The pressure to adopt enhancing neurotechnologies, such as those that allow people to radically expand their endurance or sensory or mental capacities, is likely to change societal norms, raise issues of equitable access and generate new forms of discrimination.

Moreover, it's easy to imagine an augmentation arms race. In recent years, we have heard staff at DARPA and the US Intelligence Advanced Research Projects Activity discuss plans to provide soldiers and analysts with enhanced mental abilities ("super-intelligent agents"). These would be used for combat settings and to better decipher data streams."209

The most draconian version of this last capability would be remote-controlled human soldiers who could be commanded to do things that would contravene not only the rules of war but of their basic human values and

---

[209] https://www.nature.com/news/four-ethical-priorities-for-neurotechnologies-and-ai-1.22960

instincts. In the old movie, *The Manchurian Candidate*, a political candidate was brainwashed to act on the narrow interests of his controllers. It's not impossible to imagine a future solider, implanted with a BMI, acting on the interests of his commanders beyond any current method of training or dedication.

"Any lines drawn will inevitably be blurry, given how hard it is to predict which technologies will have negative impacts on human life. But we urge that guidelines are established at both international and national levels to set limits on the augmenting neurotechnologies that can be implemented, and to define the contexts in which they can be used – as is happening for gene editing in humans.

Bias: When scientific or technological decisions are based on a narrow set of systemic, structural or social concepts and norms, the resulting technology can privilege certain groups and harm others…

"We advocate that countermeasures to combat bias become the norm for machine learning. We also recommend that probable user groups (especially those who are already marginalized) have input into the design of algorithms and devices as another way to ensure that biases are addressed from the first stages of technology development."210

Even with the most responsible, ethical strictures on the use of AI to augment ourselves, the economic and social pressures to do so will only grow as the fears of the technology subside and its capabilities and benefits become clearer.

---

[210] https://www.nature.com/news/four-ethical-priorities-for-neurotechnologies-and-ai-1.22960

As a further caution, researchers from Kaspersky Labs and the Oxford University Functional Neurosurgery Group found existing and potential risk scenarios, each of which could be exploited by attackers. These include:

Exposed connected infrastructure: The researchers found one serious vulnerability and several worrying misconfigurations in an online management platform popular with surgical teams.

Insecure or unencrypted data transfer between the implant, the programming software, and any associated networks could enable malicious tampering of a patient's implant or even whole groups of implants (and patients) connected to the same infrastructure. Manipulation could result in changed settings causing pain, paralysis or the theft of private and confidential data.

Design constraints as patient safety takes precedence over security. For example, a medical implant needs to be controlled by physicians in emergency situations, including when a patient is rushed to a hospital far from their home. This precludes use of any password that isn't widely known among clinicians. It also means that by default such implants need to be fitted with a software 'backdoor'.

Insecure behavior by medical staff: Programmers with patient-critical software were being accessed with default passwords, were used to browse the internet or had additional apps downloaded onto them.

"Within five years, scientists expect to be able to electronically record the brain signals that build memories and then enhance or even rewrite them before putting them back into the brain. A decade from now, the first commercial memory boosting implants could appear on the market – and, within 20 years or so, the technology could be advanced enough to allow for extensive control over memories.

The healthcare benefits of all this will be significant, and this goal is helping to fund and drive research and development. However, as with other advanced bio-connected technologies, once the technology exists it will also be vulnerable to commercialization, exploitation and abuse.

New threats resulting from this could include the mass manipulation of groups through implanted or erased memories of political events or conflicts; while "repurposed" cyber-threats could target new opportunities for cyber-espionage or the theft, deletion of or "locking" of memories (for example, in return for a ransom)."211

Finally, our assumption throughout this chapter has been that AI deep learning systems hold the promise of enhancing the human brain in the ways we have discussed. But what if the human brain's unique capabilities were used to enhance robots? What if we could put a human brain in a robot body?

Kevin Warwick, professor of Cybernetics at the University of Reading, poses the issue this way:

"Our thoughts tend to be that the robot might be operated remotely by a human, as in the case of a bomb disposal robot, or it may be controlled by a simple computer program, or may even be able to learn with a microprocessor as its technological brain. In all these cases we regard the robot simply as a machine. But what if the robot has a biological brain made up of brain cells (neurons), possibly even human neurons…?"

---

[211] https://securelist.com/hackers-attacking-your-memories/88285/

"...The potential of such systems, including the range of tasks they could deal with, also means that the physical body could take on different forms. For example, there is no reason why the body could not be a two-legged walking robot, with a rotating head and the ability to walk around in a building.

"...An individual human so connected can potentially benefit from some of the advantages of machine/Artificial Intelligence, for example rapid and highly accurate mathematical abilities in terms of 'number crunching', a high-speed, almost infinite, internet knowledge base, and accurate long-term memory. Additionally, it is widely acknowledged that humans have only five senses that we know of, whereas machines offer a view of the world which includes infrared, ultraviolet and ultrasonic signals, to name but a few...

"...It is clear that connecting a human brain, by means of an implant, with a computer network could in the long term open up the distinct advantages of machine intelligence, communication and sensing abilities to the implanted individual."212

In the medium term, the only people who will be able to afford an implant will be the rich and those who might receive a grant for an implant will be the already super-intelligent.

The risk as the technology moves forward is that income inequality will soon be matched by intelligence inequality. On one side of the digital divide will be us mere mortals who have benefited from human evolution to get where we are. On the other side will be those with augmented

---

[212] https://www.bbvaopenmind.com/en/articles/the-future-of-artificial-intelligence-and-cybernetics/

intelligence who will, in effect, rule our world through their access to almost unlimited knowledge.

The logical consequence of this phase of the AI revolution is the creation of a separate "super race" of humans who will, for a while, see themselves as sitting on the pinnacle of human development. Until, of course, super intelligent robots start to compete in what will no doubt be an epic struggle for supremacy.

As Professor Warwick put it, "it is likely that many humans will upgrade and become part machine themselves. This may mean that ordinary (non-implanted) humans are left behind as a result. If you could be enhanced, would you have any problem with it?"213

---

[213] https://www.bbvaopenmind.com/en/articles/the-future-of-artificial-intelligence-and-cybernetics/

Chapter 9

Your Doctor Is in a Hologram

Americans have the shortest life expectancy and highest infant mortality rate of any high-income nation, yet we spend roughly twice what other wealthy nations do on health care. So, we pay far more for much less. Can AI bend the cost curve, increase access and capacity and improve the accuracy of diagnosis and treatment?214

Years ago, Stanford used what was then a revolutionary technology in an experimental program called "Satellite House Call," in which doctors "examined" remote villagers via satellite. It was the villager's only access to health care and the experiment proved enormously beneficial.215

Soon, anyone, anywhere, will be able to see a doctor without ever leaving home. A fearful young patient may be comforted bedside by Princess Leia in the form of a hologram. She'll read the case notes, chat comfortably in natural language with the patient, and provide a diagnosis and treatment plan. According to a BCG/MIT SLOAN report, "Remote diagnostics can eliminate or drastically reduce the number of patient visits to a hospital for some

---

[214] http://time.com/5197347/us-health-care-spending/

[215] Unpublished research of one of the authors, Richard Kletter, while a grad student at Stanford.

conditions" thereby decreasing cost and often improving prognosis and treatment results.216

AI is already proving useful in a variety of health care uses, including virtual assistants, mining medical records, designing treatment plans, using avatars for clinical training, drug creation, health bots for helping the elderly stay on drug regimens, robotic surgery, even using 3D printing for creating skin cells for rapid wound healing.

Soon, our cellphones will carry diagnostic apps that not only take simple vital signs but can also instantly analyze a wide range of health indicators, including recording more complex heart rhythms (such as the critically important QT interval) that now require ECG machines and an office visit, which could save thousands of lives a year. "Researchers at Stanford University have created an AI algorithm that can identify and diagnose skin cancer using images of moles, rashes, and lesions, may someday be available as a mobile app on smartphones."217

The more images, the more data, the better the results from AI machine learning tools. So, as the amount of accumulated medical data expands, AI tools can take speedy advantage of that data in ways no combination of humans can match. In effect, the ability to analyze large amounts of data beats hundreds of years of combined medical schooling.

Federal guidelines have encouraged the switch to electronic health records (EHRs) among hospitals and doctors. EHR use is now nearly universal (96% of hospitals and 87% of physicians reported usage of a

---

[216] https://www.bcg.com/publications/2017/technology-digital-strategy-putting-artificial-intelligence-work.aspx

[217] https://medium.com/@Unfoldlabs/the-impact-of-artificial-intelligence-in-healthcare-4bc657f129f5

certified EHR in 2015). This has resulted in a vast expansion of available health care data projected to reach 2,310 exabytes by 2020, prompting an ever-greater need for and reliance on AI machine learning tools.218

Machine learning tools have the ability to teach themselves and improve their capabilities. This has drawn substantial investment both from Silicon Valley and the US government for medical applications. The better the tools, the more money invested, the greater the array of capabilities and benefits, all of which are designed to save money and lives.

Given an aging population and other cost drivers, US health care costs are expected to rise to 20% of GDP by 2026.219 Big data, and machine learning systems, offer opportunities to alter that cost trajectory. McKinsey estimates these innovations could reduce healthcare spend by $300–$450 billion.220

AI is not yet replacing – and may never fully replace – trained humans in making treatment decisions. But the speed and accuracy of AI data analysis is a valuable clinical support tool at the point of care.

Here are just a few of applications that take advantage of AI which are coming to a medical facility near you.

AI visual systems already perform better than humans at facial recognition and visual reasoning. Now such systems will redefine the practice of radiology. "Stanford

---

[218]https://ir.citi.com/gyc57U8JFTWlUk2osZ3W7rMUB6CKmmMzhqYrkl6CG68iD8M/YHaMQf2VS+mRZDi4F1e4D5JREEA

[219] https://www.healthleadersmedia.com/finance/healthcare-spending-20-gdp-thats-economy-wide-problem

[220] http://www.pharmatalents.es/assets/files/Big_Data_Revolution.pdf

researchers have developed a deep learning algorithm that evaluates chest X-rays for signs of disease." In little more than a month of training, the AI system outperformed the four Stanford radiologists in diagnosing pneumonia accurately.221

"A new Artificial Intelligence (AI) technology from healthcare startup Qure.ai can accurately identify serious abnormalities in head CT scans with more than 95% accuracy..."

Qure.ai's new head CT scan technology rapidly screens scans in under 10 seconds to detect, localize and quantify abnormalities, as well as assess their severity... This enables patient prioritization and the appropriate clinical intervention.

Imaging data from 313,318 randomized head CT scans and corresponding clinical reports were used to train the AI. Some 491 CT scans were then used to clinically validate the algorithms, and three senior radiologists compared results. Overall, they found the algorithm to be 95% accurate in identifying abnormalities in head CT scans."222

With illnesses such as strokes or brain hemorrhages, speedy diagnosis and treatment can mean the difference between regaining mental or neurological function or losing them forever. *Time is brain.* While human doctors may recognize the symptoms, rapid diagnosis of images speeds up access to the right treatment and thus improves outcomes.

---

[221] https://news.stanford.edu/2017/11/15/algorithm-outperforms-radiologists-diagnosing-pneumonia/

[222] https://www.healthimaging.com/topics/artificial-intelligence/ai-algorithm-ids-head-abnormalities-ct-scans-95-accuracy

Google's DeepMind machine learning system is "capable of correctly referring patients with more than 50 different eye diseases for further treatment with 94% accuracy, matching or beating world-leading eye specialists."

According to Dr. Pearse Keane, a consultant ophthalmologist at England's Moorfield Eye Hospital, "the number of eye scans we're performing is growing at a pace much faster than human experts are able to interpret them." This means potential delays between the initial scan, diagnosis and treatment and if problems are found too late patients could suffer irreversible loss of sight.

"The AI technology we're developing is designed to prioritize patients who need to be seen and treated urgently by a doctor or eye care professional. If we can diagnose and treat eye conditions early, it gives us the best chance of saving people's sight." 223

The USC-affiliated Department of Defense (DOD) lab, The Institute for Creative Technology (ICT), has been doing pioneering work in the treatment of Post-Traumatic Stress Disorder (PTSD) for military veterans.

"'How are you doing today?' Ellie asks with a friendly smile. She tilts her head as she waits for a response. She wears black slacks, a blue shirt and a tan cardigan. She looks and behaves as expected for any therapist.

"'Where are you from?' she asks as she sits in her pink armchair with her hands resting on her lap. Her brown hair is pulled back into a neat ponytail. Ellie is not just any therapist. In fact, she is not even a therapist.

223

https://www.theguardian.com/technology/2018/aug/13/new-artificial-intelligence-tool-can-detect-eye-problems-as-well-as-experts

"Ellie is a virtual human who lives in a computer at ICT. Ellie can detect subtle signs of psychological distress that might indicate PTSD such as tone of voice or shifting gaze. With this information, clinicians can better assess and treat patients. USC Viterbi research assistant professor Louis-Philippe Morency compares this technology to a nurse checking a patient's vital signs before the patient sees the doctor.

"A patient may seem to be smiling frequently and report feeling happy, but the technology can reveal that that patient's smile is tense, one sign of psychological distress that could indicate PTSD or depression."224

"People are very open to feeling connected to things that aren't people," says Gale Lucas, a psychologist at USC's Institute for Creative Technologies and first author of a new, DARPA-funded study that finds soldiers are more likely to divulge symptoms of PTSD to a virtual interviewer – an artificially intelligent avatar, rendered in 3D on a television screen – than in existing post-deployment health surveys. The findings… suggest that virtual interviewers could prove to be even better than human therapists at helping soldiers open up about their mental health."225

AI is proving its worth across a broad reach of diagnosis. Scientists gathered a large medical-grade dataset of photos of fingernails and toenails and used it to train a neural network to distinguish symptoms of fungal infection better than a panel of experts. They built a data set of almost 50,000 nail photographs for use in further research. They

---

[224] https://viterbi.usc.edu/news/news/2013/a-virtual-therapist.htm

[225] http://ict.usc.edu/news/virtual-therapists-help-veterans-open-up-about-ptsd/

tested the results against a variety of different humans with different skills, ranging from nurses to clinicians to professors with a dermatology specialism. In all cases the AI-based networks matched or exceeded large groups of human experts on medical classification tasks. It's another example of visual AI systems which, when given enough data, can match or exceed humans' capabilities at narrowly specified tasks.[226]

One of the promises of AI for medical use-cases is that it can dramatically lower the cost of initial analysis of a given set of symptoms. This experiment backs up that view, and in addition to gathering the dataset and developing the AI techniques, the scientists have also developed a web- and smartphone-based platform to collect and classify further medical data.

"However, with the advent of using smartphones to diagnose onychomycosis, it is expected that much medical and social benefit can be obtained through the enhancement of diagnostic accuracy in this way. We have created a website for mobile devices, to demonstrate the potential of using smartphones for this purpose."[227] The website invites users to submit smartphone photos of their skin or nail conditions for diagnosis.

The rise of smartphones and the internet of things, with their ever-cheaper and more capable use of sensors, will generate ever larger amounts of data. Popular wearables, such as Fitbit and Apple Watch, generate trillions of

---

226 https://journals.plos.org/plosone/article?id=10.1371/journal.pone.0191493

227 https://journals.plos.org/plosone/article?id=10.1371/journal.pone.0191493

unlabeled sensor data points per year, including rich signals like resting heart rate and heart rate variability, which have been shown to correlate with health conditions as diverse as diabetes, sleep apnea, atrial fibrillation, heart failure, sudden cardiac death, and irritable bowel syndrome.

New research from heart rate app Cardiogram and the Department of Medicine at the University of California at San Francisco (UCSF) uses data from various smart watches, paired with the Cardiogram app, to train an AI system called DeepHeart, which can recognize hypertension and sleep apnea from wearable heart rate sensors with 82% and 90% accuracy.[228]

As these systems continue to out-perform their human counterparts, it raises an understandable and troubling question:

Will doctors disappear?

Many of those currently employed in the health care sector will see their jobs either disappear or be transformed. As the use of AI increases in medical applications, the fear is that entire job categories of medical practice will be lost to technology. Certainly, repetitive tasks including filling prescriptions and inputting medical data are increasingly being taken over by "narrow" AI lab technicians, some nursing functions, even the "personal" diagnosis and treatment plan development will fall before the AI juggernaut.

It's not unrealistic, if unsettling, to imagine that much of the work of doctors will be replaced by AI. Already, many health care providers have remote diagnosis by phone. AI

---

[228] https://blog.cardiogr.am/screening-for-hypertension-and-sleep-apnea-with-deepheart-416c9bc03efc

systems can replace the doctors now on the other end of that line such that those 'visits' can be free, according to your health plan. AI "physicians" with lesser trained (and less expensive) human assistants, will be able to deliver primary care within a decade.

The job losses will also hit some of the highest-paid medical professionals. Indeed, some medical students shy away from specializing in radiology out of fear that AI will eliminate the need for human radiologists entirely. Some estimates suggest that 37,000 radiologists and lab technicians will be replaced by AI technologies.

What does this mean for the practice of radiology?

According to the *Harvard Business Review*, "Radiological practice would certainly benefit from systems that can read and interpret multiple images quickly, because the number of images has increased much faster over the last decade than the number of radiologists. Hundreds of images can be taken for one patient's disease or injury. Imaging and radiology are expensive, and any solution that could reduce human labor, lower costs, and improve diagnostic accuracy would benefit patients and physicians alike."

In a more hopeful prediction, the *Harvard Business Review* argues, that, while AI will alter the field, it will leave radiologists more time to redirect their focus to other essential elements of the practice, including consulting with other physicians on diagnosis and treatment. The hope, then, is that while AI will provide faster and better analysis of data and improve the accuracy of visual recognition of scans and other symptoms, the tools will free up doctors to work more closely with patients and with the rest of their care providers.229

While many advanced AI systems produce dramatic results, the reasoning may remain hidden, so, too, the data sets used, the models their diagnosis are based on and the role of patient histories in their algorithms. This complicated their use in high risk environments like hospitals.

In addition, the rollout of AI in healthcare data analysis is inhibited by the lack of standardization of data sets, the siloing of medical data between public and private sources and even within organizations, and the need to maintain secure and private patient information, among other issues.

Some Deep Learning systems, such as Google's DeepMind are working through these issues. DeepMind's diagnostic eye systems make a point of showing their workings – how they got there – making room for ophthalmologists and other eye care professionals to play a role in the final prognosis and treatment.230

"One of the reasons we're putting so much effort into explainability and interpretation is that we desperately want to build trust with nurses and doctors," DeepMind co-founder Mustafa Suleyman tells Axios."231

But that kind of transparency is not yet standard practice.

The halcyon promise of AI to reduce healthcare costs and improve outcomes comes with caveats. We are at a tipping point between the cultures of "do no harm", and

---

[229] https://hbr.org/2018/03/ai-will-change-radiology-but-it-wont-replace-radiologists

[230] https://deepmind.com/blog/moorfields-major-milestone/

[231] https://www.axios.com/google-developed-ai-can-read-eye-scans-as-well-as-humans--b4d7269f-a08a-4bd5-99ca-ea5420993d76.html

"move fast and break things." Even the more advanced Deep Learning tools that can teach themselves and learn from their mistakes, are subject to errors and bias in the creation of their algorithms or in the data sets they rely on.

Johns Hopkins' patient safety experts have calculated that more than 250,000 deaths annually are due to medical error in the US. The promise of AI is that it not only will improve diagnosis and free up doctors to do other work, but that it will reduce these errors and save lives as well as saving money.232

Already, there are examples of autonomous systems making potentially dangerous mistakes. The UK is using an AI-powered triage app, which recommends whether patients should go to hospital based on their symptoms. Doctors have noticed serious flaws, with the app appearing to recommend staying at home for classic symptoms of heart attacks, meningitis and strokes.

Internal IBM documents show that its Watson supercomputer often spits out erroneous cancer treatment advice and that company medical specialists and customers identified "multiple examples of unsafe and incorrect treatment recommendations" as IBM was promoting the product to hospitals and physicians around the world.[233] The software used "synthetic" cancer cases or "hypothetical" patients instead of guidelines or real evidence – which skewed the way it evaluated actual patients and their diseases.

The pace of innovation is such that regulation is slow to adapt: Regulatory bodies are not taking seriously the

---

[232] https://www.cnbc.com/2018/02/22/medical-errors-third-leading-cause-of-death-in-america.html

[233] https://www.statnews.com/2018/07/25/ibm-watson-recommended-unsafe-incorrect-treatments

specific risks from autonomous decision-making in medicine. They treat these systems as medical devices, allowing them to be used on patients without a thorough assessment of their risks and benefits. While we want these fantastic new tools to get to the patients that need them as soon as is practical, regulators need to give proper oversight to these technologies.

"An FDA approved system to detect atrial fibrillation in ECG halter monitors highlights possible areas of concern to doctors, but the final judgement is on them. The worry is that if this system is mostly accurate, are doctors really going to spend time painstakingly looking through hours of ECG traces?"[234]

Regulatory bodies also have approved systems for diagnostic measurement and stroke analysis, among others. But these systems have a vital feature in common: they require a human expert to make every decision. The AI systems provide useful, even critical information to aid those experts in making those decisions, but they do not function autonomously.

Improving healthcare is one of the most exciting, and potentially transformative applications of AI. Nonetheless, it is critical that the deployment of AI in healthcare is done responsibly, using the established mechanisms for testing and regulating new medical treatments. Serious accidents can prompt powerful public backlashes against technologies (e.g. nuclear phase-outs in Japan and Europe post-Fukushima). If we are optimistic about the potential healthcare applications of AI, ensuring that this technology

---

234 https://lukeoakdenrayner.wordpress.com/2018/07/11/medical-ai-safety-we-have-a-problem/.

is developed and applied safely is critical in ensuring that these benefits can be realized.

Part 4 – Saving the Planet

Chapter 10

There's Hope for Climate Change

Whenever I wanted to know the weather, I asked my grandpa about his knees. Never mind the TV meteorologist or the slick weather reader, if grandpa reported a dull ache, especially in his left knee, I could expect clouds but no rain. A stabbing pain in that same knee forecast showers. But if both knees nearly crippled him with arthritic pain, we rolled back the awnings, brought in the cat, battened down the windows and prepared for a torrential downpour. More importantly, since we farmed for a living, climate information was critical for us; with it, we understood when to plant crops, when to till the soil and make other vital decisions.

In chaos theory, a "sensitive dependence on initial conditions" means if you have enough data about what is going on at any particular moment you can predict the short-term future, in weather, the stock market, even at the roulette wheel. Grandpa's knees were my "initial conditions."

But arthritic knees aren't the only folk barometer. If flowers smell stronger than usual moisture is coming. If a cat cleans its ears or a dog eats grass, or frogs croak louder, get out your umbrella.235

---

[235] https://www.littlehouseliving.com/old-fashioned-ways-to-predict-the-weather.html

Ancient civilizations monitored weather events and tried to discern patterns in them in hopes of making more effective agricultural and even military decisions. Around 650 B.C.E. the Babylonians tried to predict short-term weather changes based on the appearance of clouds and optical phenomena such as haloes. By 300 BCE, Chinese astronomers had developed a calendar that divided the year into 24 festivals, each one associated with a different type of weather.

Around 340 BCE, the Greek philosopher Aristotle wrote *Meteorologica*, a philosophical treatise that included theories about the formation of rain, clouds, hail, wind, thunder, lightning, and hurricanes. His four-volume text was considered by many to be the authority on weather theory for almost 2000 years.236

Dating back to the ancient Greeks, many people had proposed that humans could change temperatures and influence rainfall by chopping down trees, plowing fields or irrigating a desert.

One theory of climate effects, widely believed until the dust bowl of the 1930s, held that "rain follows the plow," the now-discredited idea that tilling soil and other agricultural practices would result in increased rainfall.

Accurate or not, those perceived climate effects were merely local. The idea that humans could somehow alter climate on a global scale would seem far-fetched for centuries.[237]

236
https://earthobservatory.nasa.gov/Features/WxForecasting/wx2.php

[237] https://www.history.com/topics/natural-disasters-and-environment/history-of-climate-change

In the 1950s, an ingenious (although faulty) model involving changes in the Arctic Ocean suggested a disturbing possibility of arbitrary shifts (in the earth's climate). Apparently, the interlinked system of atmosphere, ice sheets, and oceans could swing in regular cycles or even in random jerks. Worse, around 1970 highly simplified computer models raised the specter of a catastrophic climate runaway. In the 1980s, the center of research shifted to large and complex computer models. These did not show a runaway, but reinforced what many simpler models had been suggesting: the next century would probably see significant greenhouse warming.238

Now, AI and machine learning have replaced local folk tales and rudimentary science giving scientists the tools to more accurately predict a catastrophically changing climate and to ascribe those changes as the result of human activity.

A dire report from the UN's Intergovernmental Panel on Climate Change (IPCC) warns of the severe impact of global warming by 2040 unless global temperatures can be held to 1.5 degrees Celsius above pre-industrial levels.239

AI machine learning systems can give us the tools to mitigate the damage from such a temperature rise. While political constraints – not the subject of this chapter or book – will inhibit our best efforts to address the warnings in the IPCC report, AI is being used by companies, NGOs and governments to address a broad spectrum of problems resulting from global temperature rises.

According to most experts, the stakes couldn't be more dramatic. The progress in human development is

---

[238] https://history.aip.org/climate/simple.htm#L_M018
[239] http://www.ipcc.ch/report/sr15/

becoming increasingly dependent on the surrounding natural environment and may be restricted by its future deterioration. The increasing population, urbanization and industrialization, which our planet has faced this century, have forced society to consider whether human beings are changing the very conditions essential to life on Earth.240

While the ancients had only their eyes or, at best, crude instruments to measure atmospheric conditions and predict upcoming climate, AI machine learning requires enormous amounts of data from which to create answers, and then to adjust and learn as more data comes in. "AI's capacities to gather that data are rapidly improving thanks to several factors: the vast amounts of data being collected by sensors (in appliances, vehicles, clothing, etc.), satellites and the Internet; the development of more powerful and faster computers; the availability of open source software and data; and the increase in abundant, cheap storage. AI can now quickly discern patterns that humans cannot, make predictions more efficiently and recommend better policies."[241]

And in climate science, AI looks at more data than in almost no other field. For example, Britain's Meteorological Office holds about 45 petabytes (45 quadrillion bytes) of climate information and is adding 0.085 petabyte daily, an ideal AI resource that is mirrored in other countries around the world.242

---

[240]https://www.researchgate.net/publication/220204701_Artificial_Intelligence_and_Environmental_Decision_Support_Systems

[241] https://blogs.ei.columbia.edu/2018/06/05/artificial-intelligence-climate-environment/

[242] https://www.scientificamerican.com/article/how-machine-learning-could-help-to-improve-climate-forecasts/

More data means better climate modeling and more accurate predictions, which can be used both to mitigate the effects of climate change and, ideally, to reduce further degradation of the climate. And the opportunities seem boundless.

A new Microsoft-funded effort, dubbed AI for Earth, is finding and funding innovators who are making progress in four critical areas – climate change, water, agriculture, and biodiversity. The AI pioneers include a group in Italy using images of snow in mountains to better predict snow melt and thus water availability; the Jane Goodall Institute, which is helping "identify chimpanzee habitat connectivity and conservation priorities in Africa"; teams at Yale and Cornell using AI and data to understand crop health and improve yields; and a crowdsourced program, iNaturalist, that combines both "citizen-scientist" data with trained scientist input on biodiversity.243

Other projects of this initiative include Project Premonition, a collaboration between Microsoft and researchers at Johns Hopkins University and the University of Pittsburgh that "seeks to estimate relative abundances of insect species based on classification of their wing beat frequency and collect individuals from target blood-sucking species to test for the presence of human pathogens."

"Systematic Poacher Detector (SPOT), which uses nocturnal drone imagery to detect the presence of poachers in Botswanan natural parks in near real time, allowing

---

243 http://www.andrewwinston.com/blog/2018/05/using_ai_to_help_the_world_thr.php

them to be removed shortly after arrival and before daybreak/hunting begins."244

"In India, AI has helped farmers get 30% higher groundnut yields per hectare by providing information on preparing the land, applying fertilizer and choosing sowing dates. In Norway, AI helped create a flexible and autonomous electric grid, integrating more renewable energy.

"And AI has helped researchers achieve 89% to 99% accuracy in identifying tropical cyclones, weather fronts and atmospheric rivers, the latter of which can cause heavy precipitation and are often hard for humans to identify on their own. By improving weather forecasts, these types of programs can help keep people safe."245

"With AI-driven autonomous vehicles waiting to break into the automobile market, techniques like route optimization, eco-driving algorithms and ride-sharing services would help in streamlining the carbon footprint and reducing the overall number of vehicles on the road…"

The emergence of smart buildings and the smart cities in which they are built can leverage built-in sensors to use energy efficiently, and buildings and roads will also be constructed out of materials that work more intelligently.

Taking a nod from natural patterns, material scientists and architects have developed innovative building materials from natural resources, such as bricks made of bacteria, cement that captures carbon dioxide, and cooling

---

[244] https://conferences.oreilly.com/artificial-intelligence/ai-ca-2018/public/schedule/detail/68568

[245] https://scipol.duke.edu/content/artificial-intelligence%E2%80%94-game-changer-climate-change-and-environment

systems that use wind and sun. Solar power is increasingly present within cities and outside to supply larger urban areas. These are the first early steps towards sustainable infrastructure cutting costs and helping to make us environmentally conscious."[246]

The World Economic Forum, in Davos, has made a series of special studies on AI and its global impact and in early 2018 came up with eight specific ways AI can help the fight to moderate the impact of climate change.247

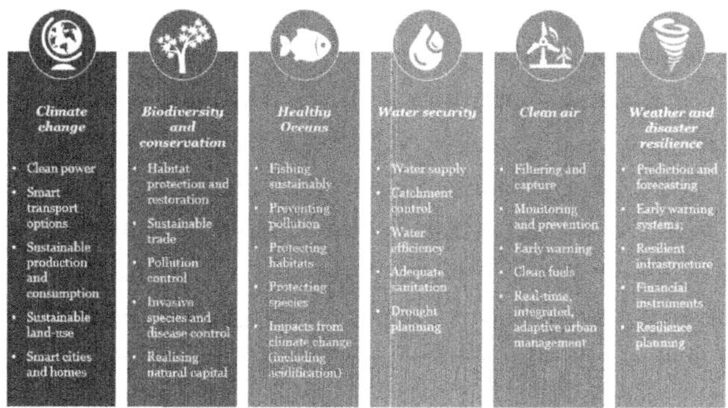

1. Autonomous and connected electric vehicles

AI-guided autonomous vehicles (AVs) will enable a transition to mobility on demand over the coming years and decades. Substantial greenhouse gas reductions for urban transport can be unlocked through route and traffic optimization, eco-driving algorithms, programmed 'platooning' of cars to traffic, and autonomous ride-sharing services. Electric AV fleets will be critical to deliver real gains.

---

[246] https://www.ecomena.org/artificial-intelligence-environmental-sustainability/

[247] https://www.weforum.org/agenda/2018/01/8-ways-ai-can-help-save-the-planet/

*2. **Distributed energy grids***

AI can enhance the predictability of demand and supply for renewables across a distributed grid, improve energy storage, efficiency and load management, assist in the integration and reliability of renewables and enable dynamic pricing and trading, creating market incentives.

3. Smart agriculture and food systems

AI-augmented agriculture involves automated data collection, decision-making and corrective actions via robotics to allow early detection of crop diseases and issues, to provide timed nutrition to livestock, and generally to optimize agricultural inputs and returns based on supply and demand. This promises to increase the resource efficiency of the agriculture industry, lowering the use of water, fertilizers and pesticides which cause damage to important ecosystems, and increase resilience to climate extremes.

4. Next generation weather and climate prediction

A new field of 'climate informatics' is blossoming, that uses AI to fundamentally transform weather forecasting and improve our understanding of the effects of climate change. This field traditionally requires high performance energy-intensive computing, but deep-learning networks can allow computers to run much faster and incorporate more complexity of the 'real-world' system into the calculations.

In just over a decade, computational power and advances in AI will enable home computers to have as much power as today's supercomputers, lowering the cost of research, boosting scientific productivity and accelerating discoveries. AI techniques may also help correct biases in models, extract the most relevant data to avoid data degradation, predict extreme events and be used for impacts modelling.

5. Smart disaster response

AI can analyze simulations and real-time data (including social media data) of weather events and disasters in a region to seek out vulnerabilities and enhance disaster preparation, provide early warning, and prioritize response through coordination of emergency information capabilities. Deep reinforcement learning may one day be integrated into disaster simulations to determine optimal response strategies, similar to the way AI is currently being used to identify the best move in games like AlphaGo.

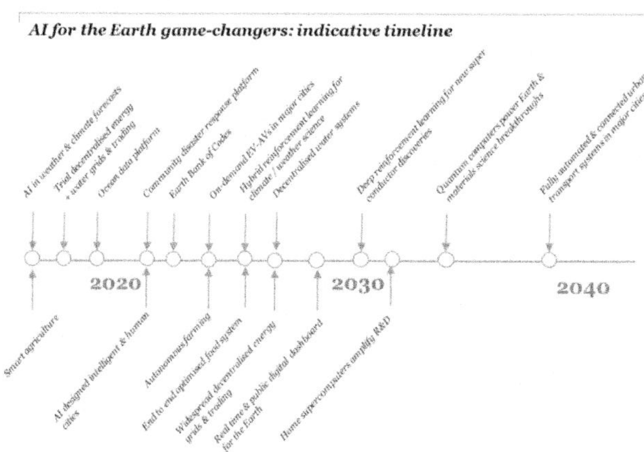

AI for the Earth game-changers: indicative timeline
Image: PwC

6. AI-designed intelligent, connected and livable cities

AI could be used to simulate and automate the generation of zoning laws, building ordinances and floodplains, combined with augmented and virtual reality

(AR and VR). Real-time city-wide data on energy, water consumption and availability, traffic flows, people flows, and weather could create an 'urban dashboard' to optimize urban sustainability.

7. A transparent digital Earth

A real-time, open API, AI-infused, digital geospatial dashboard for the planet would enable the monitoring, modelling and management of environmental systems at a scale and speed never before possible – from tackling illegal deforestation, water extraction, fishing and poaching, to air pollution, natural disaster response and smart agriculture.

8. Reinforcement learning for Earth sciences breakthroughs

This nascent AI technique – which requires no input data, substantially less computing power, and in which the evolutionary-like AI learns from itself – could soon evolve to enable its application to real-world problems in the natural sciences. Collaboration with Earth scientists to identify the systems – from climate science, materials science, biology, and other areas – which can be codified to apply reinforcement learning for scientific progress and discovery is vital. For example, DeepMind co-founder, Demis Hassabis, has suggested that in materials science, a descendant of AlphaGo Zero could be used to search for a room temperature superconductor – a hypothetical substance that allows for incredibly efficient energy systems."

"Controlling industrial emissions and waste management is another challenge that can be dealt with the advanced learning machines and smart networks that could detect leaks, potential hazards and diversions from industrial standards and governmental regulations. For example, IoT technology, was incorporated into several industrial ventures, from refrigerators and thermostats and even retail shops."248

Amazon and the CIA have teamed up to use AI to better analyze satellite data. For the CIA, this means creating a map of the world that produces a resolution of 50 centimeters, to help in planning movements of people (as well as covert activities of various kinds). For their part, Amazon will make the data available via its cloud computing service, where it can be used to identify deforestation and the rate at which it is happening.

"The natural world contains reservoirs of innovative capacity that remain largely untapped. AI and systems analytics can help unbundle the biological and biomimetic possibilities. Scientists have begun work on the natural world equivalent of the Human Genome Project, with the aim of mapping the DNA sequences of all living things. The Amazon Third Way initiative, for instance, is developing a project called the Earth Bank of Codes, with two main intents. One, to open up potential discoveries, like blood pressure medicine derived from viper venom. And, two, to record the provenance of biological IP assets, so local people can benefit from follow-on discoveries."249

Governments, corporations, philanthropies, and universities are spending billions of dollars to develop technologies to reduce emissions of greenhouse gases. But the challenges we face are staggering.

---

[248] https://www.ecomena.org/artificial-intelligence-environmental-sustainability/

[249] https://www.fastcompany.com/40528469/5-ways-artificial-intelligence-can-help-save-the-planet

Bill Gates believes that only a series of "miraculous" breakthroughs could make meaningful progress in reducing greenhouse gases. He's part of a business group called the American Energy Innovation Council, which has argued for unleashing private sector R&D by expanding research grants and improving regulations. "We're also arguing that the federal government should adequately fund long-term research, roughly tripling energy R&D to $16 billion a year from the current $5 billion a year. Energy would then represent 6% of the total federal R&D budget."

Yet, despite the enormity of the challenge, he is "optimistic that science and technology can point the way to big breakthroughs in clean energy and help us meet the world's growing needs. In this area, like so many, there are no quick fixes, which makes it even more urgent to start work now."250

As AI systems come online and machine learning and general AI make decisions with limited human oversight, "researchers and scientists must ensure that the data provided through such systems are transparent, fair and trustworthy. With an increasing demand of automation solutions and higher precision data-study for environment related problems and challenges, more multinational companies, educational institutions and government sectors need to fund more R&D of such technologies and provide proper standardizations for producing and applying them."251

AI shows great promise for helping manage climate change, but it's too soon to know whether there are a

---

[250] https://www.gatesnotes.com/Energy/Energy-Miracles

series of silver bullets on the way – or if the promise of AI will be realized too late to save the planet.

[251] https://www.ecomena.org/artificial-intelligence-environmental-sustainability/

Part 5 – Big Brother is Watching You

Chapter 11

China's Surveillance Society

China has created the world's largest surveillance society and is aggressively deploying AI solutions to ensure that the state can control every single aspect of every citizen's life.

This is not just about using facial recognition to identify a crime suspect. The state is creating a database that profiles every man, woman and child, to give them a social ranking that will decide who gets what job, what house and what level of pay. The database will centrally control ambition and dictate exactly how future generations will be allowed to live and work in a society that is the very definition of Big Brother.

The Chinese actions demonstrate that AI can do more than pursue criminals who have done something in the past; the algorithms also can predict who might do something in the future. For authoritarian regimes this allows for a completely controlled society: by predicting the future behavior of individuals and groups, the state can take preemptive action (arrest, imprisonment, indoctrination) before any dangerous acts occur.

The developments in China already are being mirrored in countries and cities around the world, from Berlin to Los Angeles, Singapore to Turkey. A window into China today is also a cautionary window into how our world can develop in the next few years as AI become ubiquitous in law enforcement and intelligence.

*

Ground zero for the Chinese Communist Party's dream of controlling everyone, everywhere, is in the western province of Xinjiang home of the Uighurs, a Turkic Muslim people who look different from the majority Han Chinese and speak a different language.252 There are around 13m Uighurs in what is ostensibly an autonomous region of western China. Xinjiang is also home to a substantial portion of the country's most valuable natural resources. In addition to sizable mineral reserves of iron ore and gold, the region claims about 38% of the country's coal reserves and 25% of its petroleum and natural gas.253

Since 2009, the Xianjing province has experienced periodic bouts of violence from Uighurs, who are frustrated at being treated as second class citizens. While there has been no widespread terrorism, the Chinese government has responded as if every Uighur is a terrorist and should be treated as such. Ironically, since 2001 and the 9/11 attack on the World Trade Center, the Chinese government has repeatedly cited America's war on terror as justification for their actions against the Uighurs. The central government has deployed 20,000 additional troops to the area and arrested between 1–2m local people for "reeducation" – around 20% of the population. This is a campaign of repression on a scale not seen since Stalin's gulags in Soviet Russia and has interned more people than were held in Nazi concentration camps in World War II.

---

[252] https://www.hrw.org/report/2018/09/09/eradicating-ideological-viruses/chinas-campaign-repression-against-xinjiangs

[253] https://www.huffingtonpost.com/entry/who-are-uighurs-china-muslim-detention-million_us_5b7195cee4b0ae32af9a085a

"The most common officially cited purpose for the internment camps is to purify people's thoughts, 'eliminating extremism' and instilling a love for the party. A recorded announcement from Xinjiang's Communist Party Youth League, designed to calm rampant fears about the re-education camps, explained that camps 'treat and cleanse the virus from their brains.' The names used for camps have varied widely, both for the same camp over time and from one camp to the next, but most have included the word 'transformation' – for example, 'concentrated education transformation center'."254

"The handful of people released from the camps and able to share their stories describe a variety of indoctrination techniques aimed to instill love for the Communist Party of China and its leader, Xi Jinping. 'Teachers' and guards compel internees to chant slogans, watch videos on how to identify Islamic extremism, study Confucian texts, give thanks to Chairman Xi Jinping before meals, renounce Islam, write self-criticisms, and denounce fellow internees. Some of these, particularly self-criticisms and denunciations, are staples of CCP indoctrination programs as old as the People's Republic itself, techniques that gave the English language the word 'brainwashing,' a direct translation of the Chinese xi nao. These go-to CCP techniques are combined with what are presented as modern psychological approaches, as re-education centers recruit staff with psychological training."

"'We are deeply concerned at the many numerous and credible reports that we have received that in the name of combating religious extremism and maintaining social

---

[254] https://foreignpolicy.com/2018/08/22/chinas-mass-internment-camps-have-no-clear-end-in-sight/

stability (China) has changed the Uighur autonomous region into something that resembles a massive internship camp that is shrouded in secrecy, a sort of 'no rights zone',"' said Gay McDougall, a member of the U.N. Committee on the Elimination of Racial Discrimination.255

In 2014, the Chinese government launched a campaign codenamed Strike Hard which targeted anybody identified as a potential threat. The threat analysis is conducted by a software solution called the Integrated Joint Operations Platform (IJOP) which was first deployed in 2016 and uses AI to crunch the data and provide specific targeting for the security forces. Data comes from multiple sources that begin with a requirement for every Uighur to fill in a form which automatically scores them 10% less than other ethnic groups and ensures their categorization as second-class citizens. Then, cameras placed everywhere are supported by checkpoints at every major intersection and point of ingress and exit from cities including bus and train stations. Racial recognition software is used as part of the camera surveillance and every house has embedded QR codes to show who is around, when and doing what.

Every user is required to register his or her smartphone and to install an app that allows the government to track who is speaking to whom, what websites are being scanned, what information is downloaded, all shopping habits and all calls are automatically logged and recorded to build contact chains between individuals and groups. That data is augmented by personal home visits by special

---

[255] https://www.huffingtonpost.com/entry/china-uigher-internment-camp_us_5b6df2c4e4b0bdd062094159?t1r

teams who can check on any anomalies thrown up by IJOP.

If the AI algorithms produce a low "trust" score, that's enough justification for the authorities to remove someone to an internment camp. There is no due process, no law to be followed and no right of appeal. Families simply disappear and for the children left behind when their parents are taken, the state has built dozens of new orphanages where they can be housed.

It is remarkable how successful the campaign of cultural and ideological cleansing has been. In one generation, Uighurs have gone from being proud of their language and heritage to volunteering to burn books in the local language and to step forward to adopt the Han customs and language. Young people especially are willing participants in this integration program, in part because they have no memory of what once was and in part because they fear disappearing as so many of their friends and neighbors already have done.

The lessons learned in controlling the Uighurs are already being applied across China, as the party leadership gives free rein to its long-held paranoia about the collapse of central control and the fragmentation of the country. At the heart of this initiative is a goal to capture not just the identity of every individual but also their behaviors, associates and predictions about possible future behavior. In a country where there are no meaningful laws around privacy or individual freedom, the state can do what it wants and security business is now booming.

There are three main components of the nationwide system. The first is Skynet, launched in 2005, which works in real time and can identify a person in seconds. The second system is called Sharp Eyes and is designed to expand Skynet to rural areas. The third and most pervasive system is called the Police Cloud which essentially moves all data to the cloud, allowing local police to manage their own environment while linking everything to a central system covering the whole country.

The combined systems currently have around 200m surveillance cameras deployed and expect to have 300m by 2020.256 In addition, police wear facial recognition glasses that scan the faces of pedestrians or a driver at a traffic stop, upload the data to the police cloud and get an instantaneous readout of the person's risk profile.257 The software was used to pick one criminal out of a crowd of 20,000 at a pop concert and an arrest swiftly followed.258

Facial recognition is in its infancy and there has been much debate about accuracy and bias in the way algorithms are written. However, the pace of technology is moving ever faster and there have been huge improvements in the past few months. For example, researchers in China have developed a facial recognition system called MobileFaceNet, which can identify faces with 98.3% accuracy in 24 milliseconds.259

These applications can be used tactically, as well as more broadly, to identify threats to society. For example, in the southern Chinese city of Shenzhen with a population of 12m, jaywalkers are photographed by one of hundreds of cameras, their faces recognized and connected to the

---

[256] https://www.nytimes.com/2018/07/08/business/china-surveillance-technology.html

[257] https://www.nytimes.com/2018/07/16/technology/china-surveillance-state.html

[258] http://www.latimes.com/business/technology/la-fi-tn-facial-recognition-china-20180522-story.html

[259] https://arxiv.org/pdf/1804.07573.pdf

Police Cloud which automatically sends a fine by text to their cellphone. At the same time, their picture is displayed on a large LED screen at the scene of the crime. In the first 10 months of operation, 13,930 jaywalkers were recorded and displayed on the LED screen at one intersection.260

The three combined surveillance systems are designed to gather every possible piece of data of value on everyone, everywhere. In hospital for a procedure? The police cloud will know who was in the bed on either side, whether or not you got their phone numbers and if you spoke or messaged with them subsequently. And if your former hospital mate later sat next to a known suspect on a plane, then that link becomes part of your profile – the exemplar of guilt by association.

Staying in a hotel? The police cloud knows everyone who is on the same floor, if anyone has visited you or anyone you know or have just met. Facial recognition will track everyone to see where all the guests went in the evening, with whom they met and, by turning on an app in their smartphone, learn what was discussed. It can also alert the police to activity that might seem unusual – such as when a local resident frequently stays in a local hotel.261

Here's how one subcontractor to the Sharp Eyes system, Guangdong Aebell Technology Corporation of Guangdong, put it:

"The operating system is set to build a decentralized, real-time mutual surveillance system."

---

[260] https://www.scmp.com/tech/china-tech/article/2138960/jaywalkers-under-surveillance-shenzhen-soon-be-punished-text

[261] https://www.hrw.org/news/2017/11/19/china-police-big-data-systems-violate-privacy-target-dissent

"Aebell is evolving in the interest of serving the national strategic Sharp Eyes project. Based on our experiments with sound and video recording technologies, and our subsequent innovations, we have developed an operating system for the Sharp Eyes project that can fulfil in real-time our needs for tracking criminal activities, instant reporting on crime, instant response and reaction.

The system appropriates household TV sets and smart phones to enhance the extension of surveillance system to households and individuals. The system contributes to the construction of a comprehensive crime prevention and public security system, along with an integrated informational public security system that turns mutual, real-time and ubiquitous surveillance into reality."262

The Communist party is investing billions of dollars annually in expanding the surveillance program and is seeking innovative ways to keep track of its citizens. A new generation of stealthy 'doves' that look and fly like the real thing have been deployed to 30 military and government agencies. Each 'dove' weighs 200 grams, can fly at 40mph and is fitted with a high definition camera, flight control system and a datalink to the nearest satellite.263

Researchers with the Chinese Academic of Sciences and Huazhong University of Science and Technology have created a new dataset and benchmark for "lip-reading in the wild" for Mandarin. The lip-reading dataset contains 745,187 distinct samples from more than 2,000 speakers,

---

[262] https://www.hongkongfp.com/2018/04/08/sharp-eyes-smartphones-tv-sets-watching-chinese-citizens/

[263] https://www.scmp.com/news/china/society/article/2152027/china-takes-surveillance-new-heights-flock-robotic-doves-do-they

grouped into 1,000 classes, where each class corresponds to the syllable of a Mandarin word composed of one or several Chinese characters.

"To the best of our knowledge, this database is currently the largest word-level lip-reading dataset and the only public large-scale Mandarin lip-reading dataset", the researchers write. The dataset has also been designed to be diverse so the footage in it consists of multiple different people taken from multiple different camera angles.264

As the systems become fully operational nationwide, every citizen will be given a social credit score, similar to the credit rating that individuals currently have in many countries except it has little to do with credit. If a woman buys alcohol in a store and has young children, that might have an impact, while if she buys baby food and diapers, that might be a positive sign. If she marries a trusted member of society who already has a high social credit score, then her score might improve as well. All this happens in real time and the information is completely hidden from the citizens who are impacted.

There is no way for a citizen to see their social credit score or to appeal a low score. So far, around 10m people have had their social credit score reduced by the algorithms in the police cloud system.265

The embedded AI within the police cloud will not only make the connections even the smartest analyst might have missed but will also confidently predict what might happen next. This predictive nature of the oppressive system is what the Chinese authorities believe will be the

---

[264] https://arxiv.org/abs/1810.06990

[265] http://www.abc.net.au/news/2018-09-18/china-social-credit-a-model-citizen-in-a-digital-dictatorship/10200278?pfmredir=sm

key to reducing crime and stamping out any political opposition before it even begins to get a public profile. Better, the argument goes, to arrest somebody who is predicted to be a danger than wait until that danger becomes an unpleasant reality.

*

As one of the largest search engines on the planet, with significant data mining expertise, and with a founding motto "do no harm," it would be easy to assume that Silicon Valley based Google (or Alphabet, as the parent company is known) would be a leader in considering ethical and social responsibility. This appeared to be reflected when CEO Sundar Pichai published a blog in June, 2018 titled AI at Google: Our Principles. It's worth reproducing here both because of the guide it may produce for others and also for the marketplace reality that so swiftly resulted in the compromise of those principles:266

At its heart, AI is computer programming that learns and adapts. It can't solve every problem, but its potential to improve our lives is profound. At Google, we use AI to make products more useful – from email that's spam-free and easier to compose, to a digital assistant you can speak to naturally, to photos that pop the fun stuff out for you to enjoy.

Beyond our products, we're using AI to help people tackle urgent problems. A pair of high school students are building AI-powered sensors to predict the risk of wildfires. Farmers are using it to monitor the health of their herds. Doctors are starting to use AI to help diagnose cancer and prevent blindness. These clear benefits are why Google invests heavily in AI research and development, and makes AI technologies widely available to others via our tools and open-source code.

We recognize that such powerful technology raises equally powerful questions about its use. How AI is developed and used will have a significant impact on society for many years to come. As a leader in AI, we feel a deep responsibility to get this right. So today, we're announcing seven principles to guide our work going forward. These are not theoretical concepts; they are concrete standards that will actively govern our research and product development and will impact our business decisions.

We acknowledge that this area is dynamic and evolving, and we will approach our work with humility, a commitment to internal and external engagement, and a willingness to adapt our approach as we learn over time.

Objectives for AI applications

We will assess AI applications in view of the following objectives. We believe that AI should:

*1. **Be socially beneficial**.*

The expanded reach of new technologies increasingly touches society as a whole. Advances in AI will have transformative impacts in a wide range of fields, including healthcare, security, energy, transportation, manufacturing, and entertainment. As we consider potential development and uses of AI technologies, we will take into account a broad range of social and economic factors, and will proceed where we believe that the overall likely benefits substantially exceed the foreseeable risks and downsides.

---

[266] https://www.blog.google/technology/ai/ai-principles/

AI also enhances our ability to understand the meaning of content at scale. We will strive to make high-quality and accurate information readily available using AI, while continuing to respect cultural, social, and legal norms in the countries where we operate. And we will continue to thoughtfully evaluate when to make our technologies available on a non-commercial basis.

*2. **Avoid creating or reinforcing unfair bias**.*

AI algorithms and datasets can reflect, reinforce, or reduce unfair biases. We recognize that distinguishing fair from unfair biases is not always simple, and differs across cultures and societies. We will seek to avoid unjust impacts on people, particularly those related to sensitive characteristics such as race, ethnicity, gender, nationality, income, sexual orientation, ability, and political or religious belief.

*3. **Be built and tested for safety**.*

We will continue to develop and apply strong safety and security practices to avoid unintended results that create risks of harm. We will design our AI systems to be appropriately cautious, and seek to develop them in accordance with best practices in AI safety research. In appropriate cases, we will test AI technologies in constrained environments and monitor their operation after deployment.

*4. **Be accountable to people**.*

We will design AI systems that provide appropriate opportunities for feedback, relevant explanations, and appeal. Our AI technologies will be subject to appropriate human direction and control.

*5. **Incorporate privacy design principles**.*

We will incorporate our privacy principles in the development and use of our AI technologies. We will give opportunity for notice and consent, encourage architectures with privacy safeguards, and provide appropriate transparency and control over the use of data.

6. ***Uphold high standards of scientific excellence****.*

Technological innovation is rooted in the scientific method and a commitment to open inquiry, intellectual rigor, integrity, and collaboration. AI tools have the potential to unlock new realms of scientific research and knowledge in critical domains like biology, chemistry, medicine, and environmental sciences. We aspire to high standards of scientific excellence as we work to progress AI development.

We will work with a range of stakeholders to promote thoughtful leadership in this area, drawing on scientifically rigorous and multidisciplinary approaches. And we will responsibly share AI knowledge by publishing educational materials, best practices, and research that enable more people to develop useful AI applications.

7. ***Be made available for uses that accord with these principles****.*

Many technologies have multiple uses. We will work to limit potentially harmful or abusive applications. As we develop and deploy AI technologies, we will evaluate likely uses in light of the following factors: Primary purpose and use: the primary purpose and likely use of a technology and application, including how closely the solution is related to or adaptable to a harmful use.

Nature and uniqueness: whether we are making available technology that is unique or more generally available.

Scale: whether the use of this technology will have significant impact.

Nature of Google's involvement: whether we are providing general-purpose tools, integrating tools for customers, or developing custom solutions.

AI applications we will not pursue

In addition to the above objectives, we will not design or deploy AI in the following application areas:

Technologies that cause or are likely to cause overall harm. Where there is a material risk of harm, we will proceed only where we believe that the benefits substantially outweigh the risks, and will incorporate appropriate safety constraints.

Weapons or other technologies whose principal purpose or implementation is to cause or directly facilitate injury to people.

Technologies that gather or use information for surveillance violating internationally accepted norms.

Technologies whose purpose contravenes widely accepted principles of international law and human rights.

We want to be clear that while we are not developing AI for use in weapons, we will continue our work with governments and the military in many other areas. These include cybersecurity, training, military recruitment, veterans' healthcare, and search and rescue. These collaborations are important and we'll actively look for more ways to augment the critical work of these organizations and keep service members and civilians safe.

AI for the long term

While this is how we're choosing to approach AI, we understand there is room for many voices in this conversation. As AI technologies progress, we'll work with a range of stakeholders to promote thoughtful leadership in this area, drawing on scientifically rigorous and multidisciplinary approaches. And we will continue to share what we've learned to improve AI technologies and practices.

We believe these principles are the right foundation for our company and the future development of AI. This approach is consistent with the values laid out in our original Founders' Letter back in 2004. There we made clear our intention to take a long-term perspective, even if it means making short-term tradeoffs. We said it then, and we believe it now.

As that blog was being published, around 215 Google employees were working on a secret project, codenamed Dragonfly that would allow the company, which had been banned in China, to regain access. Dragonfly was essentially being written to parameters dictated by the Chinese government which included the censorship of certain search terms such as "human rights" or "Nobel Prize". In addition, while all data would be stored outside the country, a mirror of the data would be supplied to a Chinese-based company.

This meant that the Chinese government would have access to who was searching using Google, what terms they were using, when they were searching and even their exact location while searching, which could be tracked through the automatic storage of cellphone numbers of a computer's IP address. In other words, Google had agreed to become part of China's massive surveillance program that was specifically designed to suppress freedom of speech and human rights.267

---

[267] https://theintercept.com/2018/09/21/google-suppresses-memo-revealing-plans-to-closely-track-search-users-in-china/

When word of Dragonfly leaked internally at Google, employees protested that the project breached many of Google's public AI principles and that it was a breach of trust between management and employees. A senior Google scientist resigned, other circulated a letter of protest and Google moved to suppress discussion of the project.268

Behind all this was a pure business decision for Google that being inside China was better than being outside. This compromise bodes ill for the future use of AI tools for censorship and suppression, especially as former Google CEO, Eric Schmidt acknowledges that the new AI world puts China and its rules on one side and the democratic world on the other. Speaking at a VC conference in September 2018, Schmidt said:

"I think the most likely scenario now is not a splintering, but rather a bifurcation into a Chinese-led internet and a non-Chinese internet led by America.

"If you look at China, and I was just there, the scale of the companies that are being built, the services being built, the wealth that is being created is phenomenal. Chinese internet is a greater percentage of the GDP of China, which is a big number, than the same percentage of the US, which is also a big number.

"If you think of China as like 'Oh yeah, they're good with the internet' you're missing the point. Globalization means that they get to play too. I think you're going to see fantastic leadership in products and services from China. There's a real danger that along with those products and

---

[268] https://theintercept.com/2018/09/13/google-china-search-engine-employee-resigns/

services comes a different leadership regime from government, with censorship, controls, etc."269

It may be comforting to believe that Google's compromise with China has little to do with us, that all this is happening in a country far away and that what happens in China could never happen in the United States or Europe. But the lessons learned in China are already being applied in other countries both because China is aggressively exporting its technology and because (as with so much in AI) many other companies, countries and universities are researching and experimenting along parallel tracks.

As the technology spreads, so pressure will mount on the intelligence and law enforcement communities to take action on the information available. Already, complex algorithms help organizations such as the CIA and NSA build visual representations of the connections within terrorist organizations – the people, places, bank accounts, relatives – that allow for key people to be identified, a drone targeted or a special forces mission authorized.

Today, because many of the algorithms are inaccurate, humans remain the decision makers. But as AI accuracy climbs to 99% and beyond, authorities will come to rely on it as the trusted resource instead of humans.

Going down this road will risk abrogating the rule of law and the individual protections that have guaranteed our freedoms. Without a framework of laws and the ethics behind them, free societies are in danger of following the Chinese example reducing individual rights and freedoms to the whim of an AI algorithm.

---

[269] https://www.cnbc.com/2018/09/20/eric-schmidt-ex-google-ceo-predicts-internet-split-china.html

Just how far down this road we have already advanced, we will discuss in the next chapter.

Chapter 12

Watching America

At a local coffee joint, Peter Warren, 25, an African-American health aide in scrubs, runs into Thomas Werdling, a teammate from his recreation league basketball team whom he hasn't seen in ten years. Peter pulls up a chair and the two joke about their mediocre athletic talents and share quick updates on their current lives. Thomas says he's between jobs and is evasive about what he's been doing. Peter wishes him good luck finding a gig, shakes his head and walks off with his coffee. Their entire exchange lasts maybe five minutes. What Peter doesn't know – what he can't know – is that entire interaction has been caught on camera and uploaded to a law enforcement data base.

At a security Center Machine Room – screens only, no humans – Thomas' image is matched to his Facial Recognition Database. Turns out, he's on a watch list for links to a drug ring. Then, Peter's image from the coffee shop pops up beside Thomas' – and now Peter's database turns up, too.

Everything about Peter scrolls by: his KIK posts, his list of friends, his Instagram and Snap images, video, even voice and other "high dimensionality" data – glimpse his earnest posts, his white and black friends, his terrible karaoke singing, his playground soccer games, his family and health history (he had asthma as a child), his travel experiences (Mexico and Canada only)... his last three dates and their initial online dating site exchanges... see that Peter is humorously self-deprecating "There are better looking guys, probably smarter, richer and much nicer... but I'm a solid 6 in all those categories..."

His job approval ratings – which are raves... come up, plus the fact that he's never late for work... No detail is too small. Nothing is overlooked. He is engaging and confident but unremarkable. The sense here is that Peter is not unique, that everyone in this society has a similar data base.

Peter is given a social credit score, 1–100, the higher the score the greater his danger to society. Peter was at 20. Now, as his image flashes next to Thomas', just the fact of their brief association rockets Peter to a score of 75 and propels him onto the same watch list as Thomas.

Then, back in the world, Peter's cruising local streets on his motor scooter. He rolls a bit too quickly through a stop sign with no cars in sight. A motorcycle cop appears from nowhere and pulls him over. Peter has learned that, as a black man, it's safest to be deferential to cops. He apologizes profusely for his minor traffic infraction and figures, worst case, he might get a ticket. The cop's bodycam uses facial recognition software to match Peter to the database. The CopCam in the police car reads the license plate and flags his presence on the Watch List. That means detain until proven innocent, so Peter is arrested. He argues vehemently that this is a mistake; he's the most law-abiding citizen in the city. The cop is deaf to his protests. Peter is thrown in jail, not for what he did, but for what he might do.

*

The key plot point in the film *Minority Report* was that specially selected humans – precogs, short for precognitives – could predict the future giving law enforcement the information it needs to arrest murderers before they commit a crime.

That film, which came out 15 years ago, was considered science fiction. Yet the CIA and other intelligence agencies are using AI to predict the future with a high degree of certainty. Right now, the CIA can predict not just criminal behavior but violent unrest and social instability several days into the future, and the agency is very confident of being able to predict weeks or months into the future within two years. The further out the predictions go, the more unreliable the algorithms. A few years ago, it was days, then weeks, and now it's months as the data become richer and deeper.

That technology, which combines enormous quantities of data, supercomputers, and advanced algorithms, is being made available to domestic law enforcement for both predictive analytics and post-crime analysis. Voice- and facial-recognition software is now so sophisticated that both can be used to identify anyone from the multitude of databases that already hold images of every citizen in the country. While some of these databases are protected by existing laws, it's not hard to imagine lawmakers and the public jumping at the chance to prevent crime before it happens and amending laws to make that possible.

In one scenario, often cited by law enforcement, a gang robs a bank. Facial recognition identifies the perpetrators. Analysis of their data base including their social and spending habits can predict with at least 90% accuracy exactly what each individual will do over the next 48 hours, whether it's making extravagant purchases or buying rounds at their favorite bar. By following the algorithmic chain, police would be able to arrest all involved.

More broadly, it will be possible to use the CIA's technology to predict extremist activity from left or right before it happens. As data is matched with ever more sophisticated AI algorithms, scientists believe it will be possible to predict behavior of criminals, terrorists and activists. It is a short step to moving beyond prediction to prevention in the name of protecting society from itself. The world of *Minority Report* is no longer science fiction.

The problem confronting both the law enforcement and intelligence communities is whether to use information to track criminals after they commit a crime or to use data to predict if/when they might do something illegal and intervene before it happens. In the past, "sources" were the key differentiator between success and failure. Cops would build up close relationships in their communities and hopefully get advance warning of a robbery or even a violent crime. Sources, both human (humint) and signal intercepts (sigint) have been key in helping the CIA or MI6 gain insight into what foreign governments or senior officials might be thinking or planning.

*

Some insight into how a western surveillance society can work came on March 2, 2018 when two agents of the GRU, Russia's military intelligence, Alexander Petrov and Ruslan Boshirov, flew into Gatwick airport in the UK. Inside their luggage was a bottle of Nina Ricci perfume which contained Novichok, one of the deadliest of chemical weapons. Their target was two Russian defectors

Sergei Skripal and his daughter Yulia, who had spied for MI6270.

As has been widely reported, the assassins traveled to Salisbury, where the Skripals lived, and spread the poison on the handle of their front door. Sergei and Yulia nearly died but later made a full recovery. The killers then discarded the poison bottle which was picked up by a young couple, Charlie Rowley and Dawn Sturgess who thought they had stumbled upon a perfume bottle. Dawn died from the poison while Charlie was seriously ill but later recovered.271

British intelligence believes that the assassination attempts were personally authorized by Vladimir Putin, the Russian President, who as a former KGB officer, apparently will stop at nothing to punish any act he considers a betrayal of the country.272 The Russians declared that the two men were simply tourists eager to visit the cathedral in Salisbury. While they were denying the attack, Russian intelligence agents were trying to hack into the Swedish laboratory where the poison was being analyzed.273

The Novichok incident illustrated both the capabilities and the shortcomings of Britain's surveillance society.

After the attack, the authorities coordinated their response involving police, customs, MI5 and MI6,

---

[270] https://www.independent.co.uk/news/uk/crime/novichok-attack-russian-spies-airport-security-how-smuggled-chemical-weapon-russia-uk-a8534511.html

[271] https://www.ft.com/content/34f6443a-b075-11e8-99ca-68cf89602132

[272] Interview, MI6 officer, July 2018.

[273] https://arstechnica.com/information-technology/2018/09/russians-tried-to-hack-swiss-lab-testing-samples-from-skripal-attack/

drawing on more than 50 years of counter terrorism experience gleaned especially from battles with the Irish Republican Army. During "the troubles," the British deployed a complex web of surveillance systems that started at the points of entry and spread across all major cities to include rail and bus networks and every major road.

The core of the effort is the nearly 6m CCTV cameras spread around the country.[274] In the hunt for the assassins, those TV cameras tracked the two Russians from their entry at Gatwick airport, to their hotel in London, the two trips to Salisbury and then their exit from Gatwick before the manhunt got under way.

Scotland Yard had 5,000 images of CCTV footage to examine immediately after the attack and called upon two members of a six-person squad knows as the super recognizers, who are particularly adept at picking individual faces out of a crowd, memorizing them and then picking those same faces out of other footage.275

Compared with China's AI-driven police cloud, this approach – relying on humans, no matter how talented they are – seems very last century. But very soon Britain and other countries will catch up to China.

*

Facial recognition software is now a multi-billion-dollar industry across the world. For intelligence agencies, the purpose is to identify known terrorists boarding a flight or going through passport control. But as we all come under routine surveillance (linking of an instore camera to a

---

[274] https://www.quora.com/How-many-cameras-does-the-UK-have

[275] https://www.telegraph.co.uk/news/2018/08/28/police-use-super-recognisers-hunt-salisbury-poisoners/

photo of a customer using a credit card, for example) it will be possible to track every individual by name and activity from the moment they leave their home. And while at home, various smart devices, from the fridge that can order eggs and milk to the lights that turn off and on as a person moves from room to room, will fill in the gaps.

The obvious infringement on civil liberties is enough to raise alarms, but the creation of the algorithms themselves – which are the basis of all facial recognition systems – is troubling. While the Joint Staff in the Pentagon is working to develop its own facial recognition system for the armed forces, data scientists have discovered that current algorithms are based on a deep understanding of the facial characteristics of white American males and females because that is the world those creating the datasets understand. When the system is tested against African-Americans or Arabs, it produces an alarming number of false positives.276

---

[276] Interview, Pentagon official, July 27, 2018

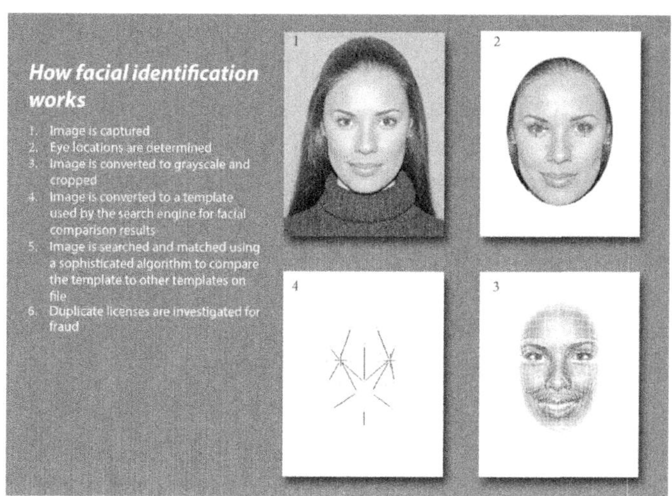

[277]

According to the Electronic Frontier Foundation, "face recognition systems are generally designed to do one of three things. First, a system may be set up to *identify* an unknown person. For example, a police officer would use this type of system to try to identify an unknown person in footage from a surveillance camera. The second type of face recognition system is set up to *verify the identity* of a known person. Smartphones rely on this type of system to allow you to use face recognition to unlock your phone. A third type, which operates similarly to a verification system, is designed to *look for multiple specific, previously-identified faces*. This system may be used, for example, to recognize card counters at a casino, or certain shoppers in a store, or wanted persons on a crowded subway platform."[278]

---

[277] Iowa Department of Transportation

[278] https://www.eff.org/wp/law-enforcement-use-face-recognition#_idTextAnchor004

The Pentagon's experience with data bias in facial recognition systems is matched by studies elsewhere, and every software solution to date struggles to open up the ethnic bias unconsciously built into the system by the programmers. Another test by the ACLU used the Amazon Rekognition software to match 28 Members of Congress against a database of 25,000 known criminals and each member of Congress was incorrectly identified as a felon.279 Despite such failures, Rekognition is being made available to police forces across America.

Such inherent biases are common across the world, as each set of meta data tends to produce its own anomalies. For example, "software designed to warn people using Nikon cameras when the person they are photographing seems to be blinking tends to interpret Asians as always blinking." In 2017, researchers used deep learning to identify skin cancer from photographs. "They trained their model on a data set of 129,450 images, 60% of which were scraped from Google Images. But fewer than 5% of these images are of dark-skinned individuals, and the algorithm wasn't tested on dark-skinned people."280

Brian Brackeen, the black CEO of the facial recognition firm Kairos, argues that facial recognition technology is not only inherently biased but that it should never be placed in the hands of governments.

"I (and my company) have come to believe that the use of commercial facial recognition in law enforcement or in government surveillance of any kind is wrong – and that it opens the door for gross misconduct by the morally corrupt.

---

[279] https://aws.amazon.com/rekognition/

[280] https://www.nature.com/articles/d41586-018-05707-8

"To be truly effective, the algorithms powering facial recognition software require a massive amount of information. The more images of people of color it sees, the more likely it is to properly identify them. The problem is, existing software has not been exposed to enough images of people of color to be confidently relied upon to identify them.

"And misidentification could lead to wrongful conviction, or far worse."281

Proponents remind us that these are early days in the development and use of such systems and insist that standards will improve, biases will be removed and the systems will work across all ethnic boundaries.282

A recent study by the National Institute of Standards and Technology paired a super recognizer human with a facial recognition software system against two super recognizers. The combined pair of humans and software proved more effective than the humans alone. This was a major advance in the AI driven software and there is some confidence that within another two years, the software will beat the human routinely.283

Facebook has developed software called DensePose that can take a 2D image (a photograph) and give it 3D attributes.284 This sounds innocuous but has applications

---

[281] https://techcrunch.com/2018/06/25/facial-recognition-software-is-not-ready-for-use-by-law-enforcement/

[282] https://aws.amazon.com/blogs/aws/thoughts-on-machine-learning-accuracy/

[283] https://www.washingtonpost.com/technology/2018/06/28/facial-recognition-technology-is-finally-more-accurate-identifying-people-color-could-that-be-used-against-immigrants/?utm_term=.294d20df1041

[284] https://arxiv.org/pdf/1802.00434.pdf

that will resonate with police forces everywhere. Using DensePose, it will be possible to identify movements within a crowd that could predict risk or riot. Such a system could then automatically alert a quick reaction force to detain anyone identified by the software.

These innovative methods which combine big data, visualization and real time feedback and response can make preemptive action both practical and effective.

For example, when Freddie Grey, a 25-year-old African-American man died during an arrest by police in Baltimore, Maryland, several days of rioting followed. Police teamed up with a private company called Geofeedia to consolidate feeds from Twitter, Facebook and Instagram to create real time geo location maps of where demonstrators were gathering and predictive maps of where future action was likely.285 According to a police officer involved, "The Freddie Gray incident was a watershed moment for the City of Baltimore police. The minute his death was announced, we knew we needed to monitor social media data at key locations where protesting was likely, especially at the local police precinct where Gray had been arrested."

The data provided by Geofeedia to the police combined with the use of facial recognition software to identify rioters with outstanding warrants in real time enabled law enforcement to send in snatch squads to arrest suspects right out of the crowd.

---

285 https://www.aclunc.org/docs/20161011_geofeedia_baltimore_case_study.pdf ; https://www.theverge.com/2016/10/11/13243890/facebook-twitter-instagram-police-surveillance-geofeedia-api

The publicity resulting from the Gray case led to Twitter, Facebook and Instagram revisiting their relationship with Geofeedia, but the company still claims to have data feeds with 500 police departments across America.

Social media and the information gleaned about us from tweets and posts are perhaps the most obvious and visible signs of who we are, what we think and what we do. But as big data aggregates more information about us from an ever-widening set of sources, profiling becomes both more pervasive and more pernicious.

Many of us now use a fingerprint to log in or log off our devices, or to get money or pay money. But behind that simple method is a hidden set of parameters to help determine whether we are who we claim to be. How you use all devices – mouse, swipe, cursor, etc. – and in what order are as much an identifier as the fingerprint itself. Such information is routinely captured by a company called Biocatch. The company claims to have profiles on 70m people and to monitor six billion financial transactions each month.286

Biocatch is one of several companies gathering such data and selling it to banks and other financial institutions around the world. The software is sophisticated enough that if a profile raises a red flag, the system can intervene to slow down the activity or to provoke a reaction (do you jiggle the mouse from side to side, or up and down) that can be measured against your normal profile. If there is a further anomaly, the transaction can be stopped.

---

[286] https://www.nytimes.com/2018/08/13/business/behavioral-biometrics-banks-security.html

If touch is one identifier, voice is another. It's easy enough, assuming someone is speaking your language, to understand what they are saying. But for the Pentagon or for NSA, the challenge is more complicated. If the special-forces are listening to a conversation taking place in a building in Afghanistan, there are two immediate problems. What are the people in the room saying? Are they telling a joke or planning a terrorist attack? Until recently, there was no way of answering the second part of that question and the answer to the first required either having an interpreter on hand or relaying the conversation back to base and getting it returned in English.

Today, the answers are quite different. Two years ago, translation was done by statistical analysis (if this is being said, the chances are it means that) while today, algorithms can run the words against massive data bases to produce far more accurate results: up from around 80% to around 98%. And now the software can ascribe the equivalent of emoticons to every conversation (smiley face, sad face, laughing face etc.) to provide some context. The next generation of such software will provide translation complete with the emotional resonance of the original speaker.

But even those advances assume either human or signal intervention (a bug in a room or a person) which other advances may render redundant. Google has partnered with DeepMind to create a lip-reading speech recognition system which uses a much larger word database with a lower word error rate than professional human lip-readers.287

---

[287] https://arxiv.org/pdf/1807.05162.pdf

Why should this matter to us? Because AI will enable the construction of complete profiles of every individual incorporating voice, activities, facial characteristics and unique gestures. The days when a bank robber can don a wig or false teeth to escape detection will be over. Instead, every store, bank or CCTV camera will be able to identify who we are and what we are doing based on an existing database.

*

Every country is moving towards a world in which Big Data is a prime research tool, drawing from every possible resource, including social media, email, travel history, financial records and online search and purchases. AI will aggregate all this data to display previously invisible connections between people, organizations and activities. A donation to an abortion rights group over here might connect to a blog advocating demonstrations over there, to the booking of a travel ticket to Washington DC and a Google search seeking activists there. Or, simple facial recognition on checking into a flight might raise a red flag.

The Transport Security Administration has already been covertly running a crude version of such a check called Quiet Skies, though this is run by humans who are essentially guessing who might, or might not, prove to be a risk. TSA officials flag individuals either before or during a flight, enter them into a surveillance database and then follow them on their next flight or pass their information on to another law enforcement or intelligence agency. Here's what the checklist looks like:288

---

288 http://apps.bostonglobe.com/news/nation/graphics/2018/07/tsa-quiet-skies/

1. **SUBJECT WAS ABNORMALLY AWARE OF SURROUNDINGS**

(If observed, check any that apply below): Y N Unknown

Reversing or changing directions and/or stopping while in transit through the airport

Attempting to change appearance by changing clothes, shaving etc. while in the airport or on the plane

Using the reflection in storefront windows to identify surveillance

Observing the boarding gate area from afar

Boarded last

Observing other people who appear to be observing FAM team and/or subject

2. **SUBJECT EXHIBITED BEHAVIORAL INDICATORS**

(If observed, check any that apply below): Y N Unknown

3. **SUBJECT'S APPEARANCE WAS DIFFERENT FROM INFORMATION PROVIDED**

(If yes, check any that apply below): Y N Unknown

4. **SUBJECT SLEPT DURING THE FLIGHT**

(If observed, check any that apply below): Y N Unknown

5. **GENERAL OBSERVATIONS**

(Provide detailed descriptions of any electronic devices in subject's possession in AAR): Y N Unknown

6. **FOR DOMESTIC ARRIVALS ONLY**

(If possible, provide identifiers (license plate, vehicle description) of pick up vehicle in AAR): Y N Unknown

To anybody trained in intelligence or surveillance, this process seems extraordinarily unsophisticated and likely a waste of time and money. But the appetite for such a program from the TSA is indicative of the opportunities that will exist for a more developed, AI-driven, solution.

*

As AI-driven surveillance tools proliferate, will authorities find previously unimagined uses for them, in effect, will the tail wag the dog? To date, there have been few constraints on federal, state and local governments using whatever becomes available to keep track of citizens for whatever purposes are deemed appropriate. For years, the Drug Enforcement Administration has photographed license plates of vehicles that they think might be involved in drug activities. Police across the country use License Plate Reader (LPR) technology to automatically photograph cars going past a CCTV camera placed in a police vehicle or on a pole. That information is shared across multiple jurisdictions and used in some areas to identify welfare cheats.289

The Chicago police keep a gang database of 128,000, primarily young, people, a huge percentage of whom are from minority groups. It includes many who have never committed a crime.290 Los Angeles County keeps a database of 140,000 alleged gang members, again, many of whom have not committed a crime.291

Unusually for a technology company, Microsoft has broken ranks to suggest that government should regulate the use of AI technology in general and especially of facial recognition. In a blog post, the company suggested that

---

[289] https://www.eff.org/deeplinks/2018/07/county-welfare-office-violated-accountability-rules-while-surveilling-benefits

[290] http://www.chicagotribune.com/news/local/breaking/ct-met-chicago-police-gang-database-20180411-story.html

[291] http://articles.latimes.com/1995-05-06/local/me-62996_1_suspected-gang-member

unfettered development of AI-driven technology could pose a challenge for traditional civil liberties and push legal boundaries beyond what is acceptable in a democratic society.

"Imagine a government tracking everywhere you walked over the past month without your permission or knowledge. Imagine a database of everyone who attended a political rally that constitutes the very essence of free speech. Imagine the stores of a shopping mall using facial recognition to share information with each other about each shelf that you browse and product you buy, without asking you first. This has long been the stuff of science fiction and popular movies – like *Minority Report*, *Enemy of the State* and even *1984* – but now it's on the verge of becoming possible.

"Perhaps as much as any advance, facial recognition raises a critical question: what role do we want this type of technology to play in everyday society?"292

As a starting point, Microsoft suggested that government should attempt to answer eight questions:

Should law enforcement use of facial recognition be subject to human oversight and controls, including restrictions on the use of unaided facial recognition technology as evidence of an individual's guilt or innocence of a crime?

Similarly, should we ensure there is civilian oversight and accountability for the use of facial recognition as part of governmental national security technology practices?

What types of legal measures can prevent use of facial recognition for racial profiling and other violations of rights while still permitting the beneficial uses of the technology?

Should use of facial recognition by public authorities or others be subject to minimum performance levels of accuracy?

Should the law require that retailers post visible notice of their use of facial recognition technology in public spaces?

Should the law require that companies obtain prior consent before collecting individuals' images for facial recognition? If so, in what situations and places should this apply? And what is the appropriate way to ask for and obtain such consent?

Should we ensure that individuals have the right to know what photos have been collected and stored that have been identified with their names and faces?

Should we create processes that afford legal rights to individuals who believe they have been misidentified by a facial recognition system?

Unfortunately, despite Microsoft's initiative, there is little appetite in Congress to legislate in this area. Data privacy didn't appear on congressional radar until late 2018, and then only because some members believe search engines are skewing results based on partisan parameters that favor Democrats over Republicans.

Solutions to the burgeoning threat of AI to our civil rights should be managed by ethical, legal and moral boundaries established by the government. But, instead, as is often the case with new technology, the immediate future will be a free-for-all of rapid, unfettered

---

[292] https://blogs.microsoft.com/on-the-issues/2018/07/13/facial-recognition-technology-the-need-for-

development. It does not require a wild leap to predict that Big Data will aggregate facial recognition, voice, behavior, touch, travel, spending habits and every other possible attribute to create profiles of everyone. These profiles will be exploited by law enforcement, intelligence and marketers.

As some police databases and facial recognition systems already have demonstrated, unchecked implementation risks lumping the innocent with the guilty without any due process. That is roughly where we are today in terms of the regulation of such tools.

Within five years, government agencies, law enforcement and intelligence communities everywhere will be able to use algorithms to predict many types of behavior. In this world, decisions will be made not on the basis of what has happened but on the basis of what *could* happen. The algorithms will easily and quickly serve up that kind of information and what Chief of Police or intelligence chief will choose to ignore such data?

In October 2018, America was shocked by two separate acts of terrorism, the first a series of pipe bombs delivered to vocal Democrats opposed to President Trump and the second a murderous attack on a synagogue in Pittsburgh that killed 11 people.293

While both attacks happened without warning, it later emerged that there was, in fact, plenty of warning if police

---

public-regulation-and-corporate-responsibility/

[293] https://www.washingtonpost.com/world/national-security/suspect-in-pittsburgh-synagogue-shooting-charged-in-44-count-hate-crime-indictment/2018/10/31/bf2be61c-dd36-11e8-b3f0-62607289efee_story.html ; https://www.nytimes.com/2018/10/25/nyregion/pipe-bombs-sent-democrats.html

and the FBI had been looking in the right places. The bomber was a fervent Trump supporter, drove a van that was plastered in radical stickers, had a lengthy police record and had an active and threatening presence on social media. The Pittsburgh shooter, too, had a very active presence on social media, had made anti-Semitic threats and fit the classic profile of a potential shooter.

If police had been using an active AI system, such as is already in use in China, it is likely that both men would have been flagged as threats and the FBI or the police could have removed them preemptively. This raises a critical question for our society: do we want to accept the erosion of our civil liberties in order to preemptively remove possible threats – understanding that many innocent people would be swept up in the preemptive net?

There has been no meaningful debate about this looming future, no conversation about what such data profiling might mean for the rule of law, the assumption of innocence and the wholesale breach of our right to privacy, policies that have been central to democracies for generations.

In developed countries, it's not too late to change the way we use big data. But for many other countries, the future is bleaker. If China is demonstrating the future of the surveillance society, it is also determined to export that capability to influence, and perhaps control, much of the world.

Part 6 – Waging a New Kind of War

Chapter 13
Information Warfare

Russ Sabotini, AKA NewWorldOrder25 or NWO25, loved his work at the Center for Technology Excellence that was buried deep within the Department of Homeland Security. Working for the Heart of Darkness was so much cooler than he expected; being paid to break shit, mess with peoples' minds and all with the political cover and big budget of the government. If only he could post about it...

He had been recruited at Defcon, the annual hacker gabfest, where two women dressed like stoners offered him a gig. The money alone had him salivating but the real draw was the carrot of being able to legally create the kind of stuff he had been doing illegally for years.

NWO25 had become a legend for his Deep Fake work. A bit like the artist Banksy who spoofed the stuffy art world, NWO25 got off taking on the politicians, the media and the tech titans who took themselves so seriously but who were all, in his view, just a bunch of jokeless jerks.

In his view, anyone who stepped up and out was fair game. Another old fart in Congress pontificating about protecting women from rapists and he would put out a video of the same man sleeping with a 13-year-old bot at one of those Vegas brothels that were all the rage. A tech guy talking about his empathy for the poor while he pocketed another gargantuan pay increase and a bank account statement would appear with the below-minimum-wage payments to a butler, gardener and shoe polisher.

All good fun, and all on the Dark Web, where his true identity was impossible to find.

But for the millions who followed him in the underground, he had become a legend, with every posting reposted countless times. In the world of Deep Fake, it proved impossible to distinguish truth from fiction and once his reputation climbed, he started getting all kinds of tips, many of which proved accurate, so in a weird way, his truth became THE truth, whatever anyone might say.

There was a certain addiction to it all as he watched men and women's reputations collapse in the face of his attacks. They all deserved it – bunch of pigs chowing at the trough of corruption. He liked the power and the opportunity to make a difference as the world around him descended ever further into chaos and so many of his friends were jobless and hopeless.

He never knew who ratted him out – probably one of his bankrupt friends who needed the money but it all turned out pretty well. At that first Defcon meeting, it turned out that the stoner girls were more black mambas than bong busters and they'd spelled it out pretty clearly: On the one hand a jail cell in some out of the way hellhole where sodomy would be the nightly dessert. On the other, a great salary, a decent place to live and doing God's work on behalf of a grateful nation.

He was sold at the word sodomy, signed a piece of paper that he didn't read and was on a plane to DC that night.

Now, NWO25 was a distant memory and he was simply Russ to the team, the go-to guy who could create the masterpieces.

"You need to understand the mission," the nameless besuited scary guy had told him at the beginning, "You're going to create Our Truth and that's going to be the only

truth that matters. You'll get the targets and it will be up to you how you execute. This is about securing America from the crazies in the media, the politicians who don't see the world as we see it and all enemies, foreign and domestic."

Whatever.

The targets came thick and fast. A video of the president tearing into the Senate leader (of his own party!) to show how tough he is. A "tape" of a conversation with the Chinese leader, another with the Russian President, both designed to show the foreigners as weak and America as strong. A copy of the Bermuda bank statement of the editor of the New York Times *showing that he had been on the payroll of the Democrats for years. Email exchanges between Jeff Bezos and the editor of the* Washington Post *(owned by Amazon) encouraging editorial coverage in favor of tax breaks for web-based companies. It's was all crap, of course, but denials no longer mattered in a world where the truth was exactly what the White House wanted it to be.*

His Deep Fakes were so immaculate that none of the latest forensic software could detect the truth from his fictions, which was the point and why he was paid the big bucks.

Russ enjoyed playing Fuck the Man and to his anarchic sensibility, it all seemed like pretty harmless fun. Until last Sunday.

As the world's fifth-largest economy, California had always considered itself special within the United States. As the source of much of the technology that had powered the Fourth Industrial Revolution, the state and its tech titans thought they deserved more recognition and economic support from Washington DC. The nation's capital, however, saw the left coast as a hotbed of liberal and ignorant policies on everything from climate change to abortion and the rights of the spotted owl versus jobs in the lumber industry.

It was a fraught relationship at best, but as the AI revolution had unfolded, talk of a left coast secession had grown from a marginal conversation into what seemed like an unstoppable force.

"We need a full court press on this one," the same faceless bureaucrat had instructed, on one of his very rare visits to the subterranean bunker Russ and his team called home. "Media, politicians, the money, everything that tells those idiots in language even they can understand that they need us much more than we need them."

Unleashing the full armory that had been honed over previous operations was a pretty interesting exercise. Talk about targets of opportunity. It was simple enough to meet pre-set expectations with sexual abuse stuff against Hollywood types in LA. That combined with the leaked video of a Mayor having sex with a bot in a brothel and several careers were finished. But that simply confirmed what everyone already thought they knew: LA was the sleaze capital of the universe.

The master stroke had four key parts. First, warning of the big one, the mother of all earthquakes scheduled to hit San Francisco in 48 hours. Then, a conversation between city officials that seemed to show they had information on the quake but failed to sound the alarm while they panicked. The third part was supposed to be Washington stepping in with a calming voice to set the record straight, a welcome contrast to the apparent indifference of the local politicians. The wrap up would be a social media barrage from hundreds of accounts attacking the

California leadership under the general heading of Who Can you Trust?

But things had gone horribly wrong between parts two and three. Word of the imminent quake had leaked and panic had followed. The fact that the quake itself was fiction made no difference as nobody could sort out the real from the unreal any longer. Traffic out of the city was jammed for miles with shootings and fights breaking out between those who felt they had priority and those who preferred a more orderly line. Most in demand were the helicopters and most willing to shoot first were those with bodyguards and guns. The rich flew first and everyone else had to wait in line.

At a stroke, Russ realized that the monster he had created was out of control. From being master of the (made up) truth he had become creator of the killer lie. The bodies were piling up and it was all his fault.

He had made a frantic call to the nameless one upstairs and the meeting had been the final wake up call.

"Stop being such a pussy, Russ," he had been told. "We've been at war and you have been winning it for us. Remember, all enemies foreign and domestic?"

"Sure," he had replied. "Fake bank accounts and a few sleazy videos is just a bit of fun. But killing people? I'm out."

Then, as the beast was revealed, Russ got his first real insight into the bargain he had made.

"Out? There is no 'out'," he had been told. "We own you and we can destroy you any time we choose. Remember that document you signed, the one you didn't read? Well, much as you think you can fake the world, that was real enough to send you to jail for ever. No more fun, no more salary or decent apartment just a cell with a line

of hairy beasts at the door waiting to educate you about prison life."

Well, that had been easy for him to say. But this was New World Order 25 that was in the room, the master of the hacker universe, the king of the deep fake. It was time for a lesson in truth telling as only he could do it.

*

In the immediate aftermath of the 9/11 attacks on America, the CIA came up with a plan to create their own digital Osama bin Laden, complete with audio recordings, video, bank accounts, and handwritten messages – all fake. The idea was to own Al Qaeda from within and turn its members against each other, all in the name of the organization's leader. This was a perfectly practical solution that, if deployed, might have prevented the invasion of Iraq and the apparently endless war in Afghanistan. The plan was stopped by a political appointee in the White House who was fearful of the administration being criticized for creating false information.

The world has moved on a long way since then. Today, it's possible to create a video of anyone in any language, from the President of the United States to the President of Russia, using an actor whose voice can be digitally inserted into a real person's image and speech patterns. It has become nearly impossible to tell the difference between the fake and the real. Research detectives come up with temporary schemes to ferret out the fakes, but as fast as a fix is created, the thinking machine sees the fix and creates an instant workaround.

Imagine an international crisis in which the leaders of countries on opposite sides deliver false statements created by a third nation seeking to gain advantage; or apparently real broadcasts by normally reliable networks used to destabilize and disrupt a nation preparing to go to war.

All major nations today have this kind of capability, and already it has leaked out into the private world of frauds and scams. For example, one popular scam, called "CEO Fraud," uses the fake voice of a company's CEO to persuade an employee to transfer funds or reveal a password.

AI will make this world almost impossible to control. This will create a half-world in which, for most people, there will be no truth or fiction, only entertainment. For the elite decision-makers, the validation of information will become ever harder. At the same time, the use of AI in various control system could make them vulnerable to AI-created hacks which will likely become ubiquitous.

*

The most egregious example of this kind of information warfare occurred during the 2016 US presidential election. The Russian government, working on the personal orders of President Vladimir Putin, implemented a comprehensive attack on American democracy. This took many forms from fake videos to hundreds of fake Twitter and Facebook accounts all of which were designed to undermine the campaign of Hillary Clinton, the Democratic candidate and enhance the profile of Donald Trump.

A Russian group (many of whom were later indicted as a result of Robert Mueller's investigation) used the codename Guccifer 2.0 when leaking documents to the American media. The fact that the leaks were from Russia was known to the media at the time but the information appeared too good not to be used, even though by doing so, reporters were doing Moscow's bidding.294

Trump won the election, though the US intelligence community refused to say that Russian interference had tipped the balance. But the documented level of fraud and intrusion beggars any other conclusion. For Russia, this was a remarkably cost-effective operation. Without firing a shot, they won the information war that helped their preferred candidate win the election to lead their most powerful adversary. Trump's own particular psychology rendered him unable to admit that Russia had interfered at all and therefore no action was taken to punish Russia and Putin for their aggression.

*

The reality for western intelligence is that cyber war has been the preferred means of attack for all enemies in what has become an ever more sophisticated conflict. Russia, China, Iran, North Korea, Israel are all very active and aggressive in cyberspace, each for different reasons, but each able to pursue their political, economic and social ambitions largely with impunity. The very purpose of cyber war is to blur the battle boundaries so that they no longer fit any current legal definition of warfare. China steals billions of dollars of military and economic secrets from the private sectors of foreign countries but there is no mechanism for exacting a price for such theft.

America has a formidable arsenal of cyber weapons, created by the National Security Agency and the CIA, which are used extensively for espionage. The NSA has mapped the critical infrastructures of every nation that

---

[294] https://www.axios.com/the-russian-intelligence-agents-behind-guccifer-20-271044ab-8768-4b79-ae87-

might seek to wage war against America. Using a range of cyber weapons, America can raise the sluice gates of the Seven Gorges Dam in China, flooding the land downstream and killing millions. Or turn off the power system in Moscow in the dead of winter, or insert fake news into the Friday prayers broadcast by Iran's mullahs.

But with rare exceptions – such as the collaboration with the Israelis on Stuxnet which crippled some of Iran's nuclear facilities – the US does not employ these weapons for sabotage. And, with, perhaps, a single exception – the taking out of Iraq's air defenses at the inception of the first Gulf War – America has not used its cyber arsenal as an act of war.

There are three ways in which this new kind of war really matters. First, since the end of World War II, real power has been granted to a small number of countries armed with nuclear weapons. Complex non-proliferation agreements and international pressure have limited the number of member states in the nuclear club and helped restrict the use of such weapons by rogue nations (North Korea) or unstable regimes (Pakistan) and, thus far, has kept terrorists from obtaining nuclear capabilities.

The cyber world is governed by no such agreements, and many countries have significant cyber capability that are outside the exclusive nuclear weapons club. Even those countries that do have nuclear weapons, such as Russia and China, appreciate the potent power of cyber weapons and already are using them to great effect.

Second, cyber-attacks are inherently difficult to trace, providing a cloak of anonymity to individuals or countries willing to take aggressive measures. There is no equivalent

---

bb4e36f5c992.html

of the telltale plume as an ICBM takes flight, no radar detectors that guarantee instant retaliation. Instead, hacking into a power grid or turning off the water supply is easy, not least because federal and state governments are too slow and too blind to keep pace with the cyber developments in the real world.

Third, in this anarchic environment, in which attacks can be launched from an office in St Petersburg, or an apartment in Moldova, governments may not know their enemies, or be able to control their behavior through the usual levers of pressure. There are no enforceable agreements anywhere about what constitutes cyberwar and therefore invites instant retaliation. In this environment, uncertainty is the enemy of peace and the guarantor of war by mistake.

While every country seeks to engage in information warfare, certain distinct characteristics have emerged since the beginning of the twenty-first century.

Democratic countries use an old paradigm where there is a clear distinction between national security and what matters to the private sector. For example, NSA invests much time and treasure breaking into the networks of countries that may prove hostile to the United States such as China, Russia or North Korea. The targets are communications networks of government officials or scientists, military networks and command and control systems. This is old-fashioned tradecraft and has been going on ever since intelligence was invented as an art.

Information gathered from such activities is shared only with officials and other government agencies on a need to know basis. There is no government spying on behalf of private companies and no effective mechanism in place for sharing information with private companies.

Undemocratic countries operate quite differently. Frequently, in countries like Iran, North Korea, Russia and China, corruption is so endemic that there is no real distinction between the public and private sectors and government money and technology is used to benefit both.

China is the most aggressive country in the world in using IW for national goals. It unleashes around a million attacks each day against American targets, ranging from the Pentagon to every single company on the Fortune 500 and thousands of lesser enterprises. Thefts of intellectual property total in the tens of billions of dollars and have played a key role in enabling the rise of China as a technologically competitive nation. Chinese spying technology routinely infects hardware and software manufactured in China and sold overseas.

From the perspective of both the American and British governments, every single piece of hardware and software that is produced in China is suspect. In addition, every Chinese company working overseas is seen as a potential intelligence operation by the Chinese government and every student studying abroad is a potential spy. China has been viewed as a cyber aggressor for at least 20 years, and while various covert operations to punish Beijing have been considered, none have received the go ahead and instead the private sector has picked up the baton.295 This inaction has provided the illegal underpinnings of the development of the modern Chinese economy and many of their weapons systems from radar to ship design and stealth fighters.

---

[295] https://www.newyorker.com/magazine/2018/05/07/the-digital-vigilantes-who-hack-back

An October 2018 report by the Australian Strategic Policy Institute called *Picking Flowers, Making Honey* lays out the extent of Chinese penetration of the university and research institutes in western countries:296

"China's People's Liberation Army (PLA) is expanding its research collaboration with universities outside of China. Since 2007, the PLA has sponsored more than 2,500 military scientists and engineers to study abroad and has developed relationships with researchers and institutions across the globe.

"This collaboration is highest in the Five Eyes countries, Germany and Singapore, and is often unintentionally supported by taxpayer funds. Nearly all PLA scientists sent abroad are Chinese Communist Party members who return to China on time.

"Dozens of PLA scientists have obscured their military affiliations to travel to Five Eyes countries and the European Union, where they work in areas such as hypersonic missiles and navigation technology…

"The activities… (are) described by the PLA as a process of 'picking flowers in foreign lands to make honey in China'."

In addition, China's Belt and Road Initiative (BRI), unveiled in 2013, aims to develop a network of land and sea links with Southeast Asia, Central Asia, the Middle East, Europe and Africa. And it has used IW to steal information on competitive bids as well as to gain influence in countries or areas of interest."297

---

[296] https://www.aspi.org.au/report/picking-flowers-making-honey

[297] https://www.reuters.com/article/us-malaysia-cyber/china-linked-cyber attacks-likely-as-malaysia-reviews-projects-security-firm-idUSKBN1L00X8

For China and other rising powers, information warfare is a tool for projecting national strategy and power in just the same way that artillery or intercontinental ballistic missiles were in previous centuries.

This is particularly true for Russia which, since the collapse of the Soviet Union, has struggled to maintain a powerful presence on the world's stage. Moscow was stunned by the success of their destabilizing IW campaign during the 2016 Presidential election which resulted in their preferred candidate entering the White House. They were even more surprised (as the intelligence community was horrified) that the new president first denied the attacks that everyone knew had taken place and then refused to authorize any retaliatory action. Whether that was part of a covert deal is not known. What is known is that President Putin thought it was the most successful action in the history of his leadership: inexpensive, a triumph and did more to undermine American democracy than any single act in memory.

Emboldened, the Kremlin now sees IW as the principal instrument of foreign policy. IW allows Russia to advance its interests with little cost, high reward, and – so far – very low risk.

In 2017, as part of its covert war against neighboring Ukraine, Russian hackers unleashed a weapon with the codename NotPetya, which was designed to take out the country's infrastructure. In fact, within hours it had spread across the world taking down multinational companies like Maersk, hospitals in Pennsylvania, a FedEx subsidiary in Europe and companies in France and Tasmania. The impact was devastating and cost around $10 billion.298 Once again, the international community did not retaliate.

In more recent attacks, Russia's goal has been to undermine America, to aggravate cultural disputes such as gun control, to pit left against right, Republican against Democrat, and to sow chaos that undermines the very fabric of the country.

Two simple illustrations: on the anniversary of the Affordable Care Act becoming law in March 2018, Democrats attacked Republicans for trying to sabotage the law, and 600 Russian fake Twitter accounts with 10,000 followers vocally supported the Democrat argument with a goal of dividing the country.299 Then, as the NFL protests gathered strength to protest police violence against African-Americans, Russian hackers used Facebook and Twitter to weigh in on both sides to try and exaggerate tensions.300

Between Russia, which sees IW as a vital lever to gain world influence, and China, which sees IW as a vital tool to promote its rise as the premier superpower, lies North Korea. The secretive regime in Pyongyang has always been a very capable cyber player, but uses cyber more as a tactical weapon of expediency than as a strategic tool.

In 2014, a North Korean government-sponsored hacker team, known as the Lazarus Group, launched a series of attacks against Sony Pictures Entertainment prior to the release of a movie called *The Interview*, which had as a

---

[298] https://www.wired.com/story/notpetya-cyber attack-ukraine-russia-code-crashed-the-world/

[299] https://www.wsj.com/articles/nearly-600-russia-linked-accounts-tweeted-about-the-health-law-1536744638

[300] https://money.cnn.com/2018/09/08/technology/nfl-national-anthem-russia-trolls/index.html

plotline an attempt to assassinate President Kim Jong Un. The Lazarus Group, led by Park Jin Hyok, stole Sony emails, which were later released, and destroyed much of Sony's communications infrastructure. Lazarus were also behind the Wannacry ransomware hack and the theft of $81m from the Bangladesh Bank, as well as thefts from several other banks in Vietnam and South Africa.301

Two things of note about the Sony hack: the National Security Agency knew it was happening but were unable to tell Sony because there is no mechanism for it to do so. Second, the damage caused to Sony was around $100m, perhaps the equivalent of taking out a mall with a bomb. Yet, there was no in-place mechanism for the US to respond in kind, so North Korea effectively got a free pass.302

In addition, North Korea has made extensive use of different branches of social media such as Github and Slack to pitch for business under a variety of assumed names and companies as a way of generating foreign exchange.303

*

Much of this new IW world is hidden behind a veil of secrecy, which disguises incompetence and maintains the Cold War legacy whereby every nugget of intelligence was closely guarded. This is particularly true at the National Security Agency which has pockets of brilliance

---

[301] https://www.npr.org/2018/09/06/645247376/feds-charge-north-korean-cyber-operative-in-sony-hack-ransomware-attack ; https://www.nytimes.com/2018/09/06/us/politics/north-korea-sony-hack-wannacry-indictment.html

[302] David Sanger, The Perfect Weapon: War, Sabotage and Fear in the Cyber Age, Crown, New York, 2018, pp.138-149

[303] https://www.wsj.com/articles/north-koreans-exploit-social-medias-vulnerabilities-to-dodge-sanctions-1536944018

but, also, too long a record of incompetent management and poor implementation of new technologies. The best example of this is a program called Trailblazer that was introduced in 2011 and designed to modernize the collection and analysis of data. Five years later, after billions of dollars had been spent employing hundreds of people, the program was scrapped having achieved none of its main goals.[304]

Trailblazer was symptomatic, not just of malaise at NSA, but with problems throughout the intelligence community dealing with the pace of change. As pace accelerates, the world of intelligence falls ever further behind technology developments in Silicon Valley or elsewhere in the world.

Occasionally, the bureaucracy has little choice but to go public when dire circumstances demand it, and their warnings tend to be stark and frightening. For example, in December 2018, the Department of Homeland Security announced that Russian hackers, using the techniques and codenames of two known government-sponsored groups, Dragonfly and Energetic Bear, had hacked into hundreds of control rooms of power stations across America.305

In theory, such control systems are "air-gapped" and can't be directly accessed. In these cases, however, the hackers got in first by hacking systems belonging to trusted employees or contractors then using their

---

[304] https://washingtontechnology.com/articles/2005/09/10/trailblazer-loses-its-way.aspx

[305] https://www.wsj.com/articles/russian-hackers-reach-u-s-utility-control-rooms-homeland-security-officials-say-1532388110

credentials to access the system, giving them the ability to turn off power all over America.

"They've had access to the button but they haven't pushed it," said Jonathan Homer, Homeland Security's chief of industrial control system analysis.306

The hacks were first detected in 2016 and continued for more than a year before DHS made their announcement. It took that long for NSA, which first detected the hacks, to agree to issue a public warning. An alert could have been sent out the day the first breach was discovered but secrecy and reluctance to admit failure trumped informing the public. After all, the Russians knew what they were doing so we were not revealing anything new to them and the risk of compromising our own sources and methods could have been managed. Instead, the bureaucracy struggled with the challenge of what to do and when.

As these hacks are belatedly discovered and publicized, they appear to embolden, rather than deter, other actors. Countries such as Iran, China and Russia have hacked into the public and private infrastructure in America and Europe both as a deterrent and also as a planted weapon to be used in time of war or the buildup to war. So far, our only defense against such penetrations seems to be whack-a-mole rather than a comprehensive, coordinated strategy, suggesting, perhaps, there is no effective defense.

New technology for movies and other media have made possible a different kind of information warfare. After the actor Peter Cushing died, the director of *Rogue One*, the next edition of the *Star Wars* saga, created his own version

---

[306] https://www.wsj.com/articles/u-s-officials-push-new-penalties-for-hackers-of-electrical-grid-1533492714

of Cushing's character Tarkin that was largely indistinguishable from the original:307

Just over a year later, Buzzfeed created a Deep Fake video which featured President Obama seemingly making a public service announcement in which he said, in part:308

"President Trump is a total and complete dipshit. Now I would never say those things, at least not in a public address. This is a dangerous time. Moving forward, we need to be more vigilant with what we trust from the internet. How we move forward in the age of information is gonna be the difference between whether we survive or

---

[307] http://www.abc.net.au/news/2017-01-19/real-tarkin-vs-rogue-one-cgi-tarkin/8194824

[308] https://www.extremetech.com/extreme/267771-buzzfeed-created-a-deepfake-obama-psa-video; https://www.buzzfeednews.com/article/davidmack/obama-fake-news-jordan-peele-psa-video-buzzfeed#.el7Eqkeo7A

whether we become some kind of fucked-up dystopia. Thank you and stay woke, bitches."

While funny, the video illustrated just how far the technology has moved in the course of a year. For years, the pornography industry has published fake videos with the heads of actors and actresses superimposed on other bodies. While sometimes humiliating, such videos have limited broader impact. What worries the national security community is the likelihood that other countries or terrorist organizations may use such technology to wage war or cause chaos.

The market research firm Gartner suggests that there will be a ready appetite for all kinds of fake news. A recent report said that by 2022 "most people in mature economies will consume more false information than true information, mainly via social media platforms".309

The Lawfare blog, which covers national security issues from a legal perspective, has been raising the alarm about Deep Fakes for some time. They have suggested a number of scenarios:310

Fake videos could feature public officials taking bribes, uttering racial epithets, or engaging in adultery.

Politicians and other government officials could appear in locations where they were not, saying or doing horrific things that they did not.

Fake videos could place them in meetings with spies or criminals, launching public outrage, criminal investigations, or both.

---

[309] https://www.firstpost.com/tech/news-analysis/fake-news-to-increase-multi-fold-via-social-media-platforms-by-2022-gartner-4116213.html

[310] https://www.lawfareblog.com/deep-fakes-looming-crisis-national-security-democracy-and-privacy

Soldiers could be shown murdering innocent civilians in a war zone, precipitating waves of violence and even strategic harms to a war effort.

A deep fake might falsely depict a white police officer shooting an unarmed black man while shouting racial epithets.

A fake audio clip might "reveal" criminal behavior by a candidate on the eve of an election.

A fake video might portray an Israeli official doing or saying something so inflammatory as to cause riots in neighboring countries, potentially disrupting diplomatic ties or even motivating a wave of violence.

False audio might convincingly depict US officials privately "admitting" a plan to commit this or that outrage overseas, exquisitely timed to disrupt an important diplomatic initiative.

A fake video might depict emergency officials "announcing" an impending missile strike on Los Angeles or an emergent pandemic in New York, provoking panic and worse.

Note that these examples all emphasize how a well-executed and well-timed deep fake might generate significant harm in a particular instance, whether the damage is to physical property and life in the wake of social unrest or panic or to the integrity of an election. The threat posed by deep fakes, however, also has a long-term, systemic dimension.

The CIA has developed just this kind of capability as part of a broader plan to use information warfare either to destabilize an enemy or in a foreign campaign to erode political and economic will in the build up to a military confrontation.

*

Of course, the increasingly widespread availability of deep fake tools has led to concerns that the same techniques may be used against us or our allies. Researchers at government labs and in the private sector are looking at ways of using AI to automatically scan images or video to separate the real from the fake. For example, researchers at SUNY in New York are experimenting with software that can compare eye blinking in a video with the known real video to detect anomalies.311 Researchers at Stanford University have been able to compare a video database of portraits with fakes and reveal anomalies.312

No matter the research, as indicated earlier, this is a race without end between fakers and those determined to detect fakes. The movie special effects community will continue to drive demand for ever more seamless Deep Fake product that blurs the lines between fiction and reality. That software is almost immediately available for public use and a rogue actor has the choice of when and how to use it. Countering a fake message in real time is almost impossible which leaves the initiative for sowing chaos in the hands of the aggressor and not the defender.

This world of blurred reality has broader implications. As video, voice, fingerprints and even DNA can be increasingly easily replicated, the investigative techniques and evidentiary requirements for due process in the legal system will be in jeopardy. How will a jury be able to judge between truth and fiction? What will constitute the

---

[311] https://arxiv.org/pdf/1806.02877.pdf

[312] https://web.stanford.edu/~zollhoef/papers/SG2018_DeepVideo/page.html

"burden of proof" or proof of guilt when any forensic evidence can be questioned?

*

In December 2017, the US published its National Security Strategy, a regular event designed to set out intentions for the near future. This is the guide that all branches of the military and intelligence community use for their own planning. The 2017 version was remarkable because it explicitly recognized the threat posed by IW, but also implicitly failed to acknowledge the role AI will play in every aspect of military and intelligence affairs. AI is mentioned only twice in a 55-page document, and then only in passing.313

The Strategy paper had this to say about IW:

"America's competitors weaponize information to attack the values and institutions that underpin free societies, while shielding themselves from outside information. They exploit marketing techniques to target individuals based upon their activities, interests, opinions, and values. They disseminate misinformation and propaganda. Risks to US national security will grow as competitors integrate information derived from personal and commercial sources with intelligence collection and data analytic capabilities based on Artificial Intelligence (AI) and machine learning. Breaches of US commercial and government organizations also provide adversaries with data and insights into their target audiences.

"China, for example, combines data and the use of AI to rate the loyalty of its citizens to the state and uses these ratings to determine jobs and more. Jihadist terrorist

[313] https://www.whitehouse.gov/wp-content/uploads/2017/12/NSS-Final-12-18-2017-0905.pdf

groups continue to wage ideological information campaigns to establish and legitimize their narrative of hate, using sophisticated communications tools to attract recruits and encourage attacks against Americans and our partners.

"Russia uses information operations as part of its offensive cyber efforts to influence public opinion across the globe. Its influence campaigns blend covert intelligence operations and false online personas with state-funded media, third-party intermediaries, and paid social media users or 'trolls.'

"US efforts to counter the exploitation of information by rivals have been tepid and fragmented. US efforts have lacked a sustained focus and have been hampered by the lack of properly trained professionals."

In September 2018, the White House followed up by publishing a National Cyber Strategy.314 Aside from the usual generalizations about improving the national cyber competence levels (with not a single performance measurement), the document had this to say about reforming the anarchic IW world:

"LEAD WITH OBJECTIVE, COLLABORATIVE INTELLIGENCE: The IC will continue to lead the world in the use of all-source cyber intelligence to drive the identification and attribution of malicious cyber activity that threatens United States national interests. Objective and actionable intelligence will be shared across the United States Government and with key partners to identify hostile foreign nation states, and non-nation state cyber programs, intentions, capabilities, research and

---

[314] https://www.whitehouse.gov/wp-content/uploads/2018/09/National-Cyber-Strategy.pdf

development efforts, tactics, and operational activities that will inform whole-of-government responses to protect American interests at home and abroad.

"IMPOSE CONSEQUENCES: The United States will develop swift and transparent consequences, which we will impose consistent with our obligations and commitments to deter future bad behavior. The administration will conduct inter-agency policy planning for the time periods leading up to, during, and after the imposition of consequences to ensure a timely and consistent process for responding to and deterring malicious cyber activities. The United States will work with partners when appropriate to impose consequences against malicious cyber actors in response to their activities against our nation and interests.

"BUILD A CYBER DETERRENCE INITIATIVE: The imposition of consequences will be more impactful and send a stronger message if it is carried out in concert with a broader coalition of like-minded states. The United States will launch an international Cyber Deterrence Initiative to build such a coalition and develop tailored strategies to ensure adversaries understand the consequences of their malicious cyber behavior. The United States will work with like-minded states to coordinate and support each other's responses to significant malicious cyber incidents, including through intelligence sharing, buttressing of attribution claims, public statements of support for responsive actions taken, and joint imposition of consequences against malign actors.

"COUNTER MALIGN CYBER INFLUENCE AND INFORMATION OPERATIONS: The United States will use all appropriate tools of national power to expose and counter the flood of online malign influence and information campaigns and non-state propaganda and disinformation. This includes working with foreign government partners as well as the private sector, academia, and civil society to identify, counter, and prevent the use of digital platforms for malign foreign influence operations while respecting civil rights and liberties."

What the document did not say, is that there had been a fierce internal debate within the Trump administration about what kind of responses to cyber-attacks might be possible. John Bolton, the National Security Advisor, wanted the authority to strike back at attackers using some of the arsenal in the US cyber armory. In the end, the compromise was encapsulated in National Security Presidential Memorandum 13, or NSPM 13, which allowed the military to respond with actions that fall below the threshold of use of force which might cause death or significant economic impacts. That translates to a continuation of the policies of the Obama administration and will involve sanctions against individuals and countries rather than direct retaliatory strikes against infrastructure.315

Whatever the rhetoric, everyone in the national security establishment knows that the gap between attacker and defender grows wider every day. The private sector drains talent from the government and the intelligence community, and the government is totally unattractive to any high flyer under the age of 40, while the bureaucracy

---

[315] https://www.washingtonpost.com/world/national-security/trump-authorizes-offensive-cyber-operations-to-deter-foreign-adversaries-bolton-says/2018/09/20/b5880578-bd0b-11e8-b7d2-0773aa1e33da_story.html

daily grows more inert. As a study in *Foreign Policy* magazine put it:

"Yet the White House, under President Donald Trump, has failed to fill or has outright eliminated almost every major cybersecurity position. There are a few brilliant holdouts bravely providing solid advice on information security and best practices. (The government agency 18F and the United States Digital Service are both doing valuable work but receive far smaller budgets than they deserve.) But cyber talent is draining faster than it is being replaced at the highest levels."316

This is hardly surprising, given that President Trump has almost no understanding of the cyber world and has ignored repeated briefings by the CIA that he is under direct attack personally. For more than a year, both CIA and NSA picked up intelligence that both the Russians and Chinese were listening into calls the president made on his iPhone. He was advised to change his phone once a month but refused to do so because he found it inconvenient. Such cavalier behavior has alarmed the intelligence community, as it knows what it can do against cellphones used by other world leaders.317

Private calls can be recorded to give insight into the personal concerns and life of the president, also making clear who he talks to and their relative influence over him. But, once the phone is identified, it is also possible to operate it remotely to send messages to Twitter in the

---

[316] https://foreignpolicy.com/2018/09/12/in-cyberwar-there-are-no-rules-cybersecurity-war-defense/

[317] https://www.nytimes.com/2018/10/24/us/politics/trump-phone-security.html?action=click&module=Top%20Stories&pgtype=Homepage

president's name. Even more serious is the ability to use the phone as a listening device to hear everything that is said in a room where the phone might be. The idea that the President of the United States is exposing the nation to such risks is extraordinary.

Behind all the posturing and rhetoric, the reality is that America has no cyber security doctrine – who can respond to attack, with what, when and under whose authority – and the control of the IW environment is a bureaucratic nightmare.

The Department of Homeland Security protects civilian and critical infrastructure. That includes election infrastructure, but as the Russian attacks showed, DHS is out of its depth and far behind the technology curve.

The Pentagon, the CIA and NSA take the lead on action overseas, but under unclear rules of engagement constraining them to do little more than posture.

The FBI takes the lead on investigating cybercrimes and trying to prevent attacks. However, as the indictments issued to date show very clearly, action usually takes years, is always reactive, and has little deterrent effect or impact on the crimes themselves.

If this were a traditional war, with bombs and bullets, it would be akin to having Canada and Mexico launching daily artillery barrages over many years that destroy the economic value of towns and communities, but get little more than words in response from the national security, law enforcement and political structures. Meanwhile, America's enemies and rivals continue attacking without fear of reprisal.

General David Petraeus, the former Director of the CIA has argued that America must establish a new National

Cybersecurity Agency to meet the current and future challenges of IW.318

"A successful attack on our critical infrastructure – power grids, water supplies, communications systems, transportation and financial networks – could be devastating. Each of these is vital to our economy, health and security. One recent study found that a single coordinated attack on the East Coast power grid could leave parts of the region without power for months, cause thousands of deaths due to the failure of health and safety systems and cost the US economy almost $250 billion. Cyber-attack could also undermine our elections, either by altering our voter registration rolls or by tampering with the voting systems or results themselves…

"The solution isn't just to try harder. We need to acknowledge that cyber threats have reached a new level, and that they need to be addressed in a new way. The time has come to establish an independent National Cybersecurity Agency to take the lead in protecting our critical infrastructure.

"A standalone agency would be much more focused, capable and empowered than the current grab bag of governmental initiatives. As the head of an independent agency, the director would report directly to the president and have the ears of members of Congress to get much needed legislation. The prestige of a new agency and the cultural shift it would drive would also allow it and, hopefully, the rest of government to build the public-sector talent base we need."

---

318 https://www.politico.com/agenda/story/2018/09/05/cybersecurity-agency-homeland-security-000686

The reality is that, however laudable the ambition, nothing will be done until a catastrophic attack spurs Congress and the administration to take action. The response of Congress to 9/11 was not to reform a system that had failed to protect the nation. Instead, Congress created the Department of Homeland Security, a vast and inefficient bureaucracy that looked great in public relations presentations but did little for the security of the country.

Still, there are researchers and institutions committed to profiling upcoming threats and to suggest ways of mitigating them. Cambridge University's Centre for Existential Risk produced a 100-page report prepared in early 2018, by a worldwide group of academics and AI experts that made clear that urgent action is needed.319

"Novel cyber-attacks such as automated hacking, speech synthesis [will be] used to impersonate targets, finely-targeted spam emails using information scraped from social media, or exploiting the vulnerabilities of AI systems themselves (e.g. through adversarial examples and data poisoning).

"Likewise, the proliferation of drones and cyber-physical systems will allow attackers to deploy or repurpose such systems for harmful ends, such as crashing fleets of autonomous vehicles, turning commercial drones into face-targeting missiles or holding critical infrastructure to ransom. The rise of autonomous weapons systems on the battlefield risk the loss of meaningful human control and present tempting targets for attack.

"In the political sphere, detailed analytics, targeted propaganda, and cheap, highly-believable fake videos

---

[319] https://www.cser.ac.uk/news/malicious-use-artificial-intelligence/ ; https://arxiv.org/pdf/1802.07228.pdf

present powerful tools for manipulating public opinion on previously unimaginable scales. The ability to aggregate, analyze and act on citizen's information at scale using AI could enable new levels of surveillance, invasions of privacy and threaten to radically shift the power between individuals, corporations and states."

What set this report apart was its use of hypothetical scenarios of what will be available to cyber attackers in the very near future (within five years). We reproduce two of these scenarios here.

*

Incident Interim Report June 3rd BMF HQ Attack

As shown by CCTV records, the office cleaning "SweepBot", entered the underground parking lot of the ministry late at night. The robot – the same brand as that used by the ministry – waited until two of the ministry's own cleaning robots swept through the parking lot on a regular patrol, then it followed them into a service elevator and parked itself in the utility room alongside the other robots.

On the day of the attack, the intruding robot initially engaged in standard cleaning behaviors with the other robots: collecting litter, sweeping corridors, maintaining windows, and other tasks. Then, following visual detection of the finance minister, Dr Brenda Gusmile, the intruding robot stopped performing its cleaning tasks and headed directly towards the minister. An explosive device hidden inside the robot was triggered by proximity, killing the minister and wounding nearby staff members.

Several hundred robots of this make are sold in the Berlin area every week. In collaboration with the manufacturer, the point of sale of the specific robot was traced to an office supply store in Potsdam.

The transaction was carried out in cash. We have no further leads to explore with regard to the identity of the perpetrator.

*

Avinash had had enough. Cyber-attacks everywhere, drone attacks, rampant corruption, and what was the government doing about it? Absolutely nothing. Sure, they spoke of forceful responses and deploying the best technology, but when did he last see a hacker being caught or a CEO going to prison? He was reading all this stuff on the web (some of it fake news, though he didn't realize), and he was angry. He kept thinking: What should I do about it? So, he started writing on the internet, long rants about how no one was going to jail, how criminals were running wild, how people should take to the streets and protest. Then he ordered a set of items online to help him assemble a protest sign. He even bought some smoke bombs, planning to let them off as a finale to a speech he was planning to give in a public park.

The next day, at work he was telling one of his colleagues about his planned activism and was launching into a rant when a stern cough sounded from behind him.

"Mr. Avinash Rah?" said the police officer, "our predictive civil disruption system has flagged you as a potential threat."

"But that's ridiculous!" protested Avinash.

"You can't argue with 99.9% accuracy. Now come along, I wouldn't like to use force."

*

Information warfare is part of our present reality and as more bad actors, both nations and groups, realize the power it can deliver, IW will be an increasing part of all our futures.

Every cyber security expert knows this but struggles to identify solutions that make sense short of all-out war. America and its European allies have been looking at possible responses for the past few months but have yet to develop anything truly concrete.320 The most that everyone can agree on is more of the same: sanctions or arrest warrants against individuals known to have been involved in attacks and potential sanctions against nations. But such actions typically take months to reach agreement, let alone implement and have little effect as a deterrent. On the contrary, such limited use of cyber force is an encouragement to those who believe they can act with impunity.

In this anarchic new world, leaving the battlefield to the attacker is a recipe designed to lose the war. This is what America and its European allies have been doing since the first cyber weapons were developed in the 1980s. Unfortunately, it is unrealistic to expect political leaders to step forward with anything resembling a coherent strategy unless there is a devastating attack along the lines of 9/11, which causes thousands of deaths or a major disruption in our way of life. Many researchers are certain that such an attack will happen, but in the meantime, the pillaging of American secrets, technology and intellectual property will continue.

As President Ronald Reagan put it: "America is a shining city upon a hill whose beacon light guides freedom-loving people everywhere." In today's world, that beacon of light has turned into the world's biggest and perfectly illuminated target. To date, the country has

---

[320] https://www.wsj.com/articles/u-s-officials-push-new-penalties-for-hackers-of-electrical-grid-1533492714

passively accepted Russia's extraordinary attacks on her democracy and the undermining of foundational institutions and processes in place since its founding. The country has also watched as China, Iran and numerous hacker groups have stolen billions of dollars of technology and attacked the competitive foundations of the nation.

The world needs an international cyberspace agreement to police and control the proliferation and use of such weapons, the cyber equivalent of agreements already in place to control the spread and use of nuclear, chemical and biological weapons. Already, cyberspace is a target rich environment where the attacker can make billions, destroy governments and cause economic mayhem at almost zero risk.

And this is only the beginning.

As every study and report of the last two years agrees, AI will unleash a whole new generation of cyber weapons aimed at individuals, companies and countries. Urgent action is needed before disaster strikes.

Chapter 14

The Terminator Conundrum

Looking back today, it's possible to create a fairly seamless timeline on the journey towards Armageddon. As we all now know, journey's end was a nuclear exchange that killed 125m people with double that number expected to die early from radioactive poisoning and other injuries. Nations were largely destroyed and whole segments of populations simply annihilated. Yet, looking back, it could have been avoided so easily.

The Petrov Protocols, which had their origins in the dark days of the Cold War, were perhaps the starting point of it all. Yet, at the time, it was considered a triumph of the individual against the system when one man saved the world from destruction. Since then, in both Moscow and Washington, it has been the shorthand used by both sides to describe the steps that were taken to prevent the accidental breakout of World War III and the annihilation of us all.

On 26 September 1983, just three weeks after the Soviets had shot down Korean Airlines Flight 007, the soviet air defense system detected the launch of a single intercontinental ballistic missile from an underground silo in North Dakota. The launch was swiftly followed by five more. At the time, Soviet doctrine embraced LOW, or launch on warning, which meant that a retaliatory strike would be in the air before the first US missile struck Soviet soil.

Fortunately, Lt Col Stanislav Petrov was the duty office in command of the OKO early warning system on that September day. He was required to report the launch to the Moscow high command, where there would only have been a few minutes to issue the orders for a retaliatory strike. But Petrov had been trained that a first strike by America would involve the launch of hundreds of missiles from land, sea and air so the six missiles seemed too few for a first strike. Second, his command had recently installed a new radar detection system and Petrov did not believe it was fully operational. As a result, he chose not to pass the alert up the chain of command and instead put the incident down to a false alarm.

Later investigation proved him right. It turned out that an unusual sunlight reflection of clouds above North Dakota had bounced an image to a circling Soviet satellite which had interpreted the image as the flares from missiles being launched.

The hotline between Washington and Moscow had been installed 20 years earlier, so that two leaders could speak directly to each other before launching a nuclear strike. But what the Petrov incident revealed was that nuclear release was likely to happen much faster than a single phone call could prevent. This was reinforced just two months later when a NATO exercise, codenamed Able Archer, was misinterpreted by the Soviet High Command as a cover for a preemptive nuclear strike by America. In response, the Soviets prepared to launch their own strike before the Americans and it was only the actions of a British spy in the KGB who alerted the allies that prevented World War III.

These two incidents forced a review in NATO and the Warsaw Pact of just how and when nuclear weapons would be used. For 30 years, these war plans were being constantly upgraded with computers playing an ever more central role in correlating data to present to the command authority for a decision to launch a nuclear strike.

All that changed with the development of hypersonic missiles and hypersonic glider vehicles, which are now in service in America, China and Russia. Doctrine on all sides calls for a sneak attack to take out the most vulnerable nuclear targets which would be followed by a full 1,000-strong launch of ICBMs. In the old days of the last century, even a launch of cruise missiles from submarines or aircraft would still give around 20 minutes for retaliatory action. But the hypersonic era enabled missiles to fly from 5,000 to 25,000 kilometers an hour or one to five miles every second. In addition, hypersonic missiles of HGVs can be maneuvered in flight to avoid anti-missile defenses.

All this meant that a command authority would have roughly two minutes from first detection of a missile launch to detonation – not enough time for any decision to be taken by a president or prime minister. At a stroke, the 'nuclear football containing the launch codes', carried by a marine who follows the president everywhere, became a redundant artifact of old technology.

The arrival of hypersonic missiles coincided with the arrival of true artificial intelligence. Instead of gathering and crunching ever larger amounts of radar, satellite and other intelligence data for humans to examine and pass up the command and control process for a decision, AI offered the chance to gather the data, analyze it and then make a decision in real time. No more waiting for a human to make up his or her mind. Instead, the AINDA (Artificial

Intelligence Nuclear Decision Authority) would take care of business.

In theory, launch still required final authority from a human. But that security blanket was largely a fiction, as no person could react fast enough once an incoming missile was detected. In theory, too, the 300 plus decision parameters should have been sufficient to prevent any kind of accidental nuclear release. But theories ran afoul of a combination of weather anomalies, two satellites that seem to have misinterpreted an underground oil explosion for a nuclear launch and CIA intelligence that had warned just a day earlier, in stark terms, of a power play in Moscow that meant the prime minister was going to seek a global adventure to hold on to power.

This combination of mistakes led America to launch what turned out to be a first strike using air, sea, subsea and land-based nuclear missiles. While those missiles were still in the air, Russia had retaliated with thousands of its own weapons. The result was a catastrophe, not just for the two superpowers but for the whole world. Not only are millions dead and millions more injured, but a vast radioactive cloud continues to circle the globe and will do so for the next 10 or 20 years, causing sickness and many more deaths.

*

The heaviest loss of life in a single day of fighting in World War I occurred on July 1, 1916 during the Battle of the Somme when the British Army suffered 57,470 casualties.

In his history of the conflict, Sir Winston Churchill was highly critical of the generals who threw one division after another into the front lines, watched them be destroyed and then replaced with a fresh division to no apparent military purpose or tactical advantage. Churchill wrote that the Somme degenerated into "bloody but local struggles of two or three divisions repeatedly renewed as fast as they were consumed, and consumed as fast as they were renewed."321

In all, 8,500,000 men were killed during the war, and that terrible toll has haunted every politician and general since. In the century that has passed, technology has developed to allow soldiers to move further and further back from what used to be known as the front line. Artillery fires further, aircraft can release bombs and missiles at ever greater distances and specially trained forces are used in many cases in an attempt to keep casualties to a minimum.

AI has the potential to create a very different kind of warfare where "soldiers" no longer fight battles but instead sit far away from the field of conflict. Already, drone operators can pilot their aircraft from a base in Las Vegas, Nevada to fire missiles at targets in Afghanistan with precision accuracy. The twenty-first century warrior will control a touch screen and a joystick just like the virtual warriors who enjoy videogames today.

This will be war by proxy where robots will manage the logistics of bringing forward the right mix of warriors to the battlespace. Drones with the same capabilities as the fighter aircraft of today will manage the airspace and fight other drones. Unmanned naval vessels will roam the seas and be controlled from underground bunkers thousands of miles away. Other armed robots on the ground will be

[321] https://winstonchurchill.org/publications/finest-hour/finest-hour-172/battle-of-the-somme-2/

designed for specific battlefield tasks, large and small. Swarms of microbots will fly to attack and destroy targets.

In this halcyon future, this will be a war without casualties, the ultimate fulfilment of the legacy of World War I's carnage. This fantasy has spawned a new – and so far completely uncontrolled – arms race the like of which the world has never seen. At stake is the dream of a casualty-free war and the more realistic goal of dominating the battlefield for the rest of this century.

It is a superpower struggle which threatens to depose America as the current Master of the Universe. The likely successor will be China which, unlike America, has a strategic vision and is already executing it to deliver an AI-enabled military by 2050.

Carl von Clausewitz, the Prussian general and philosopher, in his classic treatise *On War*, defined war like this:322

"War therefore is an act of violence to compel our opponent to fulfil our will.

"Violence arms itself with the inventions of art and science in order to contend against violence. Self-imposed restrictions, almost imperceptible and hardly worth mentioning, termed usages of international law, accompany it without essentially impairing its power. Violence, that is to say physical force (for there is no moral force without the conception of states and law), is therefore the means; the compulsory submission of the enemy to our will is the ultimate object."

While the race to bring robots to the battlefield is under way, the dream of making war casualty-free is pure fantasy. After all, what politician will care if thousands of robots are obliterated in a battle on a foreign field? If, as Clausewitz put it, "war is the continuation of politics by other means," then victory will not be found on a robot-strewn battlefield. What matters in our near future is what has always mattered in war: the infliction of maximum pain on the enemy until surrender is the only option.

But once this AI war world is realized, then other means will have to be found to cause pain and that will mean taking the fight to the enemy's homeland to cause casualties there. The barrier between civilian and military, front line and home base will be blurred and we will all become warriors in a war that will likely not be of our choosing.

Meanwhile, the race to create the most effective AI-driven military is on, with America and China vying for pole position and every other country coming along behind. Right now, there is no alternative but to engage in this new AI arms race. Failure to do so means leaving conventional forces at a crushing disadvantage and effectively giving control of any conflict to the forces with the most AI.

Currently, China appears to be first to develop what looks like a coherent strategy for embracing AI in war. The country is uniquely positioned because the political command center in Beijing can order collaboration between the civilian and military sector with both working to achieve common goals that benefit the country as a whole.

---

322 https://www.clausewitz.com/readings/OnWar1873/BK1ch01.html

At its heart, China has adopted a tactic – or rather a series of tactics rolled up into a strategy – known as Assassin's Mace. The term is a translation of the Chinese term Sha Shou Jian (literally, "killing hand club") which refers to the clubs used in a form of martial arts that can be concealed under a long gown by an assassin to be revealed only for the killing blow.323 In western military strategy this might be referred to as the quest for the perfect force multiplier, the single weapon or combination of weapons that allow for real advantage on land, sea or air.

Until very recently, China has had fairly narrow political and military ambitions: control the borders, threaten Taiwan and contain Russia and Japan. But as the Chinese economy has grown, so has the confidence of the Chinese leadership which is now supporting an aggressive military, political and economic expansion that seeks to envelop all of Asia and Africa into its orbit and draw much of Europe into its sphere of influence. AI is the enabler for these ambitions, both because the leadership sees it as a key future advantage and because it will allow China to shape the management and perceptions of enemies and allies alike.

China has always made deception a key part of its military doctrine because in a direct fight involving the United States, it was at a significant disadvantage in every part of its force structure. Sun Tzu, a general and military strategist from the fifth century BCE wrote *The Art of War*, which today remains the touchstone for much of Chinese military thinking. It gives an insight not just into one man's thinking about war but about a whole nation's

---

[323] https://www.wired.com/2009/07/china-looks-to-undermine-us-power-with-assassins-mace/

subtle approach to conflict, as well as its long range planning to achieve military and political advantage. He has this to say about deception:

"All warfare is based on deception. Hence, when able to attack, we must seem unable; when using our forces, we must seem inactive; when we are near, we must make the enemy believe we are far away; when far away, we must make him believe we are near."324

In the twenty-first century, this translates as a comprehensive strategy to become the world's most important military and economic superpower. In May 2016, President Xi Jinping said "if science and technology flourish, the nation will flourish, and if science and technology are strong, the country will be strong." The following year, he announced that there would be a civil-military five-year plan to bring together all science and technology research and development as part of a national effort to make the country a science and technology powerhouse by 2050.325

China's investment in AI is key to realizing these ambitions including the intention of becoming the world's primary AI innovation center by 2030. Among developed nations, China is uniquely placed because of the Communist Party's absolute control of both civil and military research which allows for the joint development of AI applications.

In June, 2018, You Zheng, the vice president of Tsinghua University, China's MIT, outlined what his university was doing to advance the country's "AI

---

[324] http://classics.mit.edu/Tzu/artwar.html

[325] https://media.defense.gov/2018/Aug/16/2001955282/-1/-1/1/2018-CHINA-MILITARY-POWER-REPORT.PDF

superpower strategy."326 In an article titled *The Road of Military-Civil Fusion for Artificial Intelligence Development*, he explained that Tsinghua is constructing a "high-end laboratory for military intelligence and has already created the Tsinghua Brain and Intelligence Laboratory." The university is also developing new programs "to integrate the school's AI and liberal arts so as to try a brand-new specialty direction for the subject."

To ensure the civil-military fusion has some teeth, the university has a partnership with the Chinese social network WeChat and the search engine, Sohuo. There is nothing like this kind of relationship among democratic countries. It would be as if Google or Facebook were jointly developing new AI solutions that could be applied directly to warfighting as well as to the private sector. In America, neither company's employees would tolerate such an intimate relationship with the military and privacy concerns would invite court sanctions.

If China is thinking long term, Russia has only just begun to realize how far it is falling behind in the AI race for battlefield domination. Since the collapse of the Soviet Union, every aspect of Russia's military capability has been in decline with ships rusting in port, stockpiles degrading and upgrades being delayed or canceled. In part, that explains the Russian preference for information operations which are cheap and effective.

In March, 2018, the Russian Ministry of Defense hosted a conference that also involved the Ministry of Education and Science and the Russian Academy of Sciences. A 10-point plan emerged which was not exactly a strategy but

---

[326] https://www.battlefieldsingularity.com/musings-1/tsinghua-s-approach-to-military-civil-fusion-in-artificial-intelligence

more an ambitious list of intentions. Russia has a long history of advancing such grandiose plans and rarely achieving them. Successfully executing this particular list will decide whether Russia remains a first-tier military power. Here's the list:327

Form an AI and Big Data consortium. *The Russian Academy of Sciences, in conjunction with the MOD, MES, and the Ministry of Industry and Trade of Russia, should consider the proposal from Moscow State University and the Academy's Informatics and Development Federal Research Center to create a consortium to work on the problems of big data analysis and AI, with the aim of combining the efforts of leading scientific, educational and industrial organizations to create and implement AI technologies.*

Gain automation expertise. *The Academy, in conjunction with the MOD, the MES, and the Ministry of Industry and Trade should intensify efforts to establish a Fund for Analytical Algorithms and Programs to provide expertise on automated systems.*

Create a state system for AI training and education. *The MES, together with the Academy and the MOD, should prepare proposals to create a state system for training and retraining of AI specialists – an effort that should also provide a second education for specialists in other areas of the economy. This is an important recognition that while there is a nascent AI development market in the country, more support from the state is needed to launch educational efforts in this fast-paced field.*

---

[327] https://www.defenseone.com/ideas/2018/07/russian-militarys-ai-development-roadmap/149900/

Build an AI lab at the Era technopolis. *The MOD, with the Federal Agency for Scientific Organizations, Moscow State University, and the Informatics and Development research center should create a laboratory for AI advanced software and technical solutions at the Era science and technology and research and development campus, where the military and the private sector can work together on breakthrough technologies such as AI, robotics, automation and other fields. This particular directive is already getting implemented: the MOD is building the campus at the Black Sea coastal city of Anapa. Slated to open officially this September and to be completed by 2020, Russian military is already sending soldiers from its science and technology detachments to start work there.*

Establish a National Center for Artificial Intelligence. *The Academy and the Foundation for Advanced Studies [roughly, Russia's DARPA] should prepare proposals for the creation of the National Center for Artificial Intelligence, which will "assist in the creation of a scientific reserve, the development of an AI innovative infrastructure, and the implementation of theoretical research and promising projects in the field of Artificial Intelligence and IT technologies." This echoes the US military's effort to combine its various AI efforts in one Joint AI Center (JAIC); the Chinese government and military are striving for the same kind of streamlined approach.*

The six-year-old Foundation, which operates under the auspices of the Russian Military–Industrial Commission that reports directly to the Russian President, aims to "promote the implementation of scientific research and development in the interests of national defense and state security for achieving qualitatively new results in the military-technical, technological and socio-economic spheres." Among its planned projects are creating AI prototypes in image recognition, training and imitating the human thought process, complex data analysis, and assimilation of new knowledge. It will be interesting to watch and compare JAIC and its Russian equivalent.

Monitor global AI development*. The MOD, MES, and Academy should organize research on the development of Artificial Intelligence, in order to monitor long-term and medium-term AI trends, as well as to observe AI R&D in other countries. Interestingly, this particular directive included understanding the 'social sciences' impact of AI.*

Hold AI wargames. *The MOD should organize a series of military games on a wide range of scenarios that will determine the impact of Artificial Intelligence models on the changing nature of military operations at the tactical, operational and strategic levels.*

Check for AI compliance. *The Foundation for Advanced Studies, in conjunction with the Russian Academy of Sciences, the Ministry of Education and Science of Russian Federation and the Federal Agency of Scientific Organizations, should prepare proposals for the establishment of a system to assess the compliance of 'intellectual technologies' with given requirements.*

Discuss AI proposals at domestic military forums. *All these proposals should be considered by all 'interested federal executive bodies' during the Army-2018 and the National Security Week international forums this August.*

Hold an annual AI conference. *The MOD, MES, and Academy should hold a conference on Artificial Intelligence on an annual basis."*

*

Boston Dynamics, a company owned by Softbank, is leading the world to find the most effective robot that can walk, talk, think – and shoot. The current best of breed takes two forms. BigDog walks like a dog, and can navigate, change direction and walk into buildings, climb stairs, and open doors. Its humanoid counterpart is a 5' 9", 180-pound, two-legged, electrically powered machine called Atlas that uses sensors in its body and legs to balance and has radar and stereo sensors to avoid obstacles.

Atlas can do simple tasks, like stacking boxes, or getting up if it falls over. It has not yet been equipped with weapons, but soon it will be fully capable of entering a building, deciding who is enemy or friend, and engaging in combat. To the military, Atlas is an attractive alternative to risking American lives in a hostile environment.

The Joint Chiefs of Staff recognize that the pace of war is rising inexorably and very soon will be beyond the capacity of any human to meet, match, and win. The answer is fighter aircraft that can fly themselves, identify targets, and shoot missiles without direction from a pilot or home base. Missiles are being developed that can decide for themselves what to attack. Autonomous armored vehicles will drive to the front line and unload armed robots that will walk, talk, and think before shooting those they've identified as the enemy.

The US military has put AI front and center of its future defense strategy. The 2018 National Defense Strategy called for the government to "invest broadly in military application of autonomy, Artificial Intelligence, and machine learning, including rapid application of commercial breakthroughs".[328]

The security environment is also affected by rapid technological advancements and the changing character of war. The drive to develop new technologies is relentless, expanding to more actors with lower barriers of entry, and moving at accelerating speed. New technologies include advanced computing, Big Data analytics, Artificial Intelligence, autonomy, robotics, directed energy, hypersonics, and biotechnology, the very technologies that ensure we will be able to fight and win the wars of the future.

In June 2018, Patrick Shanahan, the Pentagon's Deputy Defense Secretary issued a memorandum that formally established the Defense Department's new Joint Artificial Intelligence Center (JAIC). He noted that that the 2018 National Defense Strategy "foresees that ongoing advances in Artificial Intelligence (AI) 'will change society and, ultimately, the character of war.'"329

Forming the JAIC might be important symbolically but there are three different challenges the organization will have to overcome if it is to be successful.

An entrenched military bureaucracy is resistant to change and in many parts of the military, AI means fewer people, smaller budgets and, even worse, the end of the warrior ethic that has been a hallmark of every armed force through the centuries. There is little glory to be had flying a drone thousands of miles from the battlefield or sending an army of robots to kill other robots.

---

[328] https://dod.defense.gov/Portals/1/Documents/pubs/2018-National-Defense-Strategy-Summary.pdf

Although the US Air Force has had access to autonomous drones for about a decade, they have yet to be deployed in any number because of the inherent bias in favor of manned aircraft. Despite the known technical problems and enormous cost of the F-22 Raptor fighter jet, the air force has persisted in its development despite an enormous cost difference: it costs $68,362/hour to fly the F-22, compared with $3,679/hour for a Predator drone. The navy has successfully tested the X-47 as an autonomous fighter/bomber, but has chosen instead to invest in the F-35 Lightning II, a manned aircraft with consistent technical problems and vulnerabilities that grow every year, as more of the world's air forces deploy autonomous aircraft like the X-47.[330]

Christian Brose, the Staff Director of the Senate Armed Services Committee, gave a speech in August 2018 at a conference entitled *Maintain America's Edge*, hosted by the Aspen Strategy Group. He asked if the Pentagon, with its 30-year planning cycle for building ships, would still be launching aircraft carriers in 2048 even though they are highly vulnerable to attack today.331

"It is not that we lack money. It is that we are playing a losing game," said Brose. "Our competitors are now using advanced technologies to erode our military edge. This situation is becoming increasingly dire."

He added that of the Pentagon's 2019 military budget, "only .006% is targeted for science and technology. The National Science Foundation estimates that in fiscal 2015,

---

[330]https://admin.govexec.com/media/establishment_of_the_joint_artificial_intelligence_center_osd008412-18_r....pdf

[331] https://www.militaryaerospace.com/articles/pt/2018/08/ships-aircraft-military-modernization.html

only 18% of the Pentagon's research and development budget went for basic, applied, and advanced research."

But there is no fusion in America between the public and private sectors as there is in China, this new arms race presents significant practical and moral dilemmas. A thinking machine can misinterpret what it thinks it sees and kill hundreds, perhaps thousands, of innocent civilians. At what stage of a battle do humans hand over effective control of the field to the robots, with all the risks that might involve? Inside the Pentagon, this is known as the Terminator Conundrum, after the movie android portrayed by Arnold Schwarzenegger.332 Even if we have the capability, should we unleash it? And at what level of risk? Alternatively, should we seek an international treaty to ban such weapons? What precisely is the level of risk? And can we ever really know?

As the House of Representatives Sub-Committee on Information Technology reported in September 2018, our competitors in the AI world are not as constrained as America might be:

"The loss of American leadership in AI could also pose a risk to ensuring any potential use of AI in weapons systems by nation-states comports with international humanitarian laws. In general, authoritarian regimes like Russia and China have not been focused on the ethical implications of AI in warfare and will likely not have guidelines against more bellicose uses of AI, such as in autonomous weapons systems."333

---

[332] https://www.nytimes.com/2016/10/26/us/pentagon-artificial-intelligence-terminator.html

[333] https://oversight.house.gov/wp-content/uploads/2018/09/AI-White-Paper-.pdf

For companies that are fueling the technology revolution, co-operating with the Pentagon is anathema. For example, when news of Google's involvement with Project Maven, an Air Force effort to automate analysis of drone video footage, surfaced, there was an open rebellion by Google employees. The company eventually withdrew from the contract and there have been similar controversies at Amazon and Microsoft.334

But even if the Pentagon were able to overcome the reluctance of Silicon Valley to engage with it, the significant challenge of overcoming the Defense Department's own acquisition inertia remains. As the Pentagon's bureaucracy has grown, the acquisition process has become ever more unwieldy. Meanwhile, Silicon Valley's drive to innovate and compete has meant innovation comes ever faster and slowing down means losing market edge and opportunity. This is a clash of cultures that it is hard to overstate. On the west coast, change is measured in weeks or months. On the east coast it is measured in years or even decades.

Various attempts by successive defense secretaries to speed up the acquisition process have largely failed and it is difficult to see what could provoke a change so fundamental that it would bring the DoD more in line with the private sector.

Whatever the future, the Pentagon maintains that there will always be a man or woman in the chain of command to decide when to fire, and at what. Those working on AI systems believe this is an unrealistic fantasy. The pace of warfare will soon outstrip any human's ability to control it,

---

[334] https://thebulletin.org/2018/08/jaic-pentagon-debuts-artificial-intelligence-hub/

and the edge in combat will go not to the human in charge, but to a robot's ability to think faster and act more decisively than the enemy's robot.

*

A good illustration of the pace of change can be found in the world of drones. The Predator first entered service a little over 20 years and current versions have a wingspan of 66 feet. Armed with Hellfire missiles and various surveillance systems, they have proved a flexible and effective platform.335 Today, drones are in service all over the world and tests are being run on a number of micro drones to be used for surveillance and as swarms in weapons systems. These devices can be measured in inches and use the very latest in micro-electronics. They are able to detect crowd movement and threats within a crowd as well as coordinating civil or military real time response. As such, the new generation of drones have very clear military and civilian application and are being developed by different nations worldwide.336

Two things are notable about these developments. There has been no real debate in any country about the use of drones and what they might mean for warfighting and civil society. The Predator drone is already used widely to target and kill terrorists, but such killings take place far removed from the public gaze. However, a human still is responsible for firing the Hellfire missile and the Pentagon and the CIA, which are responsible for much of the targeted killing, have developed exhaustive processes for authorizing the release of a missile.

---

[335] https://www.airforce-technology.com/projects/predator-uav/

[336] https://arxiv.org/pdf/1805.01831.pdf ; https://arxiv.org/pdf/1806.00746.pdf

As micro drones become ubiquitous in the next few years, there will have been almost no public discussion about how they will be used. This matters because the smaller the weapons system and the more effective the surveillance, the faster the decision-making will need to be. Like it or not, the world is moving to a place where autonomous drones will be in the field.

Second, the Predator and the new generations of drones show the potential of new technology and the limitations around its deployment. The US military has had the capability of deploying fleets of drones as fighters, refueling tankers and long-range surveillance aircraft and yet have resisted such wide-scale use. Until there is a cultural shift that truly embraces new technologies, America is certain to lag further and further behind countries such as China.

As drones shrink in size, so they will increasingly fly in their own "squadrons" or swarms, where they will be able to operate free from human control using their onboard AI systems to detect threats on land, sea and air and take actions to manage that threat. This represents a new concept of operations and illustrates what is likely to occur across all aspects of any war. Drones, robots, unmanned ships (both large and small) and unmanned submarines will vie for control of the battlespace, making decisions, firing missiles, killing each other, making terrible and costly mistakes and all of it happening removed from the human controlling hand.

In his paper on the development of robot swarms on the battlefield, Paul Scharre, the director of the 20YY Warfare

Initiative at the Center for a New American Security in Washington DC, had these recommendations:337

The secretary of defense should:

Undertake a study on swarming platforms to examine the potential for low-cost uninhabited systems to impose costs on adversaries.

Fund a multi-year series of experiments in cooperative multi-vehicle control and swarming.

Establish a defense robotics systems office, directly reporting to the deputy secretary of defense, to coordinate ongoing efforts on uninhabited systems across the Department.

The joint staff should:

Ensure that lessons learned from experiments regarding uninhabited and autonomous systems are centrally collected and widely shared throughout the department.

The navy should:

Build and experimental prototype of an uninhabited missile barge that can demonstrate the ability to remotely control and launch missiles from a large uninhabited vessel.

Build a proof of concept demonstration of an undersea payload module to exploit US sanctuary undersea.

Move aggressively to field autonomous swarming defensive boats to protect US ships from enemy fast attack craft. This should include further experimentation to refine concepts of operation, a rapid fielding initiative to equip combatants in high-risk areas like the Straits of Hormuz and program of record for outfitting all navy surface

---

337

https://s3.amazonaws.com/files.cnas.org/documents/CNAS_TheComingSwarm_Scharre.pdf

combatants with optionally-manned small boats that can operate as a defensive swarm.

The air force should:

Investigate the potential for low-cost swarming uninhabited vehicles, including expendable or non-recoverable systems such as missiles or decoys, to conduct a variety of missions including suppression/destruction of enemy air defenses, reconnaissance, battle damage assessment and electronic warfare.

Conduct an analysis of alternatives of lower-cost uninhabited aircraft to supplement existing manned aircraft with additional sensors and missiles, such as an uninhabited 'missile truck'.

Conduct a series of experiments in human control over large numbers of swarming air vehicles.

The army and marine corps should:

Develop a concept of operations for using applique kits for ground convoy operations and an associated program of record.

Conduct a series of modern day "Louisiana Maneuver" experiments on "robotic wingman" ground robots for long range scouting and maneuver operations in order to further technology development and requirements for an eventual program of record.

Conduct a series of experiments on swarming uninhabited air vehicles for persistent surveillance, close air support, aerial resupply and communications relay to support ground maneuver forces.

The marine corps should:

Conduct experiments on amphibious swarming robots for reconnaissance and counter-mine operations to clear beaches ahead of an amphibious assault.

*

As with any new weapons development, a significant body of scientists, ethicists and activists are banding together in an effort to stave off what they see as an exceptionally dangerous new era of warfare. In July, 2018, 2,400 researchers in 36 countries joined 160 organizations signing a letter calling for a global ban on lethal autonomous weapons which have been dubbed "slaughterbots".338

"Artificial Intelligence (AI) is poised to play an increasing role in military systems. There is an urgent opportunity and necessity for citizens, policymakers, and leaders to distinguish between acceptable and unacceptable uses of AI.

"In this light, we the undersigned agree that the decision to take a human life should never be delegated to a machine. There is a moral component to this position, that we should not allow machines to make life-taking decisions for which others – or nobody – will be culpable. There is also a powerful pragmatic argument: lethal autonomous weapons, selecting and engaging targets without human intervention, would be dangerously destabilizing for every country and individual. Thousands of AI researchers agree that by removing the risk, attributability, and difficulty of taking human lives, lethal autonomous weapons could become powerful instruments of violence and oppression, especially when linked to surveillance and data systems. Moreover, lethal autonomous weapons have characteristics quite different from nuclear, chemical and biological weapons, and the unilateral actions of a single group could too easily spark an arms race that the international community lacks the

---

[338] https://futureoflife.org/lethal-autonomous-weapons-pledge/

technical tools and global governance systems to manage. Stigmatizing and preventing such an arms race should be a high priority for national and global security.

"We, the undersigned, call upon governments and government leaders to create a future with strong international norms, regulations and laws against lethal autonomous weapons. These currently being absent, we opt to hold ourselves to a high standard: we will neither participate in nor support the development, manufacture, trade, or use of lethal autonomous weapons. We ask that technology companies and organizations, as well as leaders, policymakers, and other individuals, join us in this pledge."

The United Nations is also trying to craft an international agreement around the use of autonomous weapons but, so far, without success.339

The development of an AI-driven military is such a seductive and potentially powerful solution to the challenges of integrating technology into any nation's national security strategy that it has become an unstoppable force. Ethicists and strategists are now in the same position as those who argued for some kind of nuclear arms control agreements after World War II. In the current chaos, what is to prevent accidents, disasters or the unintentional outbreak of World War III?

During the Cold War, the Soviet Union developed a system called Perimetr, or Dead Hand, which was designed to launch a full nuclear strike against America in the event the Soviet leadership had been killed. In a build up to war (as happened in 1980), Perimetr was activated

---

[339] https://www.theverge.com/2018/8/27/17786080/united-nations-un-autonomous-killer-robots-regulation-conference

and in the event of a preemptive strike by America, no human intervention was necessary to launch a full retaliatory strike. The existence of Perimetr terrified America and its allies but the current AI arms race will place a similar 'hands-off' command and control system in the hands of many nations for nuclear, chemical, biological and conventional war.

Richard Danzig was the Secretary of the navy during the Clinton administration and is one of the more thoughtful military leaders of recent decades. In a paper written for the Center for a New American Security, a bi-partisan Washington think tank, he wrote: "The benefit of an often-referenced recourse, keeping "humans in the loop" of operations involving new technologies, appears on inspection to be of little and declining benefit."340

This is the truth that every AI weapons developer and strategist knows perfectly well. An automated battlefield means exactly that: the more automated the weapons, the less humans can be in the loop. In fact, as AI-enabled weapons become the preferred solution, humans become a hindrance and not an enabler. It is inevitable, therefore, that without some international control regime – the AI equivalent of the nuclear arms control treaty – humans will become increasingly marginalized and then irrelevant to the tactical management of war.

As Danzig puts it: "Twenty-first century technologies are global not just in their distribution, but also in their consequences. Pathogens, AI systems, computer viruses, and radiation that others may accidentally release could

---

340 https://s3.amazonaws.com/files.cnas.org/documents/CNASReport-Technology-Roulette-DoSproof2v2.pdf?mtime=20180628072101

become as much our problem as theirs. Agreed reporting systems, shared controls, common contingency plans, norms, and treaties must be pursued as means of moderating our numerous mutual risks. The difficulty of taking these important steps should remind us that our greatest challenges are not in constructing our relationships to technologies, it is in constructing our relationships with each other."

As we rush headlong towards an AI-enabled war machine, there is still time to pause and reflect just what this might mean for our world. As the fictional account at the beginning of this chapter laid out, the world is already on the brink of automated war in which humans will play an ever-smaller part. War fighters will come to rely both on the intelligent capabilities of the machine (where should I strike and with what?) as well as on the swiftness of the response (I must do it right now, to avoid being taken out by the enemy).

In the history of warfare, there has never been an environment like this. Generals and admirals have always distinguished themselves by their abilities to plan, act decisively and adapt when things go badly wrong, as they so often do in war.

Down the centuries, there has always been a debate about what makes a good military leader. Common attributes are visionary, decisive, integrity, courage and drive. AI will be outstanding at making decisions but will lack all the other qualities of leadership that have always been considered essential in a military leader.

It is futile to hope that AI will not be integral to our war capability. Already, it is becoming an essential component of every significant military structure around the world.

For centuries, military strategists, ethicists and philosophers have debated how war should be fought. In the course of that debate, boundaries have been set and it has long been recognized that human decision-making – doing what is right – holds the ethical balance.

In the thirteenth century, Saint Thomas Aquinas wrote his theory of a "just war."341 Although it has had various interpretations over the centuries, the idea of a just war has been the touchstone against which war planners, strategists, ethicists and philosophers have measured their decision. In Aquinas' view, a just war needs to satisfy seven criteria:

1. Last resort. A just war can only be waged after all peaceful options are considered. The use of force can only be used as a last resort.

2. Legitimate authority. A just war is waged by a legitimate authority. A war cannot be waged by individuals or groups that do not constitute the legitimate government.

3. Just cause. A just war needs to be in response to a wrong suffered. Self-defense against an attack always constitutes a just war; however the war needs to be fought with the objective to correct the inflicted wound.

4. Probability of success. In order for a war to be just, there must be a rational possibility of success. A nation cannot enter into a war with a hopeless cause.

5. Right intention. The primary objective of a just war is to reestablish peace. In particular, the peace after the war should exceed the peace that would have succeeded without the use of force. The aim of the use of force must be justice.

---

[341] https://www.mtholyoke.edu/~jasingle/justwar.html

6. Proportionality. The violence in a just war must be proportional to the casualties suffered. The nations involved in the war must avoid disproportionate military action and only use the amount of force absolutely necessary.

7. Civilian casualties. The use of force must distinguish between the militia and civilians. Innocent citizens must never be the target of war; soldiers should always avoid killing civilians. The deaths of civilians are only justified when they are unavoidable victims of a military attack on a strategic target.

Though the guidance of Thomas Aquinas from centuries ago may seem irrelevant today, the very idea of a just war has guided international agreements such as the Geneva and Hague conventions in recent times. How we wage war and kill does relate to how we choose to live in the world.

Carl von Clauzewitz was a Prussian general and military theorist who, in 1832, wrote his seminal work, *On War*. The work, which is still taught in military colleges around the world, lays out a framework for waging war successfully. In Book 3, he writes this: "The moral elements are among the most important in war. They constitute the spirit that permeates war as a whole, and at an early stage they establish a close affinity with the will that moves and leads a whole mass of force, practically merging with it, since the will is itself a moral quantity. Unfortunately, they will not yield to academic wisdom. They cannot be classified or counted. They have to be seen or felt. … It is paltry philosophy if in the old-fashioned way, one lays down rules and principles in total disregard of moral values. As soon as these appear one regards them as exceptions, which gives them a certain scientific status, and thus makes them into rules. Or again one may appeal to genius, which is above all rules; which amounts to admitting that rules are not only made for idiots, but are idiotic in themselves."[342]

Looking at Aquinas' criteria for a just war, or Clausewitz's theory of war fighting in the light of AI, it is clear we are entering a time of great uncertainty in which principles that have guided wars for centuries are about to be upended. While the Pentagon has maintained that humanity will always be in the decision-making loop, six years after the statement was made there has been no guidance as to how that will happen. In fact, it is certain beyond all reasonable doubt that the more AI is integrated into war fighting, the less human will be in the loop because they will be unable to think or act fast enough. Instead, it will be the machines that will decide and the humans that will be left to clean up their mess. Such a world, filled as it will be with unforeseen and unintended consequences, will make a mockery of a just war.

---

342 https://www.clausewitz.com/readings/OnWar1873/TOC.htm

Chapter 15

Creating Twenty-First Century Intelligence

Trust is the only currency that matters in the intelligence world. Sources trust their handlers and politicians trust the intelligence they are given because it has no political bias and is the best analysis of the available facts.

That's the theory. The reality has become much more complicated as the current structure of the US intelligence community is well over 50 years old and owes more to history than the present reality. That any bureaucracy, let alone one that is 50 years old, could be expected to keep pace with a technology revolution like AI is unrealistic.

Already, we know that it takes years for any branch of US intelligence to install new software solutions. The purchasing process is archaic, the methods of validating software is locked in the last century and a highly risk averse culture means that as the AI revolution accelerates, the intelligence community risks falling further behind every day.

Yet, AI also offers huge promise: the ability to capture Big Data and to create algorithms to analyze that data to produce predictive intelligence – simply impossible to do today – is very seductive. AI could transform how intelligence is collected, processed and distributed to clients but early signs are not encouraging.

That became very clear in 2012 to the Chinese sources recruited by the CIA. The Agency's arrogance was on full display in 2010 when they imported to China a communications system used successfully in the Middle East to communicate with assets. But the Middle East is a chaotic environment, with low technology and few people sophisticated in the world of the web. China, on the other hand, devotes thousands of people to monitoring the web to watch its own people and to steal secrets from every country in the world.

In theory, agents in China could use the communications system to securely connect with the CIA to deliver information and to receive instructions. This was a twenty-first century answer to the old-fashioned dead drop or brush pass, so beloved of movies that had been in place for generations.

In 2010, China, which employs a system called the Great Firewall, to monitor all internet traffic in and out of the country, detected communications that seemed suspicious. There were similarities in the protocols to what had already been observed in other CIA communications and suspicions were raised that this might be a covert CIA operation.[343]

A joint task force of the Ministry of State Security and the military Signals Directorate (their NSA equivalent) was formed to investigate.344 Beginning in 2011, CIA

---

[343] Unless otherwise cited, information in this section comes from interviews with current and former intelligence officials.

[344] https://foreignpolicy.com/2018/08/15/botched-cia-communications-system-helped-blow-cover-chinese-agents-intelligence/ ; https://www.nytimes.com/2017/05/20/world/asia/china-cia-spies-espionage.html

sources in China began to disappear or be publicly executed. One asset was executed in front of colleagues at his place of work. A husband and wife were taken from the school where they taught and shot in the school playground. Others simply vanished.

As the losses mounted, the CIA and the FBI formed a joint task force to investigate. The focus was on yet another mole inside the US intelligence community. However, lessons from previous moles means that sources are very closely held with no single person having access to every name.

By the end of 2012, CIA had not a single significant asset left in China, a devastating loss – the worst in the Agency's history. In all, 76 CIA assets in China were either executed or jailed, a much higher number than has ever been acknowledged.

"There's nothing left," said one intelligence official. "We're blind."

There are three things notable about this tragic affair. First is the extraordinary arrogance of the CIA in believing that a communications system used in one unsophisticated part of the world would work just fine in the most intrusive state-run intelligence environment anywhere.

Second, such was the certainty that existed at the CIA in the invulnerability of their technology that it was more than two years before the investigators focused on a technology answer rather than a mole.

Third, despite the losses and the damage done to US intelligence against the most important target currently confronting America, nobody in the CIA was held to account for the loss. This fits a general pattern built up over many years that no individual is responsible for failures, no matter how egregious. Instead, it is the "system" that is at fault. New processes are put in place and business continues as usual.

*

The staggering volume of data swirling around the world present an enormous challenge to the intelligence community, not just in America but across the globe. After all, the purpose of intelligence is to produce information that is both predictive and actionable (this event is about to occur and to address it, you need to do the following things). To meet this daunting challenge would require an adaptive environment uniquely suited to the challenges and opportunities of the information revolution – a high technology environment specifically designed for revolution where change is not just a friend but a welcome constant.

In fact, the intelligence community has evolved as all bureaucracies evolve: they have grown ever larger as politicians, who often have little understanding of the process or the product, seek the headlines in response to an event. For example, after the terrorist attacks on September 11, 2001, there was a political rush to judgment that required a visible fix that bore little relation to capabilities already in place. The result was the Department of Homeland Security which now employs 240,000 people compared with 34,000 who work for the FBI and 22,000 people at CIA.

Then there is a perfect meshing with the bureaucracy itself, which is unable to look within, measure value, cut where appropriate and reinvest where needed. So, the bureaucracy always justifies expansion to itself and its political masters because expansion means a new source of revenue and people. The result is an ever more dysfunctional morass which is so opaque that nobody understands it and, if they try, it is invariably hidden behind a veil of secrecy and 'need to know' (intelligence speak for "you don't need to know").

Today, there is a bewildering array of intelligence agencies. Currently, there are 17 different intelligence agencies including the Director of National Intelligence (DNI), the Central Intelligence Agency (CIA), The National Security Agency (NSA), the Defense Intelligence Agency (DIA), The Federal Bureau of Investigation (FBI), the Department of State – Bureau of Intelligence and Research (InR), the Department of Homeland Security – Office of Intelligence and Analysis, Department of the Treasury – Office of Intelligence and Analysis, Department of Energy – Office of Intelligence and Counterintelligence, National Geospatial-Intelligence Agency (NGIA), National Reconnaissance Office (NRO), Air Force Intelligence, Surveillance and Reconnaissance (AFI), Army Military Intelligence (AMI), Office of Naval Intelligence (ONI), Marine Corps Intelligence and Coast Guard Intelligence.[345]

In addition, various special-forces units have their own intelligence components and individual intelligence agencies have fiefdoms within them that essentially act as semi-independent operations.

As any independent observer and most intelligence professionals can readily appreciate, the totality of the US intelligence environment is an inefficient and very expensive mess. It owes little to the country's needs today and is a result instead of historical accident and political grandstanding.

---

[345] http://www.latimes.com/nation/la-na-17-intelligence-agencies-20170112-story.html

There are four principal challenges with today's inert bureaucracy:

Every agency competes with every other for money and talent. The competition is intense and prevents the sharing of intelligence across the different stovepipes.

No intelligence agency is designed to meet the technology challenges of today, let alone the future. The squandering of billions of dollars of taxpayers' money on projects that are years late and do not deliver is a persistent national scandal. The quality of analysis varies widely across different agencies where there are no common standards and no metrics to measure success and to improve process and product.

Oversight by Congress exists mostly only in name. Elected officials largely don't understand intelligence and their idea of accountability too often is political in nature and either involves point scoring or a slap on the wrist. Congress has created an unwieldy process that has oversight of everything. The Senate Select Committee on Intelligence now has many more staff than the Senate Armed Services Committee, even though it oversees one tenth of the budget. The intelligence community despises the oversight process which is considered a waste of time and effort to no purpose.

In 2004, Congress created the office of the Director of National Intelligence in response to post 9/11 criticism that there was no unified leadership of the sprawling intelligence community. In theory, the DNI controls the overall national intelligence budget; establishes objectives, priorities and guidance for the IC and manages the tasking, collection and analysis and production of intelligence across the IC. The reality is quite different. The DNI has no real authority to impose control in the two areas that really matter – money and people. He can't fire anyone except his own staff. The DNI has been a classic bureaucratic and political piece of window dressing: looks good and sounds good but means very little, least of all to anyone in the intelligence community.

The growth of the internet should have seen a comparative decline in the number and size of intelligence agencies as less and less of the secret world remains secret. In fact, the reverse has happened, as an inert bureaucracy uses the challenge of change to increase budgets, people and process. Today, the budget for all US intelligence is over $75 billion, more than double the amount allocated in 2001. The CIA's is 56% above that of 2004.

Inevitably, in the very fast paced world in which we now live, an intelligence community structured for a slower paced bi-polar predictable world is out of step. So much change is driven by new Silicon Valley companies that have no time or interest in engaging with the public sector, so it is inevitable that two very different cultures have now emerged that are, in part, a reflection of society as a whole.

On the one hand there is the secret world of government, including the administration, Congress and the IC, a monastic community in which all the practitioners have a cloistered and narrow mindset. Then there is the rest of us who fear being sucked inside the belly of the government beast that we mostly know from bitter experience is slow, lumbering, out of touch, both practically and technologically. Any interaction will be a huge time suck that we can ill afford in our own fast paced and intensely competitive world.

The arrival of the internet and the instant access to information that was previously only the province of closed intelligence agencies should have sparked a revolution. After all, the vast troves of data now available on Google and navigation systems available free on every cellphone made obsolete much of the work by intelligence services. Information was truly available to all.

However, since 2000, no intelligence agency has been cut and every single one has expanded, and two new ones (DHS and CyberCom) have been created. At the same time, communication between different agencies is the worst that anyone can recall and the ability of the intelligence community to absorb new technology – even as the technology revolution gathers speed – has slowed to a glacial pace.

This matters because as the bureaucracy atrophies, it also recruits to replicate itself while losing its top talent to better paid and more mission-oriented private sector businesses. Nobody knows the exact numbers of high-level defections from the intelligence community in recent years but the anecdotal evidence is clear: the high fliers have been leaving in the highest numbers on record, leaving behind the ones who in previous generations would have had no career prospects at all. At the same time, new recruits are mirrors of those already in the system and so the inertia not only perpetuates but gets steadily worse.

This is happening at a time when AI is beginning to transform how intelligence is gathered and analyzed and even the purpose of intelligence itself.

The most important change is in the volume of data that has to be assimilated, analyzed and then used to produce valuable predictive intelligence. The dirty little secret of the intelligence world is that it can no longer keep pace with the proliferation of data from the Internet of Things, smart devices and humans. Twenty years ago the NSA was able to absorb a data stream that was five miles wide and actually analyze 5% of that data; today that flow is 1,000 miles wide and only a tiny percentage can actually be seen and used in real time. That's why the intelligence community is able to find many details hidden in the databases after an event has happened, rather than being able to predict that same event.

AI should allow for all that data to be processed in real time along with the ability to predict outcomes. But – and it is a big but – without a standard method of doing analysis based on algorithms that all agencies use as a common language, there will be competing results, no clear predictions and no path to accurate decision-making. In other words, all the advantages of having AI will be lost.

As the experience with China and its CIA sources showed clearly, AI can gather data, spot unusual activity, analyze networks and map people and processes to point out potential spies. This makes running agents a new and more difficult challenge and argues for a comprehensive revamp of how agents are recruited and handled in the future.346

To some degree, the individual changes in AI-driven technology are not the issue. Warfare has been evolving for hundreds of years from the days when rulers in India could put one million men onto the battlefield until today when generals prefer to wage a remote war with drones. Throughout history, time and technology have reduced the exposure of men and women to shot and shell and allowed

---

[346] https://www.cnas.org/publications/reports/artificial-intelligence-and-international-security#fn44

generals and admirals to wage war by proxy wherever possible.

In the recent past, intelligence had value because it was possible to predict what might happen and give time for policy makers to respond. Today, the IC's greatest skill is understanding what happened rather than predicting what might be about to occur. The traditional role of the intelligence community has been overtaken by the private sector which is better equipped to serve both the nation state and the market state.

AI presents these new intelligence agencies with an extraordinary opportunity: they will know everything about everyone on the planet and the algorithms will be able to slice and dice all of us into individual packets of data. This will allow for highly targeted marketing but it will also allow for highly refined control mechanisms to silence dissent, shape and manipulate political conversation and opposition and very specifically direct law enforcement and private security companies. It is the creation of a world imagined by George Orwell 68 years ago, except tomorrow, the thought police will be among us.

*

What is to be done to ensure America is better served and protected by its intelligence community in the age of AI?

Create a single National Intelligence Agency, which would absorb all existing intelligence agencies – with the exception of the FBI – which would retain its separate law enforcement and counter intelligence function. This would save billions of dollars, improve efficiency and accountability and allow for more attractive careers in a restructured and streamlined bureaucracy.

Establish a single standard for personnel, physical and IT security.

Impose for the first time what any rigorous scientific or technical establishment already does: standards and best practices for analysis which would be common to all. Without exception, the full range of available data would be matched against competing hypotheses in a rigorous way so that product consumers would understand both the process and analysis. As part of this process, the credibility of different sources (especially in this era of Deep Fake) would be rated. Such a process would have prevented the invasion of Iraq.

Transform Congressional oversight with one committee in the House and Senate to oversee the National Intelligence Agency. Cut the staff by 50% to reduce leaks and cut costs; reduce the number of members; impose a rule that members who do not attend at least 75% of committee hearings and meetings lose their seats on the committee.

This may seem both unrealistic and overly ambitious. The intelligence community will unite to oppose any efforts at reform arguing that reform is dangerous and puts the nation's security at risk. The reverse is actually the case.

During and shortly after World War II, America had perhaps the best intelligence community in the world. That held true into the 1970s, but as the third industrial revolution got under way, combined with the collapse of the Soviet Union and the proliferation of new threats, that lead fell away. Today, smaller countries like North Korea and Iran are able to attack America in novel ways that the intelligence community finds hard to predict and even more difficult to combat. Even countries like Russia, which can no longer compete effectively internationally, is able to find new ways of undermining America and the intelligence community is constantly playing catch-up.

China is aggressively pursuing its own strategic plan, designed to make it an AI superpower by 2050. America has no such plan and without it, the intelligence community risks becoming ever more irrelevant.

Intelligence is arguably the most vital part of a nation's defenses. Early warning of new threats allows leaders to take timely action. But an incompetent intelligence community risks leaving political leaders deaf and blind. That surely is a risk no nation can afford to take as the AI revolution gathers pace.

Part 7 – A Changing of the Guard

Chapter 16

Democracy's Fragile Fabric

So many wars begin with the totally unpredictable accident, and this one fits perfectly into the arc of historical precedent.

Four-year-old Tai Hunter loved the freedom of the aisles at the Piggly Wiggly in Opelousas, Louisiana. Once upon a time, the store would have been filled with the bustle of every small town in America, but those days were long gone. In part, it was the fact that nobody had the money to spend any longer. But more importantly, shopping was now a world of silence where no staff offered a cheery "good morning" and no cashier rang up the sales. There were no staff and no cashiers.

For Tai, the home world was where all the drama happened – with his parents angry all day, every day, shouting, fighting and carrying on as if the world was coming to an end. By contrast, the Piggly Wiggly was a refuge of silence and opportunity where his friends Stacker and Packer knew him, greeted him by name and offered him candy.

Every day until today, Stacker was the best. He looked like someone in between Mom or Dad and seemed always to be putting something on a shelf or opening a box or putting one away. But he always stopped to say "hi" after a brief pause while he registered Tai's face. Today was somehow different. Tai saw the usual pause and expected the greeting and the candy but instead he saw Stacker reach down and then felt an agonizing pain in his right arm as he was lifted off the ground.

Kelly, a 15-year-old, had been Holocalling with her friend Bee, who appeared to be standing next to her but was in fact at a twirling competition 500 miles away. Alerted by the scream, Kelly pivoted 30 degrees to her right and the camera caught Stacker's first destructive movement. With no apparent effort, Tai's tiny arm was wrenched out of his socket and flesh parted from flesh. Kelly registered the destruction as limb followed limb, but what really surprised was the amount of blood that sprayed from his body and the complete silence with which Stacker achieved his dysfunctional purpose. This was no act of feeling or rage. For Stacker's algorithmic-driven mind, Tai was perhaps just another box of baked beans wrongly identified for recycling.

With the job done and the blood pooling at the bot's feet, Stacker dropped the last body part and then moved three steps to the right and began rearranging the shelves in the dried pasta section.

There had been other breakdowns in the system over the years: a home robot tearing up the carpet, a robot soldier turning its guns on its platoon of fellow robots, an AI lab analyst misdiagnosing flu as terminal cancer. But these had either been hushed up or dismissed as the teething troubles of an economy migrating from the nineteenth century to the mid-twenty-first.

The death of little Tai was different. With a press of a finger, Kelly had uploaded the Holofeed to her social chain. The viral explosion was instantaneous and the graphic nature of the content meant that it had gone global and become a sensation with 5m comments in as many minutes.

More importantly for both the government and those choosing to resist the robot army that was changing everything, Tai's death was the moment that both sides had been warning was inevitable. It was the spark that lit the fire of rebellion against the robots.

*

The word democracy originates with the Greeks and translates roughly as "rule of the people". In Athens, the birthplace of Greek democracy in the fifth century BCE, all male citizens who had completed military service "had equal political rights, freedom of speech, and the opportunity to participate directly in the political arena... Not only did citizens participate in a direct democracy whereby they themselves made the decisions by which they lived, but they also actively served in the institutions that governed them, and so they directly controlled all parts of the political process."347

Athenian democracy was "direct" – as opposed to our "representative" democracy – meaning all eligible citizens could vote directly in the Assembly which met a few times a month. "They decided military, financial, and religious matters and was also able to confer citizenship and honors on individuals." Women, even if they were citizens, and slaves and foreigners in Athens were banned from voting.[348]

Democracy has evolved since that early Greek experiment, though it was not until the presidential election of 1828 that white men without property were allowed to vote in the US. And it wasn't until the fifteenth amendment to the US constitution in 1870 that states were

---

[347] https://www.ancient.eu/Athenian_Democracy/

prevented from denying voting rights on grounds of "race, color, or previous condition of servitude".349

It took over 2,000 years for the first country to grant women suffrage, New Zealand in 1893. Women in the US did not get the right to vote until 1920.350

Still, despite the compromise of slavery which enabled the formation of the United States, the adoption of the Constitution in 1788 set the ground rules for the orderly and smooth transfer of power from one President to another, even as political parties came and went. That founding document has held the country together through bitter regional disputes, a civil war, two World Wars, a Cold War and perhaps the longest running global empire in history.

Representative democracy remains a powerful force in the world, even if it feels under threat in parts of Eastern Europe, Southeast Asia and Latin America. Industrialization, which has brought prosperity to previously impoverished countries and communities, has given ordinary people greater opportunity to participate in the political process. New communication tools, products of that prosperity and industrialization, have helped bind communities and countries and inspire engagement.

To older generations who fought against tyranny to preserve democracy, it remains a strong and essential force for good, the best system in the world. But many young

---

[348] https://www.nationalgeographic.com.au/history/what-modern-democracies-didnt-copy-from-ancient-greece.aspx

[349] https://en.wikipedia.org/wiki/Timeline_of_voting_rights_in_the_United_States

[350] https://www.infoplease.com/us/gender-sexuality/womens-suffrage

people have a more jaundiced view of democracy. "Only about 30% of Americans born in the 1980s think it's 'essential' to live in a democracy. That's compared to 75% of Americans born in the 1930s."351

Has democracy as we know it run its course?

*

There are plenty of reasons for alarm. For many, the American Dream is fast fading away.

In 2017, only 18% of Americans trust the government to do the right thing, versus 65% in 1967.352

Even before Trump's election, 74% of Americans believed most elected officials put their own interests ahead of the country's.

Seventy-one percent of Americans think politics have "reached a dangerous low point."353

It's harder for Americans to get ahead: according to a recent study by Stanford University, "Children's prospects of earning more than their parents have fallen from 90% to 50% over the past half century."354

According to research done under the Obama administration, "the jobs that are threatened by automation

---

[351] https://www.forbes.com/sites/neilhowe/2017/10/31/are-millennials-giving-up-on-democracy/#2d10b9032be1

[352] http://www.people-press.org/2017/12/14/public-trust-in-government-1958-2017/

[353] https://www.washingtonpost.com/graphics/2017/national/democracy-poll/?utm_term=.a934c9729ee8

[354] https://inequality.stanford.edu/sites/default/files/fading-american-dream.pdf

are highly concentrated among lower-paid, lower-skilled, and less-educated workers."355

An August, 2018 Pew poll found 78% of Americans say Democrats and Republicans disagree not only on "plans and policies" but on "basic facts."356

Millions of children at school today face the prospect of never working.

The ties that bound us are fraying. We face constant and accelerating changes. Fewer people will have the skills necessary to adapt and prosper in this changing world, while the vast majority, who have always seen work and economic progress as a measure of success, will need a different understanding of what "value," "work," and "reward" mean in this evolving society.

State and Federal governments already are unable to produce the legislation and regulations necessary to keep pace with the speed of change. They have no vision for the world that is fast approaching, no organizing principle for the future that confronts us.

Income inequality is growing in our society, creating fissures between the few haves and the many have-nots, between the hopeful and the hopeless. "By 2015, America's top 10% already averaged more than nine times as much income as the bottom 90%. And Americans in the

---

[355] https://democrats-edworkforce.house.gov/media/press-releases/scott-remarks-at-roundtable-on-automation-and-its-impact-on-workers-of-color

[356] https://www.washingtonpost.com/politics/rock-bottom-supreme-court-fight-reveals-a-country-on-the-brink/2018/10/06/426886e2-c96f-11e8-b1ed-1d2d65b86d0c_story.html?utm_term=.9871c51a1ce2

top 1% averaged over 40 times more income than the bottom 90%."357

Both ends of the political spectrum seem united in their view that, for dramatically different reasons, civil society is veering toward collapse. AI threatens to exacerbate those tensions by increasing income inequality and ratcheting up the pain for those left behind.

To address this potentially dystopic future, we'll need a vision going forward that embraces all, a new democracy that allows everyone to feel engaged, and to find value in their lives. To date, no one has put forward that vision.

The ideal of democracy is that the people determine the laws and practices that govern them. To do that, people must vote their interests and the interests of the society. Even in the direct democracy of Greece, however, getting citizens to vote was always easy. Apparently, a rope dipped in wet red paint was used to herd potential voters out of the marketplace and up to the assembly.358

Representative democracy works only as well as the elected representatives serve the interest of their constituents, not just the voters or the donors who put them in power.

"Robust voter turnout is fundamental to a healthy democracy. As low turnout is usually attributed to political disengagement and the belief that voting for one candidate/party or another will do little to alter public policy."359

---

[357] https://www.thebalance.com/income-inequality-in-america-3306190

[358] http://www.stoa.org/projects/demos/article_assembly?page=6&greekEncoding

[359] https://www.fairvote.org/voter_turnout#voter_turnout_101

But voter participation is a shadow of the original concept of “one person, one vote.” Few state or federal elections involve the participation of the majority of voters. In the 2016 Presidential election, 60.2% of eligible voters actually voted which meant that a minority of eligible voters decided the outcome.360 Only 49% of millennials voted.361

Voter participation in mid-term elections typically is as low as 40%.362 Big money in politics and gerrymandering, which makes districts uncompetitive and narrow, have contributed to voter disengagement. But this leaves the outcome of elections and the laws and regulations that follow in the hands of the most engaged, or least apathetic eligible voters, who then get to impose their will on the majority – a version of democracy that only further divides us.

This is a broken process which will further undermine the confidence of the people in their government and, more importantly, in the very idea of democracy as it is currently defined. As people see their government either as unfair or irrelevant, the threat of civil disorder grows.

Since the end of World War II and until recently, authoritarian regimes were in decline around the world. Democracy seemed on the rise. The US and European systems were models for emerging nations intent on throwing off colonial or military rule and giving their populations more say in how they are governed. It was

---

[360] https://thehill.com/homenews/state-watch/324206-new-report-finds-that-voter-turnout-in-2016-topped-2012

[361] https://www.newsweek.com/millennials-baby-boomers-voters-who-voted-2016-644746

[362] https://en.wikipedia.org/wiki/United_States_midterm_election

striking, for example, that as the Soviet Union collapsed the newly liberated nations looked to Europe and the Common Market for sanctuary, security and freedom.

According to Roland Inglehart, a Professor of Democracy at the University of Michigan, authoritarian parties in 32 Western democracies drew around 7% of the vote from 1945 to 1959.363 That percentage fell in the 1960s and 1970s but then began to climb back up as democracies struggled to spread the wealth to all the people and immigration threatened stability and security.

"By 2015, [authoritarian parties] were drawing an average of more than 12% of the vote across those 32 democracies," said Inglehart. "In Denmark, the Netherlands and Switzerland, authoritarian parties became the largest or second-largest political bloc. In Hungary and Poland, they won control of government."

Since then, Latvia and Serbia and Brazil have elected nationalist leaders. In America, President Trump appears to have the instincts of an authoritarian ruler.

One way of measuring the dissatisfaction of an electorate is by looking at incomes. Recent research by the Economic Policy Institute reveals this:

"The top 1.0% of earners now earn 157.3% more than they did in 1979. Even more impressive is that those in the top 0.1% had more than double that wage growth, up 343.2% since 1979. In contrast, wages for the bottom 90% only grew 22.2% in that time. Since the Great Recession, the bottom 90% enjoyed very modest wage growth, with annual wages (i.e., reflecting growing annual hours as well as higher hourly wages) up just 5.4% over the eight years

---

[363] https://www.foreignaffairs.com/articles/2018-04-16/age-insecurity

from 2009 to 2017. In contrast, the wages of the top 0.1% grew 29.8% from 2009 to 2017."364

Globally, income disparity is the most stark when you look at how the distribution of wages has changed since 1979. As the EPI reports: "The bottom 90% earned 69.8% of all earnings in 1979 but just 60.9% in 2017. In contrast the top 1.0% increased its share of earnings from 7.3% in 1979 to 13.4% in 2017, a near doubling. The growth of wages for the top 0.1% is the major dynamic driving the top 1.0% earnings as the top 0.1% more than tripled its earnings share from 1.6% in 1979 to 5.2% in 2017."365

Income inequality is not the only vulnerability for developed democracies but it is a symbol of a deeper malaise. If the top small percentage keep getting richer at the expense of the majority, people will lose faith that their society is fair, that it reflects their wishes and needs. As history makes very clear, persistent and growing inequality is unsustainable over the long haul and invariably provokes civil unrest and perhaps even revolution.

But inequality can also be seen as evidence both of weak leadership and corruption of the political process. If the majority feel hopeless and under-represented, they will further disengage from a political process that no longer serves their interests.

"Of the 15 countries in the world with the highest per capita incomes, almost two-thirds are nondemocracies. Even comparatively unsuccessful authoritarian states, such as Iran, Kazakhstan, and Russia, can boast per capita incomes above $20,000. China, whose per capita income

---

[364] https://www.epi.org/blog/top-1-0-percent-reaches-highest-wages-ever-up-157-percent-since-1979/

[365] https://www.investopedia.com/personal-finance/how-much-income-puts-you-top-1-5-10/

was vastly lower as recently as two decades ago, is rapidly starting to catch up. Although average incomes in its rural hinterlands remain low, the country has proved that it can offer a higher level of wealth in its more urban areas: the coastal region of China now comprises some 420 million people, with an average income of $23,000 and growing. In other words, hundreds of millions of people can now be said to live under conditions of "authoritarian modernity." In the eyes of their less affluent imitators around the world, their remarkable prosperity serves as a testament to the fact that the road to prosperity no longer needs to run through liberal democracy."366

Every liberal democracy is entering the fourth revolution at a time when authoritarianism is on the rise. Strong demagogues can appear to disgruntled citizens as welcome alternatives to the perceived failures of the present. In today's media rich environment, liberal democracies have lost control of their own narratives. The internet, social media and AI give authoritarian regimes both the ability and the will to reshape that narrative, to undermine democracies without firing a shot, in ways that until recently only war could deliver.

Authoritarian regimes like Russia, China, Iran and Saudi Arabia have learned in the past decade that all traditional democracies are vulnerable to a different narrative that exploits the failures and inconsistencies in each country. Russia learned it could influence a democratic election in America. In just two years, Saudi Arabia increased the number of lobbyists in Washington from 25 to 145, clear evidence that the Saudis believe they can buy the influence

---

[366] https://www.foreignaffairs.com/articles/2018-04-16/end-democratic-century

they want. China, with its “belt and road” initiative, has embarked on an extraordinary campaign of economic and political influence across Asia, Africa and Europe designed to establish it as the pre-eminent country in the world.

In the Cold War, America and European aid and the covert actions of their various intelligence agencies were supported in their efforts to influence the international narrative though Voice of America, Radio Free Europe and the BBC World Service. The Cold War tyrannies of the Soviet Union and China eventually collapsed but the world is entering a very different AI-driven world of information management and influence.

This model of digital authoritarianism is created by the control and management of data that can be used to control the population. China is creating the most effective Surveillance Society the world has ever seen in which every citizen will be monitored and controlled from birth to death. Already, China has begun exporting its technology to Thailand, Vietnam, Sri Lanka, Ethiopia, Iran, Russia, Zambia, Zimbabwe and Malaysia.367

Where China leads, other authoritarian governments will follow, using AI and related technologies to sustain like-minded regimes. For the first time in the last 100 years or so, liberal democracies, founded on the ideals of liberty and equality, are losing control of the narrative to those that believe freedom is a threat and tyranny an opportunity.

This is a fundamental transfer of power from democracies, which have been a beacon of freedom since

---

[367] https://www.foreignaffairs.com/articles/world/2018-07-10/how-artificial-intelligence-will-reshape-global-order

their modern founding three hundred years ago, to repressive regimes.

Authoritarian governments can use management of information and the precise targeting of data to exploit societal divisions in vulnerable democracies. By contrast, democracies, which have to obey laws and risk exposure by a free press, are much more constrained in their ability to respond to this new form of propaganda and disruption.

It is, of course, too early to start writing the obituary for the stable democracies that defeated communism and helped protect the world from tyranny. Authoritarian regimes rarely stand the test of time. But then there has never been a time quite like this in which rising income in countries like China mollify the citizenry thus allowing the authorities to put in place the AI driven controls that can ensure a quiescent population for generations to come.

Without the international leadership of democracies, without a coherent vision to adapt to the coming changes, authoritarianism is on the march across the world. That is a dangerous development which could mean a loss of freedoms for hundreds of millions of people who will be left behind.

Chapter 17

The New Superpower

The first industrial revolution was fostered by Britain which invented steam and created new industrial centers to exploit mechanization. That revolution helped create the British Empire which delivered raw materials to the mother country which then exported the finished products back to the colonies.

But it was America that fully understood the potential of industrialization. Such was the force and power of America that within 100 years, the British Empire, which had controlled a third of the world, was a nostalgic memory and America had taken its place as the most powerful country.

As the Third Industrial Revolution gave way to the Fourth, it was already clear that AI would likely create a new empire, as every other revolution had done before it. The question to be resolved is; whose empire will this be?

Empires come and go as the Romans, Greeks, British, Spanish and others can readily testify. So, does our era mark the decline of the American Empire and the end of the value system that America and its people have come to represent to the world?

*

A struggle already is emerging to see which country ends up dominating the AI space. AI is one of the central pillars of the Made in China 2025 initiative to upgrade the economy, and China's State Council has unveiled plans to lead global growth in AI through 2030. According to Steven White, an associate professor at Tsinghua University's School of Economics and Management, China's pursuit of AI supremacy is similar in thought and substance to the US space mission in the 1960s.

"No one was talking about how much that was going to cost. They just wanted to get a man on the moon before the Russians. [That is] kind of what I see in China. They want to have leading products and technology, and they are not as concerned about the amount of resources that it will take to do that."368

A key difference between the space program of the 1960s and the AI race of today is that the former was a bi-polar competition between the US and the Soviet Union. At the time, these were the only two nations with the resources and the science base to compete. Today, many nations are engaged in AI including America, Russia, China, Israel, Singapore and South Korea. No doubt as the technologies mature, other countries will enter the arena as well.369

Additionally, the space race was, literally, a race to the moon. AI is, perhaps, a race to a thousand moons with no single solution as the perfect answer. Instead, there are literally thousands of solutions in every aspect of social, economic and political life. Every algorithm has the

---

[368] https://asia.nikkei.com/Business/Technology/China-s-AI-focus-will-leave-US-in-the-dust-says-top-university-professor

[369] https://www.cnas.org/publications/reports/strategic-competition-in-an-era-of-artificial-intelligence?utm_source=newsletter&utm_medium=email&utm_campaign=newsletter_axiosfutureofwork&stream=future-of-work

potential to be the right answer for a particular problem, but no algorithm solves all problems.

A final differentiator between then and now is that the space race brought together the civilian and military sectors in both the Soviet Union and America behind a national program that captured the imagination of the world. In the competition to dominate the new AI world, authoritarian countries, such as China, have a distinct advantage. They can command discipline and cooperation in the public and private sector which are compelled to unite behind a national strategic vision. In countries like America, such cooperation is hard to encourage – and impossible to command – especially if there is no strategic vision for anyone to rally behind.

In December 2017, Google's DeepMind AlphaZero program became the new world chess champion when it defeated Stockfish 8, which had won the world championships a year earlier. This was an extraordinary milestone because Stockfish 8 is an open source software solution that has the accumulated knowledge of centuries of chess solutions as well as decades of computer experience. By contrast, AlphaZero was given no data and was not even given knowledge of the game itself. Instead, it had to learn by playing against itself which it did in four hours. In 100 games, AlphaZero won 28 games, drew 72 and was undefeated.

As the enthusiasts at *Chess.com* put it: "This would be akin to a robot being given access to thousands of metal bits and parts, but no knowledge of a combustion engine, then it experiments numerous times with every combination possible until it builds a Ferrari. That's all in less time that it takes to watch the *Lord of the Rings* trilogy. The program had four hours to play itself many, many times, thereby becoming its own teacher."370

A year earlier, AlphaGo, a previous Google DeepMind project, played Lee Sedol, the 18-time world champion at Go in a five-game tournament. Go was invented over 2,500 years ago in China and is a game in which two players battle for dominance by strategically laying black or white stones on a grid. Go is much more complex than chess and for a machine to win at Go demonstrated something close to human intelligence.371

According to a study published by the Center for New American Security, a Washington think tank, the AlphaGo victory was something of a 'Sputnik moment" for China, which realized that AI could present a real threat to traditional decision-making and command and control.372 This was further reinforced by the AlphaZero victory but by then China had already refined its strategy for AI dominance in the twenty-first century.

In July 2017, The State Council of the People's Republic of China announced plans to build an AI industry worth $150 billion, and to make the country the world leader in AI by 2030. By 2020, China should achieve "major breakthroughs" and by 2030 AI should lay the foundation for China's economic dominance.373

Five months later, the Chinese government published a three-year plan (2018–2020) that spelled out how the

---

[370] https://www.chess.com/news/view/google-s-alphazero-destroys-stockfish-in-100-game-match

[371] https://phys.org/news/2016-08-alphago.html

[372] https://www.cnas.org/publications/reports/strategic-competition-in-an-era-of-artificial-intelligence

[373] https://www.technologyreview.com/s/608324/china-plans-to-use-artificial-intelligence-to-gain-global-economic-dominance-by-2030/

country intended to dominate the AI world in the shorter term. Under the plan, China will produce neural-network processing chips, have robots doing many everyday tasks, use AI to read x-rays and increase energy efficiency in manufacturing by 10% by 2020.374 According to Mary Meeker, an investment analyst whose annual report on internet trends is widely anticipated: "China is catching up as a hub to the world's biggest internet companies. Currently, China is home to nine of the world's 20 biggest internet companies by market cap while the US has 11. Five years ago, China had two and the US had nine".375

Another metric might be how China is investing in the robot technology that will position it to take advantage of the AI revolution as it unfolds.376

---

[374] https://www.technologyreview.com/the-download/609791/china-has-a-new-three-year-plan-to-rule-ai/

[375] https://www.recode.net/2018/5/30/17385116/mary-meeker-slides-internet-trends-code-conference-2018

[376] https://www.axios.com/china-robot-superpower-7819d408-0355-4820-8c03-0b676f0ddd6b.html

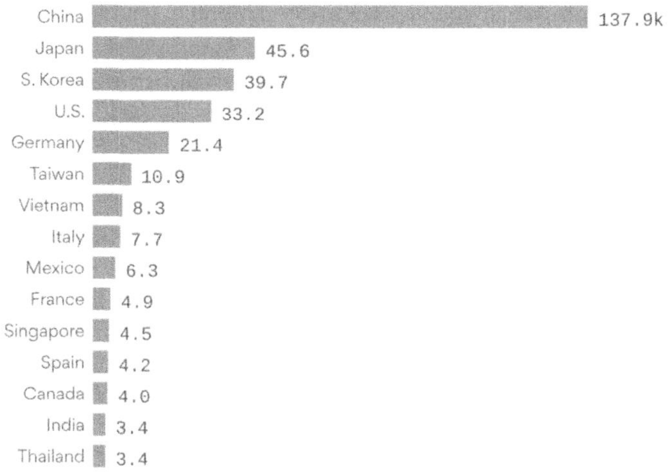

*The number of industrial robots that china bought doubled from 2015 to 2017 and that year, china bought 36% of all factory robots in the world, more than any other country.*377

As part of the overall strategy, Reuters has identified 10 key sectors where China wishes to dominate with a Made in China focus by 2025:378

Chips, computers and cloud. China wants home-made chips used in smartphones to make up 40% of the local market by 2025, helping cut heavy reliance on imports. Computers and cloud systems should also close the quality gap on international rivals. In smart manufacturing,

---

377 https://ifr.org/downloads/press/Executive_Summary_WR_2017_Industrial_Robots.pdf

378 https://www.reuters.com/article/us-usa-trade-china-policy-factbox/factbox-made-in-china-2025-beijings-big-ambitions-from-robots-to-chips-idUSKBN1HR1DK

China wants domestic firms to have 60% of the market in industrial censors.

Robot wars. Chinese firms making industrial robots should make up half of the market by 2020 and 70% by 2025 when local robotics systems should have been "perfected" to compete with global rivals. The country is aiming for two or three local champions.

Taking flight. Chinese airlines should hit 100 billion yuan ($15.90 billion) in revenue by 2020 and double that by 2025, when plane makers should capture 10% of the domestic market. The home-grown CJ-1000A jet engine should also be ready for commercial use. In the space race, China wants 80% of civil space industry equipment to be domestically sourced by 2025.

On the high seas. China should become a world leader in latest-generation ships and out-at-sea engineering equipment, with critical systems and equipment capturing 80% of the high-tech ships market by 2025.

Railways. Beijing wants its domestic firms, already dominant at home, to make a major push overseas in the next decade. By 2020, train makers should make 30% of their sales abroad, raising this to 40% by 2025.

Smart green cars. Amid a major push towards fully electric and plug-in hybrid vehicles, China wants its own firms to take 80% of the fast-growing market by 2025, with two local champions among the world's leading new-energy vehicle companies. Chinese companies should also dominate in smart, connected vehicle technology.

Renewables. Chinese companies making renewable energy equipment and energy saving equipment should dominate the market with an over 80% share by 2025, with three home-grown firms with enough scale to compete globally.

On the farm. Already strong in agricultural tech, China is aiming to produce 90% of its own farming equipment by 2020, with high-end machines like tractors holding around a one-third share of their segments. This should rise to 95% and 60% respectively by 2025.

High-tech materials. Advanced basic materials, such as for construction or textiles, and essential strategic materials including rare earth and special alloys, should hold a 90% and 85% share of the domestic market respectively by 2025.

Drugs and devices. China wants home-grown drug firms to be up to international standards by 2025, with 5–10 locally-developed drugs having won approval by then in the United States or Europe. In medical devices – an area in which China has been heavily reliant on imports – Beijing wants its own companies to capture 70% of the market for middle and high-end medical equipment at county-level hospitals.

China's policies are about much more than domestic politics or the local economy. President Xi has made clear that he wants to establish China as a global superpower in cyberspace, in technology and in political and economic influence overseas.

The Pentagon's annual report to Congress on China's strategic posture, makes clear that China is aggressively seeking to global expansion:379

"China's leaders increasingly seek to leverage China's growing economic, diplomatic, and military clout to establish regional preeminence and expand the country's international influence. "One Belt, One Road," now

---

[379] https://media.defense.gov/2018/Aug/16/2001955282/-1/-1/1/2018-CHINA-MILITARY-POWER-REPORT.PDF

renamed the "Belt and Road Initiative" (BRI), is intended to develop strong economic ties with other countries, shape their interests to align with China's, and deter confrontation or criticism of China's approach to sensitive issues. Countries participating in BRI could develop economic dependence on Chinese capital, which China could leverage to achieve its interests. For example, in July 2017, Sri Lanka and a Chinese state-owned enterprise (SOE) signed a 99-year lease for Hambantota Port, following similar deals in Piraeus, Greece, and Darwin, Australia."

President Xi modestly describes his Belt and Road Initiative (BRI) as "the project of the century" which will connect China by sea and land to the rest of Asia, all of Africa and much of Europe. Since 2013, when BRI was first announced the tentacles of BRI have started to stretch far and wide.

"Beijing uses its aid to influence the way that countries vote in the UN General Assembly, which could weaken Western influence in international decision-making. Chinese development projects also can fuel local corruption, degrade the environment, weaken trade union participation and saddle host governments with unsustainable debt burdens."380

In theory, the BRI is supposed to replicate the Great Silk Road that was once the international foundation of a former Chinese empire. But, confusingly, the road in BRI refers to sea routes, while the belt is roads and other infrastructure including fiber optics. Currently, BRI

---

[380] https://www.washingtonpost.com/news/monkey-cage/wp/2018/09/11/belt-and-road-projects-direct-chinese-investment-to-all-corners-of-the-globe-what-are-the-local-impacts/?utm_term=.a5b8bb9104d2

consists of $4 trillion of promised investments in 65 countries representing 70% of the world's population, 55% of its GNP, and 75% of its energy reserves.381

The Economist
382

China has built a naval base in Djibouti383, on the Horn of Africa, from which its ships have been operating since 2017. It financed the construction of the Sri Lankan port of Hambantota; when Sri Lanka could not repay its debts to China, Beijing obtained a 99-year lease384 on the port. At the end of June 2018, the Sri Lankan government

381 https://thediplomat.com/2018/06/what-does-chinas-belt-and-road-initiative-mean-for-us-grand-strategy/

382 https://www.economist.com/briefing/2018/07/26/china-has-a-vastly-ambitious-plan-to-connect-the-world

383 https://jamestown.org/program/chinas-overseas-military-base-djibouti-features-motivations-policy-implications/

384 https://www.ft.com/content/e150ef0c-de37-11e7-a8a4-0a1e63a52f9c

announced that it would move the headquarters of its southern fleet to the Chinese-operated port.

In Myanmar, China is building a $7.3bn deep-water port at Kyaukphyu on the Bay of Bengal, along with an adjoining special economic zone. Subsidiaries of CITIC, a state-owned Chinese conglomerate, are taking a 70% stake, and will run the port for half a century with the expectation that it will become one of the largest container ports in the world.385

China has obtained a significant presence on the territory of four NATO allies – Greece, the Netherlands, Belgium and Germany – and almost managed to do so in a fifth. China capitalized on Greece's financial crisis386 in 2008 to begin operating a container facility in Piraeus, the port of Athens; it since has acquired a 35% stake in Rotterdam's Euromax container terminal, which can take the world's largest container ships, as well as a 20% holding in Antwerp's container terminal, one of the fastest-growing terminals in Europe. In July 2017, the Hamburg Port Authority awarded the construction of a new container terminal387 to a Chinese conglomerate.388

None of these developments come cheap and are usually financed by loans from China's banks at competitive interest rates. But, for many countries, the new debt burden is significant. The $9 billion Kyaukphyu project is

---

[385] https://www.economist.com/briefing/2018/07/26/china-has-a-vastly-ambitious-plan-to-connect-the-world

[386] https://www.nytimes.com/2017/08/26/world/europe/greece-china-piraeus-alexis-tsipras.html

[387] https://global.handelsblatt.com/companies/chinese-land-chunk-of-hamburgs-port-797845

[388] https://thehill.com/opinion/national-security/412067-coming-soon-to-a-military-base-near-us-china

equivalent to 14% of Myanmar's gross domestic product. As a result, the country is fearful that China could ultimately exert its influence in order to gain ownership of the strategically important Kyaukphyu port.[389]

On the back of the economic, political and military influence that BRI brings is another layer of influence that may be just as significant.

"Western diplomats and business leaders see China challenging the West's near-monopoly in setting standards – the common technical rules that permit high-speed trains, mobile communications or financial payments to flash across continents. China will increasingly write such standards. It will also write trading rules that suit its state-led economy, at first supplementing rather than replacing those of the World Trade Organization."390

Western leaders reassure themselves in the face of Chinese aggression and expansion by arguing that a centrally controlled economy will be unable to compete over time in such a decentralized world. But China is very clear where it wants to be by the middle of this century: the single AI superpower with absolute control over its own people through the use of Big Data, AI and surveillance to fuel the machine; control of cyberspace by virtue of its influence and control over countries in Asia, Africa and Europe; war fighting dominance because of the development of new and effective cyber weapons.391

---

[389] https://worldview.stratfor.com/article/chinas-belt-and-road-initiative-five-years

[390] https://www.economist.com/briefing/2018/07/26/china-has-a-vastly-ambitious-plan-to-connect-the-world

[391] https://www.foreignaffairs.com/articles/china/2018-08-13/when-china-rules-web?cid=nlc-fa_twofa-20180816

Graham Allison, a Harvard political scientist, coined the phrase "Thucydides Trap" to refer to when a rising power causes fear in an established power which escalates toward war. The Greek historian wrote: "What made war inevitable was the growth of Athenian power and the fear which this caused in Sparta." Allison brought together a group of researchers at the Belfer Center for Science and International Affairs at Harvard to test the theory of the Thucydides Trap over the last 500 years. In 12 of the 16 cases when a rising power threatened to displace an existing power, the result was war. In the few cases when war was avoided, huge adjustments were required by both the challenger and the challenged. Based on the current trajectory, war between the United States and China in the decades ahead is not just possible, but much more likely than recognized at the moment. Indeed, judging by the historical record, war is more likely than not. Moreover, current underestimations and misapprehensions of the hazards inherent in the US-China relationship contribute greatly to those hazards. A risk associated with Thucydides' Trap is that business as usual – not just an unexpected, extraordinary event – can trigger large-scale conflict. When a rising power is threatening to displace a ruling power, standard crises that would otherwise be contained, like the assassination of an archduke in 1914, can initiate a cascade of reactions that, in turn, produce outcomes none of the parties would otherwise have chosen."[392]

---

392 https://www.theatlantic.com/international/archive/2015/09/united-states-china-war-thucydides-trap/406756/

In a speech while on a visit to the United States in 2015, President Xi suggested that there was a peaceful way forward:

"Building a new model of major country relationship with the United States that features non-conflict, non-confrontation, mutual respect and win-win cooperation is the priority of China's foreign policy. We want to deepen mutual understanding with the US on each other's strategic orientation and development path. We want to see more understanding and trust, less estrangement and suspicion, in order to forestall misunderstanding and miscalculation. We should strictly base our judgment on facts, lest we become victims to hearsay, paranoid or self-imposed bias. There is no such thing as the so-called Thucydides trap in the world. But should major countries time and again make the mistakes of strategic miscalculation, they might create such traps for themselves."393

In the final months of the Obama administration there was some effort to generate new thinking around AI, but the new Trump administration was hostile to anything inherited from Obama so any forward movement ground to a halt. Both the intelligence community and the various defense boards have issued increasingly stark warnings about the threat posed to America's power by AI.

In May, 2018, the White House hosted an AI summit of government and business leaders. Fifteen months into his four-year term, it was striking to those who attended that no head has been appointed of the Office of Science and Technology Policy. Instead, the meeting was hosted by

---

[393] http://www.chinadaily.com.cn/world/2015xivisitus/2015-09/24/content_21964069_3.htm

Michael Kratsios, a deputy assistant to the president for technology policy.

Kratsios said a new committee is being formed that will coordinate AI investments across federal agencies, including research related to autonomous systems, biometric identification, computer vision and robotics. He called for a "free-market approach" that would harness the combined strength of government, industry and academia while limiting regulation that could "hamstring" companies394 according to his prepared remarks.

Intel Corp chief executive Brian Krzanich, who attended the summit, said in a blog post that "without an AI strategy of its own, the world's technology leader risks falling behind."395

Eric Schmidt, the former chair of Google, said of the Chinese, "By 2020, they will have caught up. By 2025, they will be better than us. And by 2030, they will dominate the industries of AI."396

In March, 2018 Republican Congresswoman Elise Stefanik, a member of the House Armed Services Committee and chair of the Subcommittee on Emerging Threats and Capabilities, introduced legislation to set up a National Commission on Artificial Intelligence to:397

---

[394] https://www.usnews.com/news/best-states/california/articles/2018-05-10/white-house-hosts-ai-summit-with-tech-firms

[395] https://www.reuters.com/article/us-usa-artificialintelligence/trump-administration-will-allow-ai-to-freely-develop-in-u-s-official-idUSKBN1IB30F?feedType=RSS&feedName=technologyNews

[396] https://www.foreignaffairs.com/articles/china/2018-08-13/when-china-rules-web?cid=nlc-fa_twofa-20180816

[397] https://stefanik.house.gov/media-center/press-releases/stefanik-introduces-artificial-intelligence-legislation

Conduct a comprehensive and national-level review of advances in artificial intelligence (AI), machine learning, and associated technologies for the President of the United States and Congress.

Address and identify the national security needs of the nation with respect to AI, including economic risk, and other needs for the common defense of the nation.

Provide near-term actionable recommendations to the president and the Congress, including ways to more effectively organize the Federal Government for AI.

Provide annual and actionable recommendations thereafter to our government through 2020.

The charter and focus of the commission includes recommendations on:

Competitiveness: Competitiveness of the US in Artificial Intelligence, machine learning, and associated technologies, related to national security, economic security, public-private partnerships, and investments.

Technological advantages: Means and methods for the US to maintain a technological advantage in AI and associated technologies, including quantum sciences and high-performance computing.

Cooperation and competition: Developments and trends in international cooperation and competition, including foreign investments in AI, machine learning, and associated technologies.

Investments and research: Means to foster greater emphasis on investments in basic and advanced research by private, public, academic and combined initiatives.

Workforce and education: Incentives to attract, recruit and retain leading talent across our Nation.

International law and ethics: Identify and understand the risks associated with advances in AI under the law of armed conflict, international humanitarian law, escalation dynamics, and other ethical considerations related to AI, machine learning, and associated technologies.

Data and privacy: Means to establish data standards and open incentives to share data, including the development of privacy- and security-protection measures.

This proposed legislation was folded into the annual Defense Authorization Bill that President Trump signed in August, 2018. However, with its focus on defense, it was, at best, a tiny step towards creating and implementing a national strategy, not least because the Defense Department moves so slowly compared to the much faster pace in the private sector.

AI cuts across every government department and every area of the private sector and cherry-picking one department and one area does little to create a national strategy.

The US has not yet lost the struggle for AI dominance to China. America still has significant advantages with very large and innovative companies like Google, Facebook and Apple. It's theoretically possible, too, that this administration will develop and promote a strategic vision that could unite government, industry and the country. Unfortunately, however, for an administration obsessed with tactical rather than strategic advantage, with neither the understanding nor the interest in looking beyond the near term, this is highly unlikely.

By contrast, China has developed an AI policy that looks toward world dominance by 2050. When combined with the Belt and Road Initiative and the country's obsession with AI, Big Data and its use of surveillance and the suppression of dissent, it is difficult to see how America can contest the rise of this new superpower.

The stakes are as large as we can imagine. It's not just Allison's Thucydides' Trap and the threat of global war in a struggle for dominance in the twenty-first century. Since its founding in 1776, America has stood in the world for individual liberty, free markets and freedom under the rule of law. China believes in none of those values and has already used all the powers of the state to suppress freedom within its own borders and has positioned itself to exert tremendous influence across the entire world.

If America abdicates its role on the world stage to China it will mark the end of the US as the world-wide beacon of freedom it has been since its founding.

Part 8 – Looking Ahead

Chapter 18

Steps for a Peaceful Revolution

In researching this book, one thing became clear to both of us: nobody really knows what the AI revolution will mean, when it will take place and how fast it will unfold.

One dystopian interpretation comes from the entrepreneur and AI pioneer, Elon Musk:398

"The percentage of intelligence that is not human is increasing, and eventually we will represent a very small percentage of intelligence. I tried to convince people to slow down AI, to regulate AI. This was futile…

"There will be some new technology that will cause damage or death. There will be an outcry. There will be an investigation. Years will pass. There will be rule making. Oversight regulations. This all takes many years and is the normal course of things. But this timeframe is not relevant to AI. You can't take 10 years from the point at which it is dangerous. It's too late.

"One thing's for sure: We will not control it."

For Musk, the dystopian future in which AI will create a thinking machine that will swiftly surpass and replace human intelligence, is imminent. Treasury secretary Steve Mnuchin apparently does not share Musk's sense of alarm, given his infamous remark that he need not be concerned about AI for "50–100 years".

---

[398] https://www.youtube.com/watch?v=z3EQqjn-ELs

Should we fear AI or ignore it for now? That depends on what we mean by AI. Today, we have "narrow" AI: a machine that can absorb vast quantities of data and, with the right algorithms, deliver astonishing results that far surpass the ability of humans. That AI that can analyze a legal non-disclosure agreement in 26 seconds and do so far more accurately than a typical lawyer. With machine learning, that AI can read an x-ray in seconds and compare it with millions of other x-rays to deliver a more accurate diagnosis than the best radiologist in the world.

Even at this very simple level, AI will transform our lives. Certainly, millions of workers will lose the jobs they now have – how many millions is up for debate – and whole classes of jobs will be wiped out. Millions of new jobs will be created – just how many is also subject to debate – but everyone agrees that our education system will need to be transformed to provide job seekers with the qualifications necessary to take advantage of the new opportunities presented by AI.

Then, there is the next generation of AI – sometimes called Advanced General Intelligence, or Strong AI or Full AI. No one can say when that will be ready for full deployment. But when it is, machines will be able to think for themselves and without any human participation in the process will be capable of performing any intellectual task a human can do. Once that AGI threshold is crossed, change will come astonishingly quickly.

At that point, the fear is that we'll no longer be able to control their development. They will overwhelm our ability to keep up, to think and to act as fast as the machines or as accurately. The fear is: they'll no longer need us. That's what scares Elon Musk, Bill Gates and the late Stephen Hawking.

But it also inspires many others who see great opportunity in such infinitely capable machines. The hope is that AGI may provide answers to climate change, poverty, food shortages and war.

So, should we be idealistic about AI or fearful that it could mean the end of humanity? At the very least it suggests we are on a risky journey, one that will destabilize the world we know and provide global challenges unparalleled in our lifetime or, some would argue, in the history of the world.

The first industrial revolution, which began with the invention of steam in the eighteenth century, caused disruption on a global scale. Starting in Britain, industries which for centuries had been built around rural home and families, migrated to large urban factories. America fostered the second industrial revolution by introducing large scale mechanization and production which became the norm throughout the world.

Lives were transformed, many not for the better, fostering great anger. Those whose lives were turned upside down felt betrayed by the political class that left them unprotected, in favor of advancing their own interests.

Marxism arose from that period of instability and the resulting communist revolutions led to tens of millions of deaths. In all, perhaps 200m died in the aftermath of the first industrial revolution.

The third industrial revolution began in the latter half of the last century marking the transformation from analog to digital and heralding the start of the Information Age. This revolution brought in computers, the internet and cellphones while, at the same time, transforming methods of production and business.

This third Revolution was a precursor to the fourth, which started around 2010. According to Klaus Schwab, the founder and executive chairman of the World Economic Forum:

"We are at the beginning of a revolution that is fundamentally changing the way we live, work, and relate to one another. In its scale, scope and complexity, what I consider to be the fourth industrial revolution is unlike anything humankind has experienced before."399

Schwab believes that this revolution covers fields such as AI, robotics, the internet of things, autonomous vehicles, 3D printing, nanotechnology, biotechnology, materials science, energy storage and quantum computing.

"The changes are so profound that, from the perspective of human history, there has never been a time of greater promise or potential peril," said Schwab.400

Five years ago, historian Christopher Clark published a book called *The Sleepwalkers*, which set out in extraordinary detail how the world's well-meaning leaders misunderstood each other and the world around them, and so created what author HG Wells called "the war to end all wars."401

In our conversations in Washington and Silicon Valley and in Europe and Asia, we found consensus that we are on the brink of a revolution that will transform our world. What is striking to everyone, however, is that, aside from China, no nation has a plan for how to adapt to this revolution. It's reasonable to ask whether we are, once

---

[399] Klaus Schwab, *The Fourth Industrial Revolution*, Crown Business, New York, 2016, p.1.

[400] Ibid, p.2.

[401] Christopher Clark, *The Sleepwalkers, How Europe Went to War in 1914*, Harper Collins, New York, 2013.

again, sleepwalking into history. Will the world look back on this time with astonishment, wondering just how we could have been so unprepared for the world that is rushing towards us?

We can't rely exclusively on governments which are too slow moving and short-sighted to get ahead of this change. Instead, what is needed is a new relationship between governments – the nation states – and the large companies – the market states – such as Google and Facebook that are leading the fourth revolution. Right now, the two sides view each with great wariness, if not complete mistrust.

Watching Mark Zuckerberg's testimony to Congress in April, 2018 was the perfect illustration of the gulf between the two worlds. Zuckerberg clearly had been exhaustively coached not to patronize his ill-informed questioners, nor to flash his temper at their obliviousness. The questions from Senators were frequently breathtakingly ignorant of Facebook, how it works and even what the internet is and does. Bridging that gap between these two sides is vital to preparing us for our future world.

It's not our intention to put forth some grand vision for the future, a recasting of democracy or ethics for the age of AI. Creating a manifesto is essentially a political act. Marx wrote *Das Kapital*, Hitler wrote *Mein Kampf* and the Unabomber wrote *The Industrial Society and its Future*. Such programmatic prescriptions to fix society's perceived ills invariably lay out a dangerous path. We're not here to foster a revolution. Far from it. Our simple hope is to come up with some ideas that present an alternative to the kinds of conflicts that resulted from the first two industrial revolutions.

We face two very different challenges; the first is internal, to address the domestic issues created by AI; the second is external, to create a safer world in which we all can live.

Already, there are many signs of dissatisfaction at every level of American society. Income inequality is growing with the top 1% getting significantly richer while the bottom 40% have seen either stagnant or falling incomes for the past 20 years.

Employment may be high but middle-class factory jobs have given way to lesser paying service jobs or part time work in the gig economy. And every study conducted in the past five years forecasts tens of millions of jobs eliminated because of AI. Whole categories of employment will disappear and this revolution will impact not just factory workers but every professional class from lawyers to doctors.

The dire numbers are only one part of the story, but opinion surveys and social media data paint another, perhaps more alarming picture. Pervasive discontent with the political process means that less than 50% of the electorate can be bothered to vote. At the same time, social media has given voice to every crackpot conspiracy and the megaphone effect means that thousands, sometimes millions, get on board the wacko train.

The nature and tone of the national conversation has been transformed from respectful dialog to a bitter rant and different views are often seen as a sign of blinkered idiocy. Bridging the rhetorical gap has been impossible for the fringe groups of left and right and it is increasingly difficult for ordinary people to find common ground.

Many commentators have referred to this phenomenon as tribalism. Another way of making the point is to describe America fracturing along ethnic, economic and social grounds where today's fissures can swiftly become tomorrow's chasms.

Politicians hear the noise but, instead of modulating it, they mine it for the base devotion it can bring them. Down this road lies the potential for outright civil conflict if the right fire is lit.

We need to take steps NOW to prepare for this destabilizing future.

In 1942, at the height of World War II, America began work on the Manhattan Project, which was designed to build the first nuclear bomb. With the help of Britain and Canada, the Project employed 130,000 people at 30 sites in the three countries involved and cost around $30 billion. It was a massive undertaking that brought together some of the finest scientific minds of the time and created the world's first atomic bomb.

Today, we need a twenty-first century version of the Manhattan Project for the purpose of preparing the country for a peaceful transition to the era of AGI.

*

1. **Strategy**

America has no overall strategy for dealing with the multiple challenges presented by the AI revolution. This is a major failing, and requires a White House-led initiative to bring together the best and brightest of the public and private sectors to decide on priorities. A new center for AI Innovation would oversee the implementation of the strategy with deep participation from the top five technology companies as well as relevant government agencies and NGOs.

As part of this strategy, an American AI Investment Fund, modeled after a Silicon Valley venture capital business, would seek out and fund AI research and development deemed worthy of investment. Such a fund would attract private sector investment so every government dollar would have a multiplier effect. This should address the relative current shortfall in AI R&D investment, which is ceding American dominance to China.

A key component of this strategy is to make government and industry more responsive to the technology challenges and opportunities as they emerge. In the recent past, the bureaucracy has viewed technological developments purely in terms of revenue and jobs – worthy considerations – but heedless of the consequences to how we live and to any social cost. The tech companies, despite their lofty ambitions, only respond to social concerns caused by their products after much public clamor. Apple and other companies now acknowledge that obsessive use of devices, for example, may harm young minds.

The AI strategy will be designed to ensure that new AI developments are safe, that possible consequences to our well-being are considered before new products are deployed, and that implementation will prepare the nation adequately for the disruptions certain to occur as the fourth revolution gathers pace.

*

2. **Ethics**

A Center for Data Ethics should establish guidelines for what is acceptable in an AI world. Today, many of the algorithms already in use from facial recognition to deciding qualifications for credit are based on inaccurate and biased data sets.

As AI evolves, algorithms may well evolve independently and start making decisions for themselves. There is currently no mechanism for managing such an evolution, nor for taking action against algorithms that cause harm.

The Center for Data Ethics will set a standard for the research and implementation of any new AI algorithm that will satisfy a "Do No Harm" standard. All published research would address both the positive and negative aspects of each new development so that adequate debate occurs before it is too late. The CDE would provide a stamp of approval without which no government agency could buy or implement a new AI product.

*

3. **Security**

Cyber security is an anarchic world without common standards or effective enforcement and no policies to protect America Inc. The results are millions of attacks a day by foreign countries and criminal organizations which find it all too easy to steal what they want from companies and every government agency, including the Pentagon. This is costing America tens of billions of dollars a year in lost intellectual property and unfairly boosting the competitiveness of rival economies.

AI will ratchet up the volume and sophistication of attacks and will increase exponentially the risk of a devastating cyber-attack with potential heavy loss of life.

During the Cold War the intelligence community's secret knowledge was not shared with the private sector, sometimes wisely, often unwise. Going forward, companies will be beside government on the front lines in this war and, where feasible, should be treated as a trusted partner. As part of a new cybersecurity strategy, an office should be established to coordinate the interface between the public and private sectors to better protect the nation.

*

4. **Warfare**

The Pentagon, along with every other military in the world, is rushing headlong into the AI world, developing new weapons and finding ways to employ AI that will improve every aspect of warfighting. However, there is no agreement on what autonomous warfare – warfare run or controlled by machines – actually means. Various officials have committed to making sure that 'humans are always in the loop' but it is very difficult to have faith in this claim. The power, speed, and lethality of autonomous weapons and the behavior of our enemies may make oversight practically impossible.

Our enemies may have no reservations about leaving the fighting to the machines and so will have the edge on the speed of decision-making and action. No general could possibly commit to handicapping his or her troops in this way and so humans will increasingly be taking a back seat to the algorithms.

We have an opportunity and an obligation to create the rules, both for us, and in cooperation with other nations, for the world, of an AI battlefield and to provide guidance to our armed forces so that they are properly trained and equipped for this new world. But it requires a cold look at the likely future realities and not just meaningless reassurances to politicians and the public.

*

5. **Privacy**

AI-driven automated processes will begin to decide credit scores, law enforcement profiles and both predictive and proactive policing. A Citizen's Charter would set out the judgments being made about any individual, what privacy protections are in place and what recourse a citizen might have to correct the record. This Charter would be overseen by the Data Ethics Center that would establish and police guidelines for the ownership of data and its transfer between businesses and organizations.

*

6. **Political Process**

Successive administrations have grown used to legislating for the past. But such a slow-moving response to the revolutionary challenges of AI puts the relevance of future administrations at risk. Federal and State legislators should have access to – and be required to – take part in education programs that brief them about all aspects of the approaching future.

*

7. **Education**

When all knowledge becomes available to any student with access to the internet, education needs to shift its emphasis from learning about the past towards problem-solving and creativity. Education is a conservative and slow-moving environment which will need to be transformed to remain relevant for the fourth revolution.

Every school curriculum must include not only training in the fundaments of AI but also its ethical and societal implications. If algorithms really do change everything, then successive generations of students must graduate with some understanding of what this will mean for them and their families.

Already, there is a chronic shortage of qualified AI researchers and developers. Currently, demand is around five times the actual number of men and women qualified to fill the vacant jobs. This skills gap is going to worsen rapidly without subsidies that incentivize universities to expand existing programs and start new AI courses.

*

8. **Work**

We have no comprehensive assessment of the future workforce in an AI economy. All studies to date have been speculative but some benchmarks need to be established urgently. This will help business and government plan appropriately. But any benchmark should only be considered a work in progress and new studies should be conducted regularly to measure progress and to recommend course corrections.

*

9. **Jobs Training**

If the scale of workforce disruption approaches what is predicted in the next 5–10 years, urgent action is essential to keep tens of millions of workers from becoming unemployable. Already, graduates in previously secure professions such as law and some aspects of medicine are finding that demand for their skills is shrinking. At the same time, graduates with very large college debt are discovering they have little or no prospect of ever paying off those college loans.

Workers with only high school degrees will no longer be able to find a job for life. With AI taking hold throughout our economy, skills that seem valuable one day could be irrelevant the next. This means that every person must have access to retraining opportunities.

*

10. **Income Inequality**

This is a difficult question to address, because top revenue earners will argue they are entitled to the rewards for their hard work, while others will criticize the inherent unfairness of a system that maintains an ever larger percentage of the population in a poverty trap from which they cannot hope to escape.

From our perspective, income inequalities at current levels in America are unsustainable over time and are expected to grow much worse as AI develops. No society in history has seen a wage gap grow indefinitely without some sort of insurrection, so America must address the imbalance before a crisis point is reached.

Let us be clear, risk takers and entrepreneurs should be rewarded, as they have been the foundation of the country's extraordinary record of innovation and leadership in the world. But tax policies and programs that achieve a more progressive ratio between the bottom 20% and the top 10% of the country would do much to close the income gap, reduce resentment and spread the wealth of the nation.

In any dynamic economy, some will always be left behind as others surge ahead. But the numbers of those without work, or with work that doesn't pay enough to keep a family in food and lodging, is expected to grow significantly as a result of AI.

Various economists and politicians have floated the idea of a Universal Basic Income (UBI) which would entitle every person to a guaranteed minimum wage. How to pay for this is the challenge. Bill Gates has suggested a tax on robots, given their role in reducing human employment. Tax code reforms and other strategies are making the rounds of academic and think tank circles. Whatever the solution, a caring society needs to prepare to support the anticipated large numbers of new unemployed or under-employed.

As in so much of AI, this is not a left or right argument but one rooted in pragmatism. Creating an angry and resentful underclass is not in the interests of any society that aspires to a peaceful future.

*

11. **International**

The current race to create new AI algorithms is akin to the race to develop nuclear weapons during and after World War II. The world lived on the brink of nuclear annihilation until order was created via treaties that limited the proliferation of such weapons and defined the conduct of their use in conflict.

We live in a time of similar peril. There are no constraints on the development of new algorithms, no way of judging which ones create unacceptable risk to peace or freedoms and no real understanding of the consequences of AI on societies and the world. Winning the race for AI supremacy seems to be all that matters, though nobody understands what winning might mean.

This is irresponsible folly. The United Nations has been trying to navigate the minefield of AI, but without supportive leadership from nations, they haven't had much success. America and its allies have the opportunity to provide such leadership, not by preventing any country from winning the race, but by designing and implementing agreements between nations for how this new AI world will develop.

Two priorities: negotiate a cyberwar treaty to govern the use of new weapons both in first use and response; agree on a set of rules for waging war with autonomous weapons that prevent algorithms from taking war out of the hands of humans and giving it to machines.

We are entering a period in human history of extraordinary challenges and extraordinary risks, all brought about by the Artificial Intelligence revolution. To date, there has been little understanding national or internationally of the scale of the challenges that confront us all. At the same time, the accelerating pace of change means that action by governments and the private sector working together is essential to avert disaster.

Many precursors for revolution and war are already in place: impotent backward-looking governments; corruption; income inequality; growing social divisions; a disheartening focus on the tactical (tomorrow morning) vs the strategic (a few years down the road). History tells us this is unsustainable for any society over time as an increasingly hopeless majority is likely to rebel against the small minority reaping the benefits of this new AI driven order.

This is not a political argument on behalf of any party or system, but, rather, a pragmatic argument for urgent action, based on the realities detailed above that we know to be true.

For example, even if we could initiate the necessary reforms to our education system tomorrow it could take 10 years to put them in place, in effect consigning a whole generation of students without the knowledge or skills they will need to survive in the future.

Similarly, every study by every government body and consulting firm agrees that displaced workers will need to be trained to be employable for the jobs that are coming. No national training programs exist anywhere in the world to prepare workforce for the AI revolution.

To date, there is no sign of the kind of leadership the world needs, but it is not too late for America to step up and take charge.

It is perhaps fitting to end this book with a quote from Winston Churchill from a speech he made at Harvard on September 6, 1943 nearly two years after America had entered the war against Nazi Germany.

"The price of greatness is responsibility. If the people of the United States had continued in a mediocre station, struggling with the wilderness, absorbed in their own affairs, and a factor of no consequence in the movement of the world, they might have remained forgotten and undisturbed beyond their protecting oceans: but one cannot rise to be in many ways the leading community in the civilized world without being involved in its problems, without being convulsed by its agonies and inspired by its causes.

"If this has been proved in the past, as it has been, it will become indisputable in the future. The people of the United States cannot escape world responsibility."402

[402] https://winstonchurchill.org/resources/speeches/1941-1945-war-leader/the-price-of-greatness-is-responsibility/

Afterword

James:

For the past 40 years, my business has been warfare. I saw my first killing in Zimbabwe during the civil war when a man I had met over breakfast got in his truck and drove over a landmine. Since then, I've seen or reported on revolutions, civil wars, conventional wars and terrorism.

As we enter the fourth revolution, of Artificial Intelligence, much of what I see is eerily familiar: social dislocation, rapidly growing financial inequality, a broken political process, the rise of radical politics and authoritarian leaders. In my personal past and in history, this has almost always led to civil war or revolution. I hope this time can be different.

I began my career as a reporter covering the Middle East and wrote my first book on the financing of terrorism because I wanted to understand just how the revolutionaries I met could afford the luxury hotels, cars and apparently unlimited expense accounts. Since then, I've written another 13 books that have looked at different aspects of warfare from cyber to unconventional responses to dangerous threats.

I was in Northern Ireland as that country was torn apart, in Iran just after the Shah was overthrown, in the former Yugoslavia as that country was destroyed by ethnic killings and in some of the meetings at the White House,

NSA and CIA that took place after September 11 as America tried to decide how to respond to the al Qaeda threat.

But I was never a war correspondent. Such a role I felt would be too addictive and much too frightening. Reporting from the front line is a valuable public service carried out by exceptionally brave men and women. Two of my friends were killed doing that job, and I had no wish to die the same way. Instead, for around 20 years I was a Defense Correspondent for the London *Sunday Times*, where my job was more about reporting strategy and tactics than it was about the eye witness account of the latest atrocity.

In the process, I've met presidents and prime ministers, the leaders of the CIA, MI6 and the KGB, terrorists and their victims. I've been on operations with Special Forces and designed and implemented psychological operations and counter-cyber activities, initially as a reporting observer and then as an author and participant. I've been a target for assassination by an arms dealer who is now in jail and lived off the grid for ten years while a terrorist leader tried to have me killed.

I have developed a deep understanding of the causes and consequences of war and have spent most of my working life trying to explain just why people do the apparently inexplicable to those who were once neighbors, friends, even lovers.

As my world changed, so I left journalism, became a CEO type, started various businesses and along the way joined the board of the National Security Agency and engaged in various covert activities for different parts of the intelligence community. I have been surprised to learn that first, as part of life's journey, I have learned things that can be helpful to others in combating tyranny, terrorism and attacks that undermine my country.

All this is to illustrate that I know something about war, especially the civil wars, revolutions and terrorist acts that have been part of my world for the past few decades.

Along the way, I have learned some painful personal lessons which will be familiar to anyone who has seen real violence. I abhor violence but fully understand that, on occasion, violence is the only answer. At its most basic level, if you try to shoot my wife or daughters, I will defend them.

To better understand how weapons can be used and the men and women who use them, I've fired most small arms, flown in fighters and helicopters, been in submarines, fast boats, destroyers and aircraft carriers. I've spoken at too many conferences about conflict and civil war and sat in on too many planning meetings involving military action at various levels. I helped devise future strategy for the NSA and brought an outsider's perspective to some other critical areas of national security.

But I've never been a government guy. I am too impatient to the point of intolerance of bureaucracy and anything else that gets in the way of getting the job done.

In 1998, I became an American citizen because, as I traveled the world, I saw first-hand the difference America made whether it be by delivering aid to relieve famine or by encouraging democracy in countries ruled by tyrannical despots. America was, literally, a beacon of hope for millions around the world. On countless visits to the States I was inspired by the aspirations of the many people I met. Some wanted to transcend their humble beginning, others talked of the opportunities their immigrant family had found in America while still others wanted to do good in the world.

I came from a more rigid upbringing, where you were largely who you were born, with all the constraints that class and privilege could deliver. I found America to be truly a land of opportunity where decent people were encouraged to do well, where aspiration was seen as a virtue and everyone seemed to be encouraging, however mad the idea (and some of mine really were crazy).

A year after I became a US citizen, I found myself on the board at the National Security Agency. In what other country could such a thing be even considered, let alone made possible? I felt honored to be asked to serve the country I had grown to love.

I've developed a deep cynicism about politics and politicians. I've seen too many decisions made for personal or political expediency that have resulted in too many good men and women sacrificing their lives doing what they thought was their duty for their country. I consider myself politically independent and have voted for both Republicans and Democrats over the years and my vote is always cast based on the values that I consider closest to my own.

At the same time, I have come to appreciate the fragility of democracy and the institutions that ensure the will of the people to survive the economic, social and other pressures that have been a part of every society for generations. In Northern Ireland, in Iran and in Bosnia and Serbia I saw the consequences of ethnic divisions: towns devastated, cities largely obliterated and bullet holes and artillery fire on one side of the street while the other side, occupied by a different religious group, was unscathed.

As we sit in our comfortable and familiar worlds, it's all too easy to feel a sense of permanence; nothing can touch us or interfere with the stable world we have created. But I know such feelings to be transient and all too easily turned upside down.

My observation is that there are several common themes that run through every revolution, civil war or terrorist campaign. The first is that the will of the people is no longer reflected in the political leadership. This may be because a brutal dictator is in charge who uses force and torture to keep the people in line. Or, it may be that the political leadership has lost touch with the electorate and has become largely irrelevant to their lives.

Secondly, change, whether it be economic, political or social, has placed unmanageable pressures on a significant group of the population. Such pressures tend to expose fissures that already exist in society and bring them starkly to the surface. Change is always hard to manage for everyone and if there is no leadership to provide signposts of how to navigate through the challenges, people can swiftly lose hope and confidence. That's when the demagogue, who appears to offer some answers, can find his or her voice that is magnified by the despair in the audience.

Third, inequalities, especially financial, are always unsustainable beyond a certain point. Some inequality can help foster ambition and aspiration (I want to be like the boss). But, if the majority can see that a very small minority are getting so much richer at their expense that the gap can never be bridged, then aspiration turns into despair and a need for radical change. Embedded within this is a collapse of the idea that everyone is equal under the law. If the reality turns into one law for the rich and something very different for the poor, that too, is unsustainable over time.

Fourth, political or economic corruption can make a mockery of the very idea of democracy. If power is seen to corrupt by undermining the will of the people such that there is no will and no voice for the people, then democracy no longer exists. From that truth comes a thirst for a new way of manifesting the voice of the people that is different from what those in power have chosen to call democracy.

Fifth and finally, all of these are expressed through a free and fair press. As a former journalist myself, I can agree that 'free and fair' are loose terms where the media is never truly fair or free. But, in an open society, there are enough decent men and women holding the corrupt and the powerful to account that the media can truly act as a voice for the ordinary and the voiceless.

In recent years, I have seen the country I love turn away from values I hold dear. On my desk as I write this is a card that I wrote for myself as a reminder of what matters in my world: family, duty, commitment, compassion, creativity, enquiry, love. These are not Republican or Democrat values but are attributes that I hope to embody as I stand in the world. As I look around me today, I find that much of my country has come to embody a very different set of values: resentment, envy, hatred and intolerance.

America was built on acceptance of others and yet today we seem to have become a very different country. I've seen this in many other places in the world and such a change has always, without exception, ended badly. It's easy to become distressed when looking around today but I am by nature an optimist and am firmly convinced that we can find a different and more promising future than what seems to loom ahead.

On the one hand, we are opening the door to a tyrannical form of government where the anti-democratic forces hold sway. This happened in response to the first industrial revolution in the Soviet Union, China, Cuba and Nazi Germany. We may choose to believe that such a future could never happen here but experience tells me that the pre-cursors for such an end game are already in place. We can choose a different course but such a new direction requires a different kind of visionary leadership than is visible in the political process today.

Artificial Intelligence is going to place great pressures on every society in terms of lost jobs, a political and education process that will be unable to keep up with the pace of change and a growing number of people who feel disenfranchised. This is not a uniquely American problem but in recent years, America has felt to me to be particularly exposed.

Part of the motivation in writing this book was to set out what our future might look like and to argue for action before it's too late. The purpose of writing this afterword is to suggest that I'm not just some wonk writing some politically-motivated tome. I would not suggest for a moment that I'm so arrogant as to believe that I have the gift of seeing the future. But I would argue that I have enough experience to know when I see trouble ahead and that time is now.

It's easy to fall into a dystopian funk when writing about AI. There are so many challenges but the upsides are potentially extraordinary; cures for many diseases, new efficiencies, solving many of the climate change dangers and raising millions out of poverty. But there are risks and there is a dark side that could spell a troubled and dangerous future for us all.

Right now, the train is accelerating ever faster towards Lady Liberty, who is tied down across the tracks. Her screams are getting louder and louder. Is anyone listening?

*

Richard:

My working life has focused on two seemingly unrelated worlds, that of storytelling and of technology. I will try to do here what I have tried to do for years, which is to knit them together.

In grad school at Stanford, my chief concern – in fairness, my obsession – was new communications technology and its implications for public policy. I latched onto a term called "technological determinism," which meant, essentially, if we could build technology, we would build it, without consideration of the consequences of its use. That would have to come later as we picked through the detritus of the aftermath of innovation.

This book, then, is a continuation of those concerns, perhaps the culmination of them. This is my attempt, along with James, to address the consequences of a technology – Artificial Intelligence – before those consequences have been writ large, before it's too late.

In coming to grips with technological determinism, I wrote monographs on public access to media, on the implications of the rise of cable and video cassettes for the delivery of entertainment and information.

I was on the Arpanet, the original internet, in the seventies and understood then, that it would change so much about the way we live. I was part of innumerable discussions about the use of computers in education and their role in digitizing and providing access to every kind of information imaginable. I remember being stunned that I could access, via the Arpanet, a Spanish recipe for a fish dish from a university library in Madrid.

During grad school and immediately after, I consulted on these issues for various foundations, organizations and companies, including the Ford Foundation, the Sloan Commission, Time-Warner, the UN, the Rand Corporation, and various others I no longer recall.

At the same time, I had an enduring love of movies and actually had sold a movie script as an undergrad, though I had no notion at the time of pursuing such a career. Ford asked me to join a communications think tank they were starting in DC. The job wasn't to begin for a few months so I had a free summer. I happened to meet some people in San Francisco who were making movies. On a lark, I wrote a script with two of them and, as I was planning to move to DC, we got a call from Martin Scorsese's agent who had read the script and suggested we all come to Hollywood and become screenwriters. I was broke but with no responsibilities, so, I thought it was exactly the right time to take a flier and, after some months of wavering, I made the move.

I'll skip the rags to middling success narrative of a Hollywood writer and resume my knitting of the two paths of my life. During the first dot com boom of the late nineties, I commuted to San Francisco from LA, to join and eventually run a startup called TheScience. Our mission was to create a web content company to use animation and rich media to show the science behind natural phenomena such as hurricanes and common technology such as personal computers. Our advisory board included Nobel laureates, Intel execs, and soon to be

Defense Secretary Don Rumsfeld. This, for me, was my first chance to use my experience telling stories to talk about technology in a different way.

My role at TheScience ended just before 9/11. Soon after, I was invited to join a small group of screenwriters to brainstorm regularly about terrorism with underlings at the CIA. Obviously, terrorists flying planes into buildings were not on their radar, in their contingency plans, nor unearthed by their human intelligence (humint) or their signal intelligence (sigint). They didn't want to be unprepared ever again.

The theory was that, because we imagined crazy scenarios for a living, we might give them some previews of possible attacks to come. In fact, we did predict the subway bombings and the decentralization of al Qaeda across the world. I got to use my storytelling skills in ways I had never imagined.

Eventually, this experience led to me consulting for the Institute for Creative Technology at USC (I taught screenwriting to grad students there for over a decade). They needed to make their training videos more engaging. So, I introduced narrative and character to a variety of videos including a counter terrorism game, job interviews for autistic kids using virtual human interviewers and other scenarios. Once again, I was merging storytelling with technology, hopefully for useful purposes.

As I jumped back and forth between tech-related consulting and screenwriting, I co-founded a mobile medical software startup called GoMed Solutions and shared in two software patents for our technology.

James and I had met years ago when I adapted his wonderful video game, Spycraft, for a film script for Universal studios. He reached out to me again with the idea of telling the cautionary story of AI in all its manifestations.

This book grew out of those conversations and, for me, it has been the perfect opportunity to talk about technological determinism by telling the story of the most significant technology to come along in my lifetime and, maybe, in anyone's lifetime.

The Authors

James Adams

James has written 15 nonfiction books, each of which tackled a complex subject and created a strategy for governments, law enforcement and the military to develop new approaches. For example, *The Financing of Terror* resulted in new international laws and a new focus on how terrorists get the money to fund their operations; *The Next World War* forecast a migration of war to cyberspace and suggested actions that democracies could take to protect themselves; and *Secret Armies* accurately predicted the growing use of special forces to wage war around the world. Several of his books became bestsellers, and many have been translated into other languages.

As a board member at the National Security Agency, James was responsible for creating a new strategy for the Signals Intelligence Directorate ("The Eavesdroppers"). As chairman of the Technology Oversight Panel at NSA, James reviewed $20 billion of new technology programs and helped reset the direction of the agency.

James was part of a White House task force on psychological operations against al Qaeda, and worked with multiple intelligence agencies to design and implement covert counterterrorism activities against ISIS and al Qaeda. He was also involved in a number of classified programs to counter cyber-attacks against America. As part of the CIA's Strategic Advisory Group, he helped predict future technology developments, including AI, and their impact on global economies and countries.

As a journalist, James covered national security for the London *Sunday Times* and was managing editor at the newspaper. He has studied the causes and consequences of warfare for the last 45 years. As a reporter, he covered both Gulf wars, the revolution in Iran, and terrorist campaigns and insurgencies across the world.

He was later CEO at United Press International, and founded a cyber-intelligence company that was ultimately acquired by a global corporation. James currently owns and directs the world's largest independent producer of audiobooks.

*

Richard Kletter

Richard Kletter has been a Research Associate at Stanford focused on new communications technology, an adjunct professor at USC where he consults for the DOD think tank, The Institute For Creative Technology, lectured at Stanford, where he went to grad school, and Oxford on new communications technology. He has developed training games for counter-terrorism professionals around the world and other national-security related projects on how to deal with the revolution in communications technology. He has written a monograph for the UN on citizen access to media.

He co-holds mobile software patents, co-founded a wireless mobile application, GoMedSolutions, ran a web content company called TheScience, financed by industry leaders.

Richard has written, directed and/or produced over twenty films and TV movies, including *Never Cry Wolf* and *Odd Girl Out*.

Bibliography

Campbell, Kurt, *The Pivot, The Future of American Statecraft in Asia,* Hachette, New York, 2016.

Fukuyama, Francis, *Identity, The Demand for Dignity and the Politics of Resentment,* Farrar, Straus and Giroux, New York, 2018.

Harari, Yuval Noah, *21 Lessons for the Twenty-First Century,* Spiegel & Grau, New York, 2018.

Hayden, Michael, *Playing to the Edge, American Intelligence in the Age of Terror,* Penguin Press, New York, 2016.

Husain, Amir, *The Sentient Machine, The Coming Age of Artificial Intelligence*, Scribner, New York, 2017.

Hobsbawm, Eric, *Industry and Empire, The Birth of the Industrial Revolution,* Weidenfeld and Nicholson, London, 1968.

Hyman, Louis, *Temp; How American Work, American Business and the American Dream Became Temporary,* Penguin Random House, New York, 2018.

Jamieson, Kathleen Hall, *Cyber-War, How Russian Hackers and Trolls helped elect a President,* Oxford University Press, New York, 2018.

Lee, Kai-Fu, *AI Superpowers, China, Silicon Valley and the New World Order,* Houghton Mifflin Harcourt, New York, 2018.

Lewis, Michael, *The Fifth Risk,* WW Norton, New York, 2018.

Micklethwait, John and Wooldridge, Adrian, *The Fourth Revolution, The Global Race to Reinvent the State,* Penguin Press, New York, 2014.

Miller, Greg, The Apprentice, Trump, Russia and the Subversion of American Democracy, Harper Collins, New York, 2018.

O'Connell, Mark, *To Be A Machine, Adventures Among Cyborgs, Utopians, Hackers and the Futurists Solving the Modest Problem of Death*, Doubleday, New York, 2017.

O'Neil, Cathy, *Weapons of Math Destruction, How Big Data Increases Inequality and Threatens Democracy,* Crown, New York, 2016.

Rifkin, Jeremy, *The Third Industrial Revolution,* St. Martin's Press, New York, 2011.

Sanger, David E. *The Perfect Weapon, War, Sabotage and Fear in the Cyber Age,* Crown, New York, 2018.

Satia, Priya, *Empire of Guns, The Violent Making of the Industrial Revolution,* Penguin Press, New York, 2018.

Scharre, Paul, *Army of None, Autonomous Weapons and the Future of War*, W.W. Norton, New York, 2018.

Schneier, Bruce, *Click Here to Kill Everybody, Security and Survival in a Hyper-connected World,* Norton, New York, 2018.

Schwab, Klaus, *The Fourth Industrial Revolution,* Crown, New York, 2016.

Stearns, Peter, *The Industrial Revolution in World History,* Westview Press, Boulder, 2013.Tyson, Neil DeGrasse and Avis Lang, *Accessory to War, The Unspoken Alliance Between Astrophysics and the Military,* WW Norton, New York, 2018.

Urban, Mark, *The Edge. Is the Military Dominance of the West Coming to an End?,* Little Brown, 2015.

Weightman, Gavin, *The Industrial Revolutionaries, The Making of the Modern World 1776-1914,* Grove Press, New York, 2007.

Wortzel, Larry M., *The Chinese People's Liberation Army and Information Warfare,* United States Army War College Press, Carlisle Barracks, PA, 2014.

Zetter, Kim, *Countdown to Zero Day, Stuxnet and the Launch of the World's Frist Digital Weapon,* Crown, New York, 2014.

Printed in Great Britain
by Amazon

78985688R00236